Chinese Classics: Chinese-English Series

MENCIUS

Volume Two

Chinese Classics : Chinese-English Series

MENCIUS
Volume Two

Translated by
D.C. Lau

The Chinese University Press
Hong Kong

International Standard Book Number: 962-201-313-9

The Chinese University Press
The Chinese University of Hong Kong
SHATIN, N. T., HONG KONG

Typesetting by
The Chinese University Press (English text)
Wonderful Typesetting Co. (Chinese text)
Printing by
Caritas Printing Training Centre

CONTENTS

Book V · Part A 萬章章句上 178
Part B 萬章章句下 200

Book VI · Part A 告子章句上 222
Part B 告子章句下 242

Book VII · Part A 盡心章句上 264
Part B 盡心章句下 286

Appendix 1 The Dating of Events in the Life of Mencius 309

Appendix 2 Early Traditions about Mencius 316

Appendix 3 The Text of the *Mencius* 321

Appendix 4 Ancient History as Understood by Mencius 324

Appendix 5 On Mencius' Use of the Method of Analogy in Argument 334

Appendix 6 Some Notes on the *Mencius* 357

Works Cited 377

Index of Proper Names 379

MENCIUS 孟子

萬章章句上

1.　萬章問曰：“舜往[1]于田，號泣于[2] 旻天，何爲其號泣也？”

　　孟子曰：“怨慕也。”

　　萬章曰：“‘父母愛之，喜而不忘；父母惡之，勞而不怨。’然則舜怨乎？”

　　曰：“長息問於公明高曰：‘舜往于田，則吾旣得聞命矣；號泣于[2] 旻天，于[2] 父母，則吾不知也。’公明高曰：‘是非爾所知也。’夫公明高以孝子之心爲不若是恝，我竭力耕田，共爲子職而已矣，父母之不我愛，於我何[3]哉？帝使其子九男二女，百官牛羊倉廩備，以事舜於畎畝之中，天下之士多就之者，帝將胥天下而遷之焉。爲不順於父母，如窮人無所歸。天下之士悅之，人之所欲也，而不足以解憂；好色，人之所欲，妻帝之二女，而不足以解憂；富，人之所欲，富有天下，而不足以解憂；貴，人之所欲，貴爲天子，而不足以解憂。人悅之、好色、富貴，無足以解憂者，惟順於父母可以解憂。人少，則慕父母；知好色，則慕少艾；有妻子，則慕妻子；仕則慕君，不得於君則熱中。大孝終身慕父母。五十而慕者，予於大舜見之矣。”

[1] 《廣雅疏證》云：‘往者，勞也。’（頁106）

[2] 三‘于’字並借作‘呼’。（說見《經義述聞》頁1229）

[3] ‘何’下疑應有‘有’字。I.B. 5 ‘於王何有’即其比。

BOOK V · PART A

1. Wan Chang asked, 'While toiling in the fields, Shun wept and wailed, calling upon merciful Heaven. Why did he weep and wail?'

'He was complaining and yearning at the same time,' answered Mencius.

' "When one is loved by one's parents, though pleased, one must not forget oneself; when one is disliked by them, though distressed, one must not bear them any grudge."[1] Are you saying that Shun bore a grudge against his parents?'

'Ch'ang Hsi said to Kung-ming Kao, "That Shun toiled in the fields I now understand, but that he should have wept and wailed, calling upon merciful Heaven and calling upon father and mother, I have not understood." Kung-ming Kao said, "That is something beyond your comprehension." Now Kung-ming Kao did not think that a son could be so complacent as to say, all that is required of me is that I should do my best in tilling the fields and discharge the duties of a son, and if my parents do not love me, what is that to me? The Emperor[2] sent his nine sons, and two daughters, together with the hundred officials, taking with them the full quota of cattle and sheep and provisions, to serve Shun in the fields. Most of the Gentlemen of the Empire placed themselves under him, and the Emperor was about to hand the Empire over to him. But because he was unable to please his parents, Shun was like a man in extreme straits with no home to go back to. Every man wants to be liked by the Gentlemen of the Empire, yet this was not sufficient to deliver him from anxiety; beautiful women are also something every man desires, yet the bestowal of the Emperor's two daughters on Shun as wives was not sufficient to deliver him from anxiety; wealth is something every man wants, yet the wealth of possessing the whole Empire was not sufficient to deliver him from anxiety; rank is something every man wants, yet the supreme rank of Emperor was not sufficient to deliver him from anxiety. None of these things was sufficient to deliver him from anxiety which the pleasure of his parents alone could relieve. When a person is young he yearns for his parents; when he begins to take an interest in women, he yearns for the young and beautiful;

2.　萬章問曰：“詩云，‘娶妻如之何？必告父母。’信斯言也，宜
莫如舜。舜之不告而娶，何也？”

　　孟子曰：“告則不得娶。男女居室，人之大倫也。如告，則廢人
之大倫，以懟父母，是以不告也。”

　　萬章曰：“舜之不告而娶，則吾既得聞命矣；帝之妻舜而不告，
何也？”

　　曰：“帝亦知告焉則不得妻也。”

　　萬章曰：“父母使舜完廩，捐階，瞽瞍焚廩。使浚井，出，從而
揜之。象曰：‘謨蓋都君咸我績，牛羊父母，倉廩父母，干戈朕，琴
朕，弤朕，二嫂使治朕棲。’象往入舜宮，舜在牀琴。象曰：‘鬱陶
思君爾。’忸怩。舜曰：‘惟茲臣庶，汝其于予治。’不識舜不知象
之將殺己與？”

　　曰：“奚而不知也？象憂亦憂，象喜亦喜。”

　　曰：“然則舜偽喜者與？”

when he has a wife, he yearns for his wife; when he enters public life he yearns for his prince and becomes restless if he is without one. A son of supreme dutifulness yearns for his parents all his life. In Shun I have seen an example of a son who, even at the age of fifty, yearned for his parents.'

[1] This seems to be a saying of Tseng Tzu's. It is to be found in chapter 24 of the *Li chi* (*Li chi chu shu*, 48. 6a) and chapter 52 of the *Ta Tai li chi* (4. 11a).
[2] i.e., Yao.

2. Wan Chang asked, 'The *Odes* say,

> How does one take a wife?
> By first telling one's parents.[3]

If that were truly so, it would seem that Shun's example was not to be followed. Why did Shun marry without telling his parents?'

'Because he would not have been allowed to marry if he had told them. A man and woman living together is the most important of human relationships. If he had told his parents, he would have to put aside the most important of human relationships and this would result in bitterness against his parents. That is why he did not tell them.'

'The reason why Shun married without telling his parents is now clear to me. But why did the Emperor give Shun his daughters in marriage without telling Shun's parents?'

'The Emperor was also aware that telling them would have prevented the marriage from taking place.'

'Shun's parents sent him to repair the barn. Then they removed the ladder and the Blind Man set fire to the barn. They sent Shun to dredge the well, set out after him and blocked up the well over him. Hsiang[4] said, "The credit for plotting against the life of Shun goes to me. The cattle and sheep go to you, father and mother, and the granaries as well. But the spears go to me, and the lute and the *ti* bow as well. His two wives should also be made to look after my quarters." Hsiang went into Shun's house and there Shun was, seated on the bed playing on the lute. Hsiang, in some embarrassment, said, "I was thinking of you." Shun said, "I am thinking of my subjects. You can help me in the task of government." I wonder if Shun was unaware of Hsiang's intention to kill him.'

曰：“否；昔者有饋生魚於鄭子產，子產使校人畜之池。校人烹之，反命曰：‘始舍之，圉圉焉；少則洋洋焉；攸然而逝。’子產曰：‘得其所哉！得其所哉！’校人出，曰：‘孰謂子產智？予既烹而食之，曰，得其所哉，得其所哉。’故君子可欺以其方，難罔以非其道。彼以愛兄之道來，故誠信而喜之，奚僞焉？”

3. 萬章問曰：“象日以殺舜爲事，立爲天子則放之，何也？”

孟子曰：“封之也；或曰，放焉。”

萬章曰：“舜流共工于幽州，放驩兜于崇山，殺三苗于三危，殛鯀于羽山，四罪而天下咸服，誅不仁也。象至不仁，封之有庳。有庳之人奚罪焉？仁人固如是乎——在他人則誅之，在弟則封之？”

曰：“仁人之於弟也，不藏怒焉，不宿怨焉，親愛之而已矣。親之，欲其貴也；愛之，欲其富也，封之有庳，富貴之也。身爲天子，弟爲匹夫，可謂親愛之乎？”

“敢問或曰放者，何謂也？”

'How could he be unaware? He was worried when Hsiang was worried, and pleased when Hsiang was pleased.'

'In that case did Shun just pretend to be pleased?'

'No. Once, someone presented a live fish to Tzu-ch'an of Cheng. Tzu-ch'an told his fish-keeper to keep it in the pond. But the keeper cooked the fish and came back to report to Tzu-ch'an. "When I first let go of it," said he, "it was still sickly, but after a while it came to life and swam away into the distance." "It is in its element! It is in its element!" said Tzu-ch'an. On coming out, the keeper said, "Who says that Tzu-ch'an is wise? I cooked and ate the fish and he said, 'It is in its element! It is in its element!' " That only goes to show that a gentleman can be taken in by what is reasonable, but cannot be easily hoodwinked by the wrong method. He, Hsiang, came as a loving brother, and so Shun honestly believed him and was pleased. What need was there for pretence?'

[3] Ode 101.
[4] Shun's younger brother.

3. Wan Chang said, 'Hsiang devoted himself every day to plotting against Shun's life. Why did Shun only banish him when he became Emperor?'

'He enfeoffed him,' said Mencius. 'Some called this banishment.'

'Shun banished Kung Kung to Yu Chou,' said Wan Chang, and Huan Tou to Mount Ch'ung; he banished San Miao to San Wei and killed Kun on Mount Yü. On these four culprits being punished, the people in the Empire bowed to his will with admiration in their hearts. That was because he punished the wicked. Hsiang was the most wicked of them all, yet he was enfeoffed in Yu Pi. What wrong had the people of Yu Pi done? Is that the way a benevolent man behaves? Others he punishes, but when it comes to his own brother he enfeoffs him instead.'

'A benevolent man never harbours anger or nurses a grudge against a brother. All he does is to love him. Because he loves him, he wishes him to enjoy rank; because he loves him, he wishes him to enjoy wealth. To enfeoff him in Yu Pi was to let him enjoy wealth and rank. If as Emperor he were to allow his brother to be a nobody, could that be described as loving him?'

'May I ask what you meant by saying that some called this

曰：“象不得有爲於其國，天子使吏治其國而納其貢稅焉，故謂
之放。豈得暴彼民哉？雖然，欲常常而見之，故源源而來，‘不及貢，
以政接于有庳。’此之謂也。”

4. 咸丘蒙問曰：“語云，‘盛德之士，君不得而臣，父不得而子。’
舜南面而立，堯帥諸侯北面而朝之，瞽瞍亦北面而朝之。舜見瞽瞍，
其容有蹙。孔子曰：‘於斯時也，天下殆哉，岌岌乎！’不識此語誠
然乎哉？”

    孟子曰：“否；此非君子之言，齊東野人之語也。堯老而舜攝也。
堯典曰，‘二十有八載，放勳乃徂落，百姓如喪考妣，三年，四海遏
密八音。’孔子曰：‘天無二日，民無二王。’舜既爲天子矣，又帥
天下諸侯以爲堯三年喪，是二天子矣。”

    咸丘蒙曰：“舜之不臣堯，則吾既得聞命矣。詩云，‘普天之下，
莫非王土；率土之濱，莫非王臣。’而舜既爲天子矣，敢問瞽瞍之非
臣如[1]何？”

    [1] ‘如’讀爲‘而。’

banishment?'

'Hsiang was not allowed to take any action in his fief. The Emperor appointed officials to administer the fief and to collect tributes and taxes. For this reason it was described as banishment. Hsiang was certainly not permitted to ill-use the people. Shun frequently wanted to see him and so there was an endless flow of tributes streaming in.

> Before tribute was due,
> Yu Pi was received on account of affairs of state.[5]

This describes what happened.'

[5] It is possible that this quotation is from one of the lost chapters of the *Book of History*.

4. Hsien-ch'iu Meng asked, 'As the saying goes,

> A man of abundant virtue
> Cannot be treated as a subject by the prince,
> Nor can he be treated as a son by his father.

Shun stood facing south, while Yao stood facing north,[6] at the head of the feudal lords, paying homage to him. The Blind Man likewise stood facing north, paying homage to him. Shun saw the Blind Man and a distressed look came over his face. Confucius commented, "At that moment the Empire was precariously balanced." I wonder if this was really so?'

'No,' said Mencius. 'These are not the words of a gentleman but of a rustic from Eastern Ch'i.

'When Yao was old, Shun acted as regent. The *Yao tien* says,

> After twenty-eight years, Fang Hsün[7] died. The hundred officials mourned for him in the manner of mourning for a parent. For three years all musical instruments were silenced.[8]

According to Confucius, "There cannot be two kings for the people just as there cannot be two suns in the heavens." If Shun had already become Emperor, then for him to lead the feudal lords in the observance of three years' mourning for Yao would have meant two emperors.'

'That Shun did not treat Yao as a subject,' said Hsien-ch'iu

曰:"是詩也,非是之謂也;勞於王事而不得養父母也。曰,'此莫非王事,我獨賢勞也。'故說詩者,不以文害辭,不以辭害志。以意逆志,是爲得之。如以辭而已矣,雲漢之詩曰,'周餘黎民,靡有孑遺。'信斯言也,是周無遺民也。孝子之至,莫大乎尊親;尊親之至,莫大乎以天下養。爲天子父,尊之至也;以天下養,養之至也。詩曰,'永言孝思,孝思維則。'此之謂也。書曰,'祗載見瞽瞍,夔夔齊栗,瞽瞍亦允若。'是爲父不得而子也?"

Meng, 'is now clear to me. But the *Odes* say,

> There is no territory under Heaven
> Which is not the king's;
> There is no man on the borders of the land
> Who is not his subject.[9]

Now after Shun became Emperor, if the Blind Man was not his subject, what was he?'

'This is not the meaning of the ode, which is about those who were unable to minister to the needs of their parents as a result of having to attend to the king's business. They were saying, "None of this is not the king's business. Why are we alone over-burdened?" Hence in explaining an ode, one should not allow the words to obscure the sentence, nor the sentence to obscure the intended meaning. The right way is to meet the intention of the poet with sympathetic understanding. If one were merely to take the sentences literally, then there is the ode *Yün han* which says,

> Of the remaining multitudes of Chou
> Not a single man survived.[10]

If this is taken to be literal truth, it would mean that not a single Chou subject survived.

'The greatest thing a dutiful son can do is to honour his parents, and the greatest thing he can do to honour his parents is to let them enjoy the Empire. To be the father of the Emperor is the highest possible honour. To give him the enjoyment of the Empire is to give him the greatest enjoyment. The *Odes* say,

> He was always filial,
> And, being filial, he was a model to others.[11]

This describes well what I have said.

'The *Book of History* says

> He went to see the Blind Man in the most respectful frame of mind, in fear and trembling, and the Blind Man, for his part, became amenable.[12]

Can this be described as "Nor can he be treated as a son by his father"?'

---

[6] The sovereign faces south while his subjects face north.
[7] Yao's name.

5.　　萬章曰：“堯以天下與舜，有諸？”

　　孟子曰：“否；天子不能以天下與人。”

　　“然則舜有天下，孰與之？”

　　曰：“天與之。”

　　“天與之者，諄諄然命之乎？”

　　曰：“否；天不言，以行與事示之而已矣。”

　　曰：“以行與事示之者，如之何？”

　　曰：“天子能薦人於天，不能使天與之天下；諸侯能薦人於天子，不能使天子與之諸侯；大夫能薦人於諸侯，不能使諸侯與之大夫。昔者，堯薦舜於天，而天受之；暴之於民，而民受之；故曰，天不言，以行與事示之而已矣。”

　　“曰：敢問薦之於天，而天受之；暴之於民，而民受之，如何？”

　　曰：“使之主祭，而百神享之，是天受之；使之主事，而事治，百姓安之，是民受之也。天與之，人與之，故曰，天子不能以天下與人。舜相堯二十有八載，非人之所能爲也，天也。堯崩，三年之喪畢，舜避堯之子於南河之南，天下諸侯朝覲者，不之堯之子而之舜；訟獄者，不之堯之子而之舜；謳歌者，不謳歌堯之子而謳歌舜，故曰，天也。夫然後之中國，踐天子位焉。而[1]居堯之宮，逼堯之子，是篡也，非天與也。太誓曰，‘天視自我民視，天聽自我民聽，’此之謂也。”

　　[1] ‘而’ 讀爲 ‘如’。

[8] The *Shu ching*, 3. 18b.
[9] Ode 205.
[10] Ode 258.
[11] Ode 243.
[12] From a lost chapter.

5. Wan Chang said, 'Is it true that Yao gave the Empire to Shun?'

'No,' said Mencius. 'The Emperor cannot give the Empire to another.'

'In that case who gave the Empire to Shun?'

'Heaven gave it him.'

'You say Heaven gave it him. Does this mean that Heaven gave him detailed and minute instructions?'

'No. Heaven does not speak but reveals itself through its acts and deeds.'

'How does Heaven do this?'

'The Emperor can recommend a man to Heaven but he cannot make Heaven give this man the Empire; just as a feudal lord can recommend a man to the Emperor but he cannot make the Emperor bestow a fief on him, or as a Counsellor can recommend a man to a feudal lord but cannot make the feudal lord appoint him a Counsellor. In antiquity, Yao recommended Shun to Heaven and Heaven accepted him; he presented him to the people and the people accepted him. Hence I said, "Heaven does not speak but reveals itself by its acts and deeds." '

'May I ask how he was accepted by Heaven when recommended to it and how he was accepted by the people when presented to them?'

'When he was put in charge of sacrifices, the hundred gods enjoyed them. This showed that Heaven accepted him. When he was put in charge of affairs, they were kept in order and the people were content. This showed that the people accepted him. Heaven gave it to him, and the people gave it to him. Hence I said, "The Emperor cannot give the Empire to another." Shun assisted Yao for twenty-eight years. This is something which could not be brought about by man, but by Heaven alone. Yao died, and after the mourning period of three years, Shun withdrew to the south of Nan Ho, leaving Yao's son in possession of the field, yet the feudal lords of the Empire coming to pay homage and those who

6.　萬章問曰：“人有言，‘至於禹而德衰，不傳於賢，而傳於子。’有諸？”

　　孟子曰：“否，不然也；天與賢，則與賢；天與子，則與子。昔者，舜薦禹於天，十有七年，舜崩，三年之喪畢，禹避舜之子於陽城，天下之民從之，若堯崩之後不從堯之子而從舜也。禹薦益於天，七年，禹崩，三年之喪畢，益避禹之子於箕山之陰。朝覲訟獄者不之益而之啓，曰，‘吾君之子也。’謳歌者不謳歌益而謳歌啓，曰，‘吾君之子也。’丹朱之不肖，舜之子亦不肖。舜之相堯、禹之相舜也，歷年多，施澤於民久。啓賢，能敬承繼禹之道。益之相禹也，歷年少，施澤於民未久。舜、禹、益相去久遠，其子之賢不肖，皆天也，非人之所能爲也。莫之爲而爲者，天也；莫之致而至者，命也。匹夫而有天下者，德必若舜禹，而又有天子薦之者，故仲尼不有天下。繼世以有天下，天之所廢，必若桀紂者也，故益、伊尹、周公不有天下。伊尹相湯以王於天下，湯崩，太丁未立，外丙二年，仲壬四年，太甲顛覆湯之典刑，伊尹放之於桐，三年，太甲悔過，自怨自艾，於桐處仁遷義，三年，以聽伊尹之訓己也，復歸于亳。周公之不有天下，猶益之於夏、伊尹之於殷也。孔子曰，‘唐虞禪，夏后殷周繼，其義一也。’”

were engaged in litigation went to Shun, not to Yao's son, and ballad singers sang the praises of Shun, not of Yao's son. Hence I said, "It was brought about by Heaven." Only then did Shun go to the Central Kingdoms and ascend the Imperial throne. If he had just moved into Yao's palace and ousted his son, it would have been usurpation of the Empire, not receiving it from Heaven. The *T'ai shih* says,

> Heaven sees with the eyes of its people. Heaven hears with the ears of its people.[13]

This describes well what I meant.'

[13] From the lost chapter of the *Book of History* though incorporated into the spurious *T'ai shih* of the present text. (*Shu ching*, II. 10a)

6. Wan Chang asked, 'It is said by some that virtue declined with Yü who chose his own son to succeed him, instead of a good and wise man. Is this true?'

'No,' said Mencius. 'It is not. If Heaven wished to give the Empire to a good and wise man, then it should be given to a good and wise man. But if Heaven wished to give it to the son, then it should be given to the son. In antiquity, Shun recommended Yü to Heaven, and died seventeen years later. When the mourning period of three years was over, Yü withdrew to Yang Ch'eng, leaving Shun's son in possession of the field, yet the people of the Empire followed him just as, after Yao's death, the people followed Shun instead of Yao's son. Yü recommended Yi to Heaven, and died seven years later. When the mourning period of three years was over, Yi withdrew to the northern slope of Mount Ch'i, leaving Yü's son in possession of the field. Those who came to pay homage and those who were engaged in litigation went to Ch'i[14] instead of Yi, saying, "This is the son of our prince." Ballad singers sang the praises of Ch'i instead of Yi, saying, "This is the son of our prince." Tan Chu[15] was depraved, as was the son of Shun. Over a period of many years Shun assisted Yao, and Yü assisted Shun. Thus the people enjoyed their bounty for a long time. Ch'i was good and capable, and able to follow in the footsteps of Yü. Yi assisted Yü for only a few years, and the people had not enjoyed his bounty for long. Shun and Yü differed from Yi greatly in the

7. 萬章問曰："人有言，'伊尹以割烹要湯，'有諸？"

　　孟子曰："否，不然；伊尹耕於有莘之野，而樂堯舜之道焉。非其義也，非其道也，祿之以天下，弗顧也；繫馬千駟，弗視也。非其義也，非其道也，一介不以與人，一介不以取諸人。湯使人以幣聘之，囂囂然曰：'我何以湯之聘幣爲哉？我豈若處畎畝之中，由是以樂堯舜之道哉？'湯三使往聘之，既而幡然改曰：'與我處畎畝之中，由是以樂堯舜之道，吾豈若使是君爲堯舜之君哉？吾豈若使是民爲堯舜之民哉？吾豈若於吾身親見之哉？天之生此民也，使先知覺後知，使

length of time they assisted the Emperor, and their sons differed as radically in their moral character. All this was due to Heaven and could· not have been brought about by man. When a thing is done though by no one, then it is the work of Heaven; when a thing comes about though no one brings it about, then it is decreed.

'A common man who comes to possess the Empire must not only have the virtue of a Shun or a Yü but also the recommendation of an Emperor. That is why Confucius never possessed the Empire. On the other hand, he who inherits the Empire is only put aside by Heaven if he is like Chieh or Tchou. That is why Yi, Yi Yin and the Duke of Chou never came to possess the Empire. T'ang came to rule over the Empire through the assistance of Yi Yin. When T'ang died, T'ai Ting did not succeed to the throne.[16] Wai Ping ruled for two years, and Chung Jen for four. Then T'ai Chia upset the laws of T'ang, and Yi Yin banished him to T'ung. After three years. T'ai Chia repented and reproached himself, and, while in T'ung, reformed and became a good and dutiful man. After another three years, since he heeded the instruction of Yi Yin, he was allowed to return to Po. That the Duke of Chou never came to possess the Empire is similar to the case of Yi in Hsia and that of Yi Yin in Yin. Confucius said, "In T'ang and Yü[17] succession was through abdication, while in Hsia, Yin and Chou it was hereditary. The basic principle was the same." '

[14] Yü's son.
[15] Yao's son.
[16] Through an early death.
[17] T'ang is here the name of Yao's dynasty, not to be confused with the founder of the Yin or Shang dynasty, while Yü is here the name of Shun's dynasty, not to be confused with the founder of the Hsia dynasty.

7. Wan Chang asked, 'It is said by some that Yi Yin tried to attract the attention of T'ang by his culinary abilities. Is this true?'

'No,' said Mencius. 'It is not. Yi Yin worked in the fields in the outskirts of Yu Hsin, and delighted in the way of Yao and Shun. If it was contrary to what was right or to the Way, were he given the Empire he would have ignored it, and were he given a thousand teams of horses he would not have looked at them. If it was contrary to what was right· or to the Way, he would neither give away a mite nor accept it. When T'ang sent a messenger with

先覺覺後覺也。予，天民之先覺者也；予將以斯道覺斯民也。非予覺之，而誰也？’思天下之民匹夫匹婦有不被堯舜之澤者，若己推而內之溝中。其自任以天下之重如此，故就湯而說之以伐夏救民。吾未聞枉己而正人者也，況辱己以正天下者乎？聖人之行不同也，或遠，或近；或去，或不去；歸潔其身而已矣。吾聞其以堯舜之道要湯，未聞以割烹也。伊訓曰：‘天誅造攻自牧宮，朕載自亳。’”

8. 萬章問曰：“或謂孔子於衞主癰疽，於齊主侍人瘠環，有諸乎[1]？”

　　孟子曰：“否，不然也；好事者爲之也。於衞主顏讎由。彌子之妻與子路之妻，兄弟也。彌子謂子路曰：‘孔子主我，衞卿可得也。’子路以告。孔子曰：‘有命。’孔子進以禮，退以義，得之不得曰‘有

presents to invite him to court, he calmly said, "What do I want T'ang's presents for? I much prefer working in the fields, delighting in the way of Yao and Shun." Only after T'ang sent a messenger for the third time did he change his mind and say, "Is it not better for me to make this prince a Yao or a Shun than to remain in the fields, delighting in the way of Yao and Shun? Is it not better for me to make the people subjects of a Yao or a Shun? Is it not better for me to see this with my own eyes? Heaven, in producing the people, has given to those who first attain understanding the duty of awakening those who are slow to understand; and to those who are the first to awaken the duty of awakening those who are slow to awaken. I am among the first of Heaven's people to awaken. I shall awaken this people by means of this Way. If I do not awaken them, who will do so?' When he saw a common man or woman who did not enjoy the benefit of the rule of Yao and Shun, Yi Yin felt as if he had pushed him or her into the gutter. This is the extent to which he considered the Empire his responsibility.[18] So he went to T'ang and persuaded him to embark upon a punitive expedition against the Hsia to succour the people. I have never heard of anyone who can right others by bending himself,[19] let alone someone who can right the Empire by bringing disgrace upon himself. The conduct of sages is not always the same. Some live in retirement, others enter the world; some withdraw, others stay on; but it all comes to keeping their integrity intact. I have heard that Yi Yin attracted the attention of T'ang by the way of Yao and Shun, but I have never heard that he did it by his culinary abilities. The *Yi hsün*[20] says,

The punishment of Heaven began in the Mu Palace of Chieh. I came on the scene only at the city of Po.'

---

[18] Cf. V. B. 1.
[19] Cf. III. A. 1.
[20] A lost chapter of the *Book of History*.

8. Wan Chang asked, 'According to some, when he was in Wei Confucius' host was Yung Chü, and in Ch'i the royal attendant Chi Huan. Is this true?'

'No,' said Mencius. 'It is not. These were fabrications by people with nothing better to do. In Wei, Confucius' host was Yen

命'。而主癰疽與侍人瘠環,是無義無命也。孔子不悅於魯衞,遭宋桓司馬將要而殺之,微服而過宋。是時孔子當阨,主司城貞子,爲陳侯周臣。吾聞觀近臣,以其所爲主;觀遠臣,以其所主。若孔子主癰疽與侍人瘠環,何以爲孔子?"

[1] '有諸' 見 1.A.7;1.B.1;2,8;2.B.8,9;5.A.5,6,7;6.B.2,均無 '乎' 字。此處 '乎' 字蓋衍文《說苑·至上篇》。第八章引此文,'有諸' 下無 '乎' 字,'不然' 下無 '也' 字,與上下二章文例相同。

9. 萬章問曰:"或曰,'百里奚自鬻於秦養牲者五羊之皮食牛以要秦繆公。' 信乎?"

孟子曰:"否,不然;好事者爲之也。百里奚,虞人也。晉人以垂棘之璧與屈產之乘假道於虞以伐虢。宮之奇諫,百里奚不諫。知虞公之不可諫而去之秦,年已七十矣;曾不知以食牛干秦繆公之爲汙也,可謂智乎?不可諫而不諫,可謂不智乎?知虞公之將亡而先去之,不可謂不智也。時舉於秦,知繆公之可與有行也而相之,可謂不智乎?相秦而顯其君於天下,可傳於後世,不賢而能之乎?自鬻以成其君,鄉黨自好者不爲,而謂賢者爲之乎?"

Ch'ou-yu. The wife of Mi Tzu was a sister of the wife of Tzu-lu. Mi Tzu said to Tzu-lu, "If Confucius will let me play host to him, the office of Minister in Wei is his for the asking." Tzu-lu reported this to Confucius who said, "There is the Decree."[21] Confucius went forward in accordance with the rites and withdrew in accordance with what was right, and in matters of success or failure said, "There is the Decree." If, in spite of this, he accepted Yung Chü and the royal attendant Chi Huan as hosts, then he would be ignoring both what is right and the Decree.

'When Confucius met with disfavour in Lu and Wei, there was the incident of Huan Ssu-ma of Sung who was about to waylay and kill him, and he had to travel through Sung in disguise. At that time Confucius was in trouble, and he had as host Ssu-ch'eng Chen-tzu and took office with Chou, Marquis of Ch'en.

'I have heard that one judges courtiers who are natives of the state by the people to whom they act as host, and those who have come to court from abroad by the hosts they choose. If Confucius had chosen Yung Chü and the royal attendant Chi Huan as hosts, he would not have been Confucius.'

[21] 'When a thing is done though by no one, then it is the work of Heaven; when a thing comes about though no one brings it about, then it is decreed.' (V. A. 6)

9. Wan Chang asked, 'Some say that Po-li Hsi sold himself to a keeper of cattle in Ch'in for five sheep skins, and tended cattle to attract the attention of Duke Mu of Ch'in. Is this true?'

'No,' said Mencius. 'It is not. These were fabrications by people who had nothing better to do. Po-li Hsi was a native of Yü. Chin offered the jade of Ch'ui Chi and the horses of Ch'ü in exchange for permission to send troops through the territory of Yü to attack Kuo. Kung chi Ch'i advised against accepting the gift while Po-li Hsi remained silent. He knew that the ruler of Yü was beyond advice and left for Ch'in. He was seventy then. If at that age he did not know that it was undignified to secure a chance to speak to Duke Mu of Ch'in through feeding cattle, could he be called wise? Yet can he be called unwise when he remained silent, knowing that advice would be futile? He certainly was not unwise when he left in advance, knowing the ruler of Yü to be heading for disaster. Again, can he be said to be unwise when, after being raised to

Ch'ou-yu. The wife of Mi Tzu was a sister of the wife of Tzu-lu. Mi Tzu said to Tzu-lu, "If Confucius will let me play host to him, the office of Minister in Wei is his for the asking." Tzu-lu reported this to Confucius who said, "There is the Decree." Confucius went forward in accordance with the rites and withdrew in accordance with what was right, and in matters of success or failure said, "There is the Decree." If, in spite of this, he accepted Yung Chü and the royal attendant Chi Huan as hosts, then he would be ignoring both what is right and the Decree.

"When Confucius met with disfavour in Lu and Wei, there was the incident of Huan Ssu-ma of Sung who was about to waylay and kill him, and he had to travel through Sung in disguise. At that time Confucius was in trouble, and he lived as host Ssu-ch'eng Chen-tzu and took office with Chou, Marquis of Ch'en.

"I have heard that one judges courtiers who are natives of the state by the people to whom they act as host, and those who have come to court from abroad by the hosts they choose. If Confucius had chosen Yung Chü and the royal attendant Chi Huan as hosts, he would not have been Confucius."

When a thing is done though by no one, that is the work of Heaven; when it comes about though no one brings it about, then it is decreed. (V, A, 6)

9 Wan Chang asked, "Some say that Pe-li Hsi sold himself to a keeper of cattle in Ch'in for five sheep skins, and tended cattle, to attract the attention of Duke Mu of Ch'in. Is this true?"

"No," said Mencius, "it is not. These were fabrications by people who had nothing better to do. Po-li Hsi was a native of Yü. Chin offered the jade of Ch'ui Chi and the horses of Ch'ü in exchange for permission to send troops through the territory of Yü to attack Kuo. Kung chih Ch'i advised against accepting the gift while Po-li Hsi remained silent. He knew that the ruler of Yü was beyond advice and left for Ch'in. He was seventy then. If at that age he did not know that it was undignified to seek a chance to speak to Duke Mu of Ch'in through feeding cattle, could he be called wise? Yet can he be called unwise when he remained silent knowing that advice would be futile? He certainly was not unwise when he left, in advance, knowing the ruler of Yü to be heading for disaster. Again, can he be said to be unwise when, after being raised to office in Ch'in, he decided to help Duke Mu, seeing in him a man capable of great achievement? As prime minister of Ch'in, he was responsible for the distinction his prince attained in the Empire, and posterity has found him worthy of being remembered. Was this the achievement of a man with no ability? To sell oneself into slavery in order to help one's prince towards achievement is what even a self-respecting villager would not do. Are you saying that it is the act of a good and wise man?'

萬章章句下

1.　孟子曰：“伯夷，目不視惡色，耳不聽惡聲。非其君不事；非其民不使。治則進，亂則退。橫政之所出，橫民之所止，不忍居也。思與鄉人處，如以朝衣朝冠坐於塗炭也。當紂之時，居北海之濱，以待天下之清也。故聞伯夷之風者，頑夫廉，懦夫有立志。

“伊尹曰：‘何事非君？何使非民？’治亦進，亂亦進，曰：‘天之生斯民也，使先知覺後知，使先覺覺後覺。予，天民之先覺者也。予將以此道覺此民也。’思天下之民匹夫匹婦有不與被堯舜之澤者，若己推而內之溝中——其自任以天下之重也〔如此[1]〕。

“柳下惠不羞汙君，不辭小官。進不隱賢，必以其道。遺佚而不怨，阨窮而不憫。與鄉人處，由由然不忍去也。‘爾為爾，我為我，雖袒裼裸裎於我側，爾焉能浼我哉？’故聞柳下惠之風者，鄙夫寬，薄夫敦。

“孔子之去齊，接淅而行；去魯，曰，‘遲遲吾行也，去父母國之道也。’可以速而速，可以久而久，可以處而處，可以仕而仕，孔子也。”

[1] 按此文又見《萬章上》。彼處作：‘思天下之民匹夫匹婦有不被堯舜之澤者，若己推而內之溝中。其自任以天下之重如此。’（V.A.7）此文蓋誤脫‘如此’二字。今據補。（《萬章》文，‘重’下疑亦應有‘也’字。）

BOOK V · PART B

1. Mencius said, 'Po Yi would neither look at improper sights with his eyes nor listen to improper sounds with his ears. He would only serve the right prince and rule over the right people. He took office when order prevailed and relinquished it when there was disorder.[1] He could not bear to remain in a place where the government took outrageous measures and unruly people were to be found. To be in company with a fellow-villager was, for him, just like sitting in mud or pitch while wearing a court cap and gown.[2] He happened to live during the time of Tchou, and he retired to the edge of the North Sea[3] to wait for the murky waters of the Empire to return to limpidity. Hence, hearing of the way of Po Yi, a covetous man will be purged of his covetousness and a weak man will become resolute.[4]

'Yi Yin said, "I serve any prince; I rule over any people. I take office whether order prevails or not."[5] Again, he said, "Heaven, in producing the people, has given to those who first attain understanding the duty of awakening those who are slow to understand; and to those who are the first to awaken the duty of awakening those who are slow to awaken. I am amongst the first of Heaven's people to awaken. I shall awaken this people by means of this Way." When he saw a common man or woman who did not enjoy the benefit of the rule of Yao and Shun, Yi Yin felt as if he had pushed him or her into the gutter. This is the extent to which he considered the Empire his responsibility.[6]

'Liu Hsia Hui was not ashamed of a prince with a tarnished reputation, neither did he disdain a modest post.[7] When in office, he did not conceal his own talent, and always acted in accordance with the Way. When he was passed over he harboured no grudge, nor was he distressed even in straitened circumstances. When he was with a fellow-villager he simply could not tear himself away. "You are you and I am I. Even if you were to be stark naked by my side, how could you defile me?"[8] Hence hearing of the way of Liu Hsia Hui, a narrow-minded man will become tolerant and a mean man generous.

'When he left Ch'i, Confucius started after emptying the rice

孟子曰：“伯夷，聖之清者也；伊尹，聖之任者也；柳下惠，聖
之和者也；孔子，聖之時者也。孔子之謂集大成。集大成也者，金聲
而玉振之也。金聲也者，始條理也；玉振之也者，終條理也。始條理
者，智之事也；終條理者，聖之事也[2]。智，譬則巧也；聖，譬則力
也。由射於百步之外也，其至，爾力也；其中，非爾力也。”

[2] 馬王堆出土《老子甲本》卷後古佚書有：‘君子之爲善也，有與始也，有與終也。
君子之爲德也，有與始也，無與終也。金聲而玉振之，有德者也。金聲，善也；玉
言（玉振）聖也。善，人道也，德（聖），〔天〕道〔也〕。〔唯〕有德者然筍（后）
能金聲而玉振之。’可與《孟子》文相發明（參龐朴《帛書五行篇研究》，頁34）。

2.　北宮錡問曰：“周室班爵祿也，如之何？”

孟子曰：“其詳不可得聞也，諸侯惡其害己也，而皆去其籍；然

from the steamer, but when he left Lu he said, "I proceed as slowly as possible." This is the way to leave the state of one's father and mother.[9] He was the sort of man who would hasten his departure or delay it, would remain in a state, or would take office, all according to circumstances."[10]

Mencius added, 'Po Yi was the sage who was unsullied; Yi Yin was the sage who accepted responsibility; Liu Hsia Hui was the sage who was easy-going; Confucius was the sage whose actions were timely. Confucius was the one who gathered together all that was good. To do this is to open with bells and rally with jade tubes.[11] To open with bells is to begin in an orderly fashion; to rally with jade tubes is to end in an orderly fashion. To begin in an orderly fashion pertains to wisdom while to end in an orderly fashion pertains to sageness. Wisdom is like skill, shall I say, while sageness is like strength. It is like shooting from beyond a hundred paces. It is due to your strength that the arrow reaches the target, but it is not due to your strength that it hits the mark.'

[1] Cf. II. A. 2.
[2] It is difficult to see why Po Yi should object to the company of a fellow-villager as such. This passage is found also in II. A. 9 where the text reads, 'Po Yi . . . would not take his place at the court of an evil man, nor would he converse with him. For him to do so would be like sitting in mud or pitch wearing a court cap and gown. He pushed this dislike for evil to the extent that, if a fellow-villager in his company had his cap awry, he would walk away without even a backward look, as if afraid of being defiled.' We can see that the text in the present section is corrupt, with the result that it is wrong on three counts. First, it was being at the court of an evil man and conversing with him that was for Po Yi like sitting in mud or pitch while wearing court cap and gown. Second, he only objected to the company of a fellow-villager who had his cap awry. Third, all he did was walk away in disgust.
[3] Cf. IV. A. 13 and VII. A. 22.
[4] For this remark about the effect of Po Yi on certain types of people and for a similar remark about Liu Hsia Hui further on, cf. VII. B. 15.
[5] Cf. II. A. 2.
[6] This passage is also found in V. A. 7. The last sentence of the present section is defective and has been emended in the light of V. A. 7.
[7] Cf. VI. B. 6.
[8] Cf. II. A. 9.
[9] Cf. VII. B. 17.
[10] Cf. II. A. 2.
[11] This refers to music.

2. Po-kung Ch'i asked, 'What was the system of rank and income like under the House of Chou?'

而軻也嘗聞其略也。天子一位，公一位，侯一位，伯一位，子、男同一位，凡五等也。君一位，卿一位，大夫一位，上士一位，中士一位，下士一位，凡六等。天子之制，地方千里，公侯皆方百里，伯七十里，子、男五十里，凡四等。不能五十里，不達於天子，附於諸侯，曰附庸。天子之卿受地視侯，大夫受地視伯，元士受地視子、男。大國地方百里，君十卿祿，卿祿四大夫，大夫倍上士，上士倍中士，中士倍下士，下士與庶人在官者同祿，祿足以代其耕也。次國地方七十里，君十卿祿，卿祿三大夫，大夫倍上士，上士倍中士，中士倍下士，下士與庶人在官者同祿，祿足以代其耕也。小國地方五十里，君十卿祿，卿祿二大夫，大夫倍上士，上士倍中士，中士倍下士，下士與庶人在官者同祿，祿足以代其耕也。耕者之所獲，一夫百畝；百畝之糞[1]，上農夫食九人，上次食八人，中食七人，中次食六人，下食五人。庶人在官者，其祿以是爲差。」

---

[1] 《禮記・王制》作‘百畝之分。’（《禮記注疏》卷十一頁五下）此處蓋借‘糞’爲‘分。’（說見錢大昕《十駕齋養新錄》頁56。）

Mencius answered, 'This cannot be known in detail, for the feudal lords destroyed the records, considering the system to be detrimental to themselves. But I have heard a brief outline of it.

'The Emperor, the duke, the marquis and the earl each constituted one rank, while the viscount and the baron shared the same rank, thus totalling five grades. The ruler, the Minister, the Counsellor, the Gentlemen of the First, the Second and the Third Grades each constituted one rank, totalling six grades.

'The territory under the direct jurisdiction of the Emperor was a thousand *li* square, under a duke or a marquis one hundred *li* square, under an earl seventy *li* square, while under a viscount or a baron it was fifty *li* square, totalling four grades. Those who held territories under fifty *li* square had no direct access to the Emperor. They had to affiliate themselves to a feudal lord and were known as "dependencies".

'The Minister of the Emperor enjoyed a territory comparable to a marquis; the Counsellor of the Emperor enjoyed a territory comparable to an earl; the Senior Gentleman of the Emperor enjoyed a territory comparable to a viscount or a baron.

'The territory of a large state was a hundred *li* square, and its ruler enjoyed an income ten times that of a Minister, a Minister four times that of a Counsellor, a Counsellor twice that of a Gentleman of the First Grade, a Gentleman of the First grade twice that of a Gentleman of the Second Grade, a Gentleman of the Second Grade twice that of a Gentleman of the Third Grade, and a Gentleman of the Third Grade the same as a Commoner who was in public service, in other words, an income in place of what he would get from cultivating the land.

'The territory of a medium state was seventy *li* square, and its ruler enjoyed an income ten times that of a Minister, a Minister three times that of a Counsellor, a Counsellor twice that of a Gentleman of the First Grade, a Gentleman of the First Grade twice that of a Gentleman of the Second Grade, a Gentleman of the Second Grade twice that of a Gentleman of the Third Grade, and a Gentleman of the Third Grade the same as a Commoner who was in public service, in other words, an income in place of what he would get from cultivating the land.

'The territory of a small state was fifty *li* square, and its ruler

3.　萬章問曰：“敢問友。”

孟子曰：“不挾長，不挾貴，不挾兄弟而友。友也者，友其德也，不可以有挾也。孟獻子，百乘之家也，有友五人焉：樂正裘，牧仲，其三人，則予忘之矣。獻子之與此五人者友也，無獻子之家者也。此五人者，亦有獻子之家，則不與之友矣。非惟百乘之家爲然也，雖小國之君亦有之。費惠公曰，‘吾於子思，則師之矣；吾於顏般，則友之矣；王順、長息則事我者也。’非惟小國之君爲然也，雖大國之君亦有之。晉平公之於亥唐也，入云則入，坐云則坐，食云則食；雖蔬食菜羹，未嘗不飽，蓋不敢不飽也。然終於此而已矣。弗與共天位也，弗與治天職也，弗與食天祿也，士之尊賢者也，非王公之尊賢也。舜尚見帝，帝館甥于貳室，亦饗舜，迭爲賓主，是天子而友匹夫也。用下敬上，謂之貴貴；用上敬下，謂之尊賢。貴貴尊賢，其義一也。”

enjoyed an income ten times that of a Minister, a Minister twice that of a Counsellor, a Counsellor twice that of a Gentleman of the First Grade, a Gentleman of the First Grade twice that of a Gentleman of the Second Grade, a Gentleman of the Second Grade twice that of a Gentleman of the Third Grade, and a Gentleman of the Third Grade the same as a Commoner who was in public service, in other words, an income in place of what he would get from cultivating the land.

'What a farmer got was what he reaped from a hundred *mu* of land, the allocation of each man. With an allocation of a hundred *mu*, a farmer could feed nine persons, eight persons, seven persons, six persons, or five persons, according to his grading as a farmer. The salary of a Commoner who was in public service was also graded accordingly.'

3. Wan Chang asked, 'May I ask about friendship?'

'In making friends with others,' said Mencius, 'do not rely on the advantage of age, position or powerful relations. In making friends with someone you do so because of his virtue, and you must not rely on any advantages you may possess.

'Meng Hsien Tzu was a noble with a hundred chariots. He had five friends, including Yüeh-cheng Ch'iu and Mu Chung—the names of the other three I have forgotten. Hsien Tzu had these five as friends because they lacked his position. If these five had had his position, they would not have accepted him as a friend. This applies not only to a noble with a hundred chariots, but also to rulers of small states. Duke Hui of Pi said, "Tzu-ssu I treat as a teacher; Yen Pan I treat as a friend; as for Wang Shun and Ch'ang Hsi, they are men who serve me." Not only does this apply to rulers of small states, but sometimes also to rulers of large states. Take Duke P'ing of Chin and Hai T'ang for instance. He entered when Hai T'ang said "Enter", sat down when Hai T'ang said "Sit down", and ate when Hai T'ang said "Eat", and he ate his fill even when the fare was unpolished rice and vegetable broth, because he did not dare do otherwise. But Duke P'ing went no further than this. He did not share with Hai T'ang his position, his duties, or his revenue—all given to him by Heaven. This is the honouring of good and wise men by a Gentleman, not the honouring of good

4.　萬章曰：“敢問交際何心也？”

孟子曰：“恭也。”

曰：“‘卻之卻之爲不恭’，何哉？”

曰：“尊者賜之，曰，‘其所取之者義乎，不義乎？’而後受之，以是爲不恭，故弗卻也。”

曰：“請無以辭卻之，以心卻之，曰，‘其取諸民之不義也，’而以他辭無受，不可乎？”

曰：“其交也以道，其接也以禮，斯孔子受之矣。”

萬章曰：“今有禦人於國門之外者，其交也以道，其餽也以禮，斯可受禦與？”

曰：“不可；康誥曰：‘殺越人于貨，閔不畏死，凡民罔不譈。’是不待教而誅者也。殷受夏，周受殷，所不辭也；於今爲烈，如之何其受之？”

曰：“今之諸侯取之於民，猶禦也。苟善其禮際矣，斯君子受之，敢問何說也？”

and wise men by kings and dukes.

'Shun went to see the Emperor, who placed his son-in-law in a separate mansion. He entertained Shun but also allowed himself to be entertained in return. This is an example of an Emperor making friends with a common man.

'For an inferior to show deference to a superior is known as "honouring the honoured"; for a superior to show deference to an inferior is known as "honouring the good and wise". These two derive, in fact, from the same principle.'

4. Wan Chang asked, 'In social intercourse, what, may I ask, is the correct attitude of mind?'

'A respectful attitude of mind,' said Mencius.

'Why is it said, "Too insistent a refusal constitutes a lack of respect"?'

'When a superior honours one with a gift, to accept it only after one has asked the question "Did he or did he not come by it through moral means?" is to show a lack of respect. This is why one does not refuse.'

'Cannot one refuse, not in so many words, but in one's heart? Thus while saying to oneself, "He has taken this from the people by immoral means," one offers some other excuse for one's refusal.'

'When the superior makes friends with one in the correct way and treats one with due ceremony, under such circumstances even Confucius would have accepted a gift.'

'Suppose a man waylays other men outside the gates to the capital. Can one accept the loot when the robber makes friends with one in the correct way and treats one with due ceremony?'

'No. The *K'ang kao* says,

He who murders and robs and is violent and devoid of the fear of death is detested by the people.[12]

One can punish such a person without first attempting to reform him. This is a practice which the Yin took over from the Hsia and the Chou from the Yin without question. Such robbery flourishes more than ever today. How can it be right to accept the loot?'

'Now the way feudal lords take from the people is no different

曰：“子以爲有王者作，將比今諸侯而誅之乎？其敎之不改而後誅之乎？夫謂非其有而取之者盜也，充類至義之盡也。孔子之仕於魯也，魯人獵較，孔子亦獵較。獵較猶可，而況受其賜乎？”

曰：“然則孔子之仕也，非事道與？”

曰：“事道也。”

“事道奚獵較也？”

曰：“孔子先簿正祭器，不以四方之食供簿正。”

曰：“奚不去也？”

曰：“爲之兆也。兆足以行矣，而不行，而後去，是以未嘗有所終三年淹也。孔子有見行可之仕，有際可之仕，有公養之仕。於季桓子，見行可之仕也；於衞靈公，際可之仕也；於衞孝公，公養之仕也。”

5.   孟子曰：“仕非爲貧也，而有時乎爲貧；娶妻非爲養也，而有時乎爲養。爲貧者，辭尊居卑，辭富居貧。辭尊居卑，辭富居貧，惡乎宜乎？抱關擊柝。孔子嘗爲委吏矣，曰，‘會計當而已矣。’嘗爲乘田矣，曰，‘牛羊茁壯長而已矣。’位卑而言高，罪也；立乎人之本朝，而道不行，恥也。”

from robbery. If a gentleman accepts gifts from them so long as the rites proper to social intercourse are duly observed, what is the justification?'

'Do you think that if a true King should arise he would line up all the feudal lords and punish them? Or do you think he would try reforming them first before resorting to punishment? To say that taking anything that does not belong to one is robbery is pushing moral principles to the extreme. When Confucius held office in Lu, the people of Lu were in the habit of fighting over the catch in a hunt to use as sacrifice, and Confucius joined in the fight. If even fighting over the catch is permissible, how much more the acceptance of a gift.'

'In that case, did not Confucius take office in order to further the Way?'

'Yes. He did.'

'If he did, why did he join in the fight over the catch?'

'The first thing Confucius did was to lay down correct rules governing sacrificial vessels, ruling out the use of food acquired from the four quarters in such vessels.'

'Why did he not resign his office?'

'He wanted to make a beginning. When this showed that a ban was practicable, and in spite of this it was not put into effect, he resigned. In this way Confucius never remained at any court for as long as three years. Confucius took office sometimes because he thought there was a possibility of practising the Way, sometimes because he was treated with decency, and sometimes because the prince wished to keep good people at his court. That he took office with Chi Huan Tzu was an example of the first kind; with Duke Ling of Wei, the second kind; and with Duke Hsiao of Wei, of the last kind.'

[12] See *Shu ching*, 14. 8b.

5. Mencius said, 'Poverty does not constitute grounds for taking office, but there are times when a man takes office because of poverty. To have someone to look after his parents does not constitute grounds for marriage, but there are times when a man takes a wife for the sake of his parents. A man who takes office

6.　萬章曰："士之不託諸侯，何也？"

孟子曰："不敢也。諸侯失國，而後託於諸侯，禮也；士之託於諸侯，非禮也。"

萬章曰："君餽之粟，則受之乎？"

曰："受之。"

"受之何義也？"

曰："君之於氓也，固周之。"

曰："周之則受，賜之則不受，何也？"

曰："不敢也。"

曰："敢問其不敢何也？"

曰："抱關擊柝者皆有常職以食於上。無常職而賜於上者，以爲不恭也。"

曰："君餽之，則受之，不識可常繼乎？"

曰："繆公之於子思也，亟問，亟餽鼎肉。子思不悅。於卒也，摽使者出諸大門之外，北面稽首再拜而不受，曰：'今而後知君之犬馬畜伋。'蓋自是臺¹無餽也。悅賢不能舉，又不能養也，可謂悅賢乎？"

---

¹ '臺'借爲'始。'（說見楊樹達《積微居小學金石論叢》頁213-4）

because of poverty chooses a low office in preference to a high one, an office with a small salary to one with a large salary. In such a case, what would be a suitable position to choose? That of a gate-keeper or of a watchman. Confucius was once a minor official in charge of stores. He said, "All I have to do is to keep correct records." He was once a minor official in charge of sheep and cattle. He said, "All I have to do is to see to it that the sheep and cattle grow up to be strong and healthy." To talk about lofty matters when in a low position is a crime. But it is equally shameful to take one's place at the court of a prince without putting the Way into effect.'

6. Wan Chang said, 'Why is it a Gentleman does not place himself under the protection of a feudal lord?'

'He does not presume to do so,' said Mencius. 'According to the rites, only a feudal lord who has lost his state places himself under the protection of another. It would be contrary to the rites for a Gentleman to place himself under the protection of a feudal lord.'

'But if the ruler gives him rice,' said Wan Chang, 'would he accept it?'

'Yes.'

'On what principle does he accept it?'

'A prince naturally gives charity to those who have come from abroad to settle.'

'Why is it that one accepts charity but refuses what is bestowed on one?'

'One does not dare presume.'

'Why does one not dare presume?'

'A gate-keeper or a watchman accepts his wages from the authorities because he has regular duties. For one who has no regular duties to accept what is bestowed on him is for him to show a lack of gravity.'

'If it is permissible to accept gifts from the ruler. I wonder if one could count on their continuance?'

'Duke Mu frequently sent messengers to ask after Tzu-ssu, every time making gifts of meat for the tripod. Tzu-ssu was displeased and in the end ejected the messenger from the front door, faced north, knocked his head twice on the ground and refused, saying,

曰：“敢問國君欲養君子，如何斯可謂養矣？”

曰：“以君命將之，再拜稽首而受。其後廩人繼粟，庖人繼肉，
不以君命將之。子思以爲鼎肉使己僕僕爾亟拜也，非養君子之道也。
堯之於舜也，使其子九男事之，二女女焉，百官牛羊倉廩備，以養舜
於畎畝之中，後舉而加諸上位，故曰，王公之尊賢者也。”

7. 萬章曰：“敢問不見諸侯，何義也？”

    孟子曰：“在國曰市井之臣，在野曰草莽之臣，皆謂庶人。庶人
不傳質爲臣，不敢見於諸侯，禮也。”

    萬章曰：“庶人，召之役，則往役；君欲見之，召之、則不往見
之，何也？”

    曰：“往役，義也；往見，不義也。且君之欲見之也，何爲也哉？”

    曰：“爲其多聞也，爲其賢也。”

"Only now do I realize that the prince treats me in the way he treats his horses and hounds." Presumably it was only after this that no more gifts were made. If, in spite of one's claim to like good and wise men, one is able neither to raise them to office nor to take care of them, can one be truly said to like such men?'

'If the ruler of a state wishes to take care of good and wise men, how should this be done?'

'Gifts are made at the outset in the name of the prince, and the recipient accepts them after knocking his head twice on the ground. After this is done, the granary keeper presents grain and the cook presents meat, and these gifts are no longer made in the name of the prince. In Tzu-ssu's view, to make him bob up and down rendering thanks for the gifts of meat for the tripod was hardly the right way to take care of a gentleman. In the case of Yao, he sent his nine sons to serve Shun and gave him his two daughters as wives. After this, the hundred officials provided Shun with cattle and sheep and granaries for his use while he worked in the fields. And then Yao raised Shun to high office. Hence the phrase, "the honouring of the good and wise by kings and dukes".[13]

[13]Cf. V. B. 3.

7. Wan Chang said, 'May I ask on what grounds does one refuse to meet feudal lords?'

'Those who live in the capital,' said Mencius, 'are known as "subjects of the market place", while those who live in the out-skirts are known as "subjects in the wilds". In both cases the reference is to Commoners. According to the rites, a Commoner does not dare present himself to a feudal lord unless he has handed in his token of allegiance.'

'When a Commoner,' said Wan Chang, 'is summoned to corvée he goes to serve. Why then should he refuse to go when he is summoned to an audience?'

'It is right for him to go and serve, but it is not right for him to present himself. Moreover, for what reason does the prince wish to see him?'

'For the reason that he is well-informed or that he is good and wise.'

曰：“為其多聞也，則天子不召師，而況諸侯乎？為其賢也，則吾未聞欲見賢而召之也。繆公亟見於子思，曰：‘古千乘之國以友士，何如？’子思不悅，曰：“古之人有言曰，事之云乎，豈曰友之云乎？’子思之不悅也，豈不曰，‘以位，則子，君也；我，臣也；何敢與君友也？以德，則子事我者也，奚可以與我友？’千乘之君求與之友而不可得也，而況可召與？齊景公田，招虞人以旌，不至，將殺之。‘志士不忘在溝壑，勇士不忘喪其元。’孔子奚取焉？取非其招不往也。”

曰：“敢問招虞人何以？”

曰：“以皮冠，庶人以旃，士以旂，大夫以旌。以大夫之招招虞人，虞人死不敢往；以士之招招庶人，庶人豈敢往哉？況乎以不賢人之招招賢人乎？欲見賢人而不以其道，猶欲其入而閉之門也。夫義，路也；禮，門也。惟君子能由是路，出入是門也。詩云，‘周道如底，其直如矢；君子所履，小人所視。’”

'If it is for the reason that he is well-informed, even the Emperor does not summon his teacher, let alone a feudal lord. If it is for the reason that he is a good and wise man, then I have never heard of summoning such a man when one wishes to see him. Duke Mu frequently went to see Tzu-ssu. "How did kings of states with a thousand chariots in antiquity make friends with Gentleman?" he asked. Tzu-ssu was displeased. "What the ancients talked about," said he, "was serving them, not making friends with them." The reason for Tzu-ssu's displeasure was surely this. "In point of position, you are the prince and I am your subject. How dare I be friends with you? In point of virtue, it is you who ought to serve me. How can you presume to be friends with me?" If the ruler of a state with a thousand chariots cannot even hope to be friends with him, how much less can he hope to summon such a man. Duke Ching of Ch'i went hunting and summoned his gamekeeper with a pennon. The gamekeeper did not come, and the Duke was going to have him put to death. "A man whose mind is set on high ideals never forgets that he may end in a ditch; a man of valour never forgets that he may forfeit his head." What was it that Confucius found praiseworthy in the gamekeeper? His refusal to answer to a form of summons to which he was not entitled.'[14]

'May I ask with what should a gamekeeper be summoned?'

'With a leather cap. A Commoner should be summoned with a bent flag, a Gentleman with a flag with bells and a Counsellor with a pennon. When the gamekeeper was summoned with what was appropriate only to a Counsellor, he would rather die than answer the summons. How would a Commoner dare to answer when he is summoned with what is appropriate only to a Gentleman? How much more would this be the case when a good and wise man is summoned with what is appropriate only to one who is neither good nor wise! To wish to meet a good and wise man while not following the proper way is like wishing him to enter while shutting the door against him. Rightness is the road and the rites are the door. Only a gentleman can follow this road and go in and out through this door. The *Odes* say,

> The highway is like a grindstone.
> Its straightness is like an arrow.

萬章曰：“孔子，君命召，不俟駕而行；然則孔子非與？”
曰：“孔子當仕有官職，而以其官召之也。”

8   孟子謂萬章曰：“一鄉之善士斯友一鄉之善士，一國之善士斯友
一國之善士，天下之善士斯友天下之善士。以友天下之善士爲未足，
又尙論古之人。頌其詩，讀其書，不知其人，可乎？是以論其世也。
是尙友也。”

9.   齊宣王問卿。孟子曰：“王何卿之問也？”
王曰：“卿不同乎？”
曰：“不同；有貴戚之卿，有異姓之卿。”
王曰：“請問貴戚之卿。”
曰：“君有大過則諫；反覆之而不聽，則易位。”
王勃然變乎色。
曰：“王勿異也。王問臣，臣不敢不以正對。”

It is walked on by the gentleman
And Looked up to by the small man.'[15]

Wan Chang said, 'Confucius, when summoned by his prince, would set off without waiting for horses to be yoked to his carriage.[16] In that case was Confucius wrong in what he did?'

'Confucius was in office and had specific duties, and he was summoned in his official capacity.'

[14]Cf. III. B. 1.
[15]Ode 203.
[16]The *Analects of Confucius*, X. 20. Also cf. II. B. 2 where this is quoted as part of a ritual text.

8. Mencius said to Wan Chang, 'The best Gentleman of a village is in a position to make friends with the best Gentlemen in other villages; the best Gentleman in a state, with the best Gentlemen in other states; and the best Gentleman in the Empire, with the best Gentlemen in the Empire. And not content with making friends with the best Gentlemen in the Empire, he goes back in time and communes with the ancients. When one reads the poems and writings of the ancients, can it be right not to know something about them as men? Hence one tries to understand the age in which they lived. This can be described as "looking for friends in history".'

9. King Hsüan of Ch'i asked about ministers.

'What kind of ministers,' said Mencius, 'is Your Majesty asking about?'

'Are there different kinds of ministers?'

'Yes. There are ministers of royal blood and those of families other than the royal house.'

'What about ministers of royal blood?'

'If the prince made serious mistakes, they would remonstrate with him, but if repeated remonstrations fell on deaf ears, they would depose him.'

The King blenched at this.

'Your Majesty should not be surprised by my answer. Since you asked me, I dared not give you anything but the proper answer.'

王色定，然後請問異姓之卿。

曰："君有過則諫，反覆之而不聽，則去。"

Only after he had regained his composure did the King ask about ministers of families other than the royal house.

'If the prince made mistakes, they would remonstrate with him, but if repeated remonstrations fell on deaf ears, they would leave him.'

告子章句上

1.　告子曰：“性猶杞柳也，義猶桮桊也；以人性爲仁義，猶以杞柳爲桮桊。”

　　孟子曰：“子能順杞柳之性而以爲桮桊乎？將戕賊杞柳而後以爲桮桊也？如將戕賊杞柳而以爲桮桊，則亦將戕賊人以爲仁義與？率天下之人而禍仁義者，必子之言夫！”

2.　告子曰：“性猶湍水也，決諸東方則東流，決諸西方則西流。人性之無分於善不善也，猶水之無分於東西也。”

　　孟子曰：“水信無分於東西，無分於上下乎？人性之善也，猶水之就下也。人無有不善，水無有不下。今夫水，搏而躍之，可使過顙；激而行之，可使在山。是豈水之性哉？其勢則然也。人之可使爲不善，其性亦猶是也。”

3.　告子曰：“生之謂性。”

　　孟子曰：“生之謂性也，猶白之謂白與？”

　　曰：“然。”

　　“白羽之白也，猶白雪之白；白雪之白猶白玉之白與？”

　　曰：“然。”

　　“然則犬之性猶牛之性，牛之性猶人之性與？”

BOOK VI · PART A

1. Kao Tzu said, 'Human nature is like the *ch'i* willow. Dutifulness is like cups and bowls. To make morality out of human nature is like making cups and bowls out of the willow.'

'Can you,' said Mencius, 'make cups and bowls by following the nature of the willow? Or must you mutilate the willow before you can make it into cups and bowls? If you have to mutilate the willow to make it into cups and bowls, must you, then, also mutilate a man to make him moral? Surely it will be these words of yours men in the world will follow in bringing disaster upon morality.'

2. Kao Tzu said, 'Human nature is like whirling water. Give it an outlet in the east and it will flow east; give it an outlet in the west and it will flow west. Human nature does not show any preference for either good or bad just as water does not show any preference for either east or west.'

'It certainly is the case,' said Mencius, 'that water does not show any preference for either east or west, but does it show the same indifference to high and low? Human nature is good just as water seeks low ground. There is no man who is not good; there is no water that does not flow downwards.

'Now in the case of water, by splashing it one can make it shoot up higher than one's forehead, and by forcing it one can make it stay on a hill. How can that be the nature of water? It is the circumstances being what they are. That man can be made bad shows that his nature is no different from that of water in this respect.'

3. Kao Tzu said, 'The inborn is what is meant by "nature".'

'Is that,' said Mencius, 'the same as "white is what is meant by 'white' "?'[1]

'Yes.'

'Is the whiteness of white feathers the same as the whiteness of white snow and the whiteness of white snow the same as the whiteness of white jade?'

'Yes.'

4.　告子曰：“食色，性也。仁，內也，非外也；義，外也，非內也。”
　　孟子曰：“何以謂仁內義外也？”
　　曰：“彼長而我長之，非有長於我也；猶彼白而我白之，從其白
於外也，故謂之外也。”
　　曰：“異於白，〔白[1]〕馬之白也，無以異於白人之白也；不識長
馬之長也，無以異於長人之長與？且謂長者義乎？長之者義乎？”
　　曰：“吾弟則愛之，秦人之弟則不愛也，是以我爲悅[2]者也，故謂
之內。長楚人之長，亦長吾之長，是以長爲悅[2]者也，故謂之外也。”
　　曰：“耆秦人之炙，無以異於耆吾炙，夫物則亦有然者也，然則
耆炙亦有外與？”

[1] 按文義‘白’字當重，今據補。（說見俞樾《羣經平議》（《續皇清經解》卷千三百
九十四，頁十七。））
[2] 兩‘悅’字並讀爲‘說’。

5.　孟季子問公都子曰：“何以謂義內也？”
　　曰：“行吾敬，故謂之內也。”
　　“鄉人長於伯兄一歲，則誰敬？”
　　曰：“敬兄。”

'In that case, is the nature of a hound the same as the nature of an ox and the nature of an ox the same as the nature of a man?'

[1] In *'sheng chih wei hsing'* ('the inborn is what is meant by "nature" '), the two words *'sheng'* and *'hsing'*, though slightly different in pronunciation, were probably written by the same character in Mencius' time. This would make the statement at least tautological in written form and so parallel to *'pai chih wei pai'* ('white is what is meant by "white" ').

4. Kao Tzu said, 'Appetite for food and sex is nature. Benevolence is internal, not external; rightness is external, not internal.'

'Why do you say,' said Mencius, 'that benevolence is internal and rightness is external?'

'That man there is old and I treat him as elder. He owes nothing of his elderliness to me, just as in treating him as white because he is white I only do so because of his whiteness which is external to me. That is why I call it external.'

'The case of rightness is different from that of whiteness. "Treating as white" is the same whether one is treating a horse as white or a man as white. But I wonder if you would think that "treating as old" is the same whether one is treating a horse as old or a man as elder? Furthermore, is it the one who is old that is dutiful, or is it the one who treats him as elder that is dutiful?'

'My brother I love, but the brother of a man from Ch'in I do not love. This means that the explanation lies in me. Hence I call it internal. Treating an elder of a man from Ch'u as elder is no different from treating an elder of my own family as elder. This means that the explanation lies in their elderliness. Hence I call it external.'

'My enjoyment of the roast provided by a man from Ch'in is no different from my enjoyment of my own roast. Even with inanimate things we can find cases similar to the one under discussion. Are we, then, to say that there is something external even in the enjoyment of roast?'

5. Meng Chi-tzu asked Kung-tu Tzu, 'Why do you say that rightness is internal?'

'It is the respect in me that is being put into effect. That is why I say it is internal.'

'If a man from your village is a year older than your eldest

"酌則誰先？"

曰："先酌鄉人。"

"所敬在此，所長在彼，果在外，非由內也。"

公都子不能答，以告孟子。

孟子曰："'敬叔父乎？敬弟乎？'彼將曰，'敬叔父。'曰，'弟為尸，則誰敬？'彼將曰，'敬弟。'子曰，'惡在其敬叔父也？'彼將曰，'在位故也。'子亦曰，'在位故也。庸敬在兄，斯須之敬在鄉人。'"

季子聞之，曰："敬叔父則敬，敬弟則敬，果在外，非由內也。"

公都子曰："冬日則飲湯，夏日則飲水，然則飲食亦在外也？"

6. 公都子曰："告子曰：'性無善無不善也。'或曰：'性可以為善，可以為不善；是故文武興，則民好善；幽厲興，則民好暴。'或曰：'有性善，有性不善；是故以堯為君而有象；以瞽瞍為父而有舜；以紂為兄之子，且以為君，而有微子啟、王子比干。'今曰'性善'，然則彼皆非與？"

brother, which do you respect?'

'My brother.'

'In filling their cups with wine,[2] which do you give precedence to?'

'The man from my village.'

'The one you respect is the former; the one you treat as elder is the latter. This shows that it is in fact external, not internal.'

Kung-tu Tzu was unable to find an answer and gave an account of the discussion to Mencius.

Mencius said, '[Ask him,] "Which do you respect, your uncle or your younger brother?" He will say, "My uncle." "When your younger brother is impersonating an ancestor at a sacrifice, then which do you respect?" He will say, "My younger brother." You ask him, "What has happened to your respect for your uncle?" He will say, "It is because of the position my younger brother occupies." You can then say, "[In the case of the man from my village] it is also because of the position he occupies. Normal respect is due to my elder brother; temporary respect is due to the man from my village." '

When Meng Chi-tzu heard this, he said, 'It is the same respect whether I am respecting my uncle or my younger brother. It is, as I have said, external and does not come from within.'

'In winter,' said Kung-tu Tzu, 'one drinks hot water, in summer cold. Does that mean that even food and drink can be a matter of what is external?'

[2] i.e., at a village gathering where precedence is in accordance with seniority.

6. Kung-tu Tzu said, 'Kao Tzu said, "There is neither good nor bad in human nature," but others say, "Human nature can become good or it can become bad, and that is why with the rise of King Wen and King Wu, the people were given to goodness, while with the rise of King Yu and King Li, they were given to cruelty." Then there are others who say, "There are those who are good by nature, and there are those who are bad by nature. For this reason, Hsiang could have Yao as prince, and Shun could have the Blind Man as father, and Ch'i, Viscount of Wei and Prince Pi Kan could have Tchou as nephew as well as sovereign."[3] Now you say human

孟子曰："乃若其情，則可以爲善矣，乃所謂善也。若夫爲不善，非才之罪也。惻隱之心，人皆有之；羞惡之心，人皆有之；恭敬之心，人皆有之；是非之心，人皆有之。惻隱之心，仁也；羞惡之心，義也；恭敬之心，禮也；是非之心，智也。仁義禮智，非由外鑠[1]我也，我固有之也，弗思耳矣。故曰，'求則得之，舍則失之。'或相倍蓰而無筭者，不能盡其才者也。詩曰，'天生蒸民，有物有則。民之秉彝，好是懿德。'孔子曰：'爲此詩者，其知道乎！故有物必有則；民之秉彝也，故好是懿德。'"

[1] 按《爾雅・釋詁》云：'鑠，美也。'（《爾雅注疏》卷二頁三下），又《文選》注引郭璞《方言注》云：'鑠，言光明也。'（《文選》卷五十八頁二下）

7.　孟子曰："富歲，子弟多賴；凶歲，子弟多暴，非天之降才爾殊也，其所以陷溺其心者然也。今夫麰麥，播種而耰之，其地同，樹之時又同，浡然而生，至於日至之時，皆熟矣。雖有不同，則地有肥磽，雨露之養、人事之不齊也。故凡同類者，舉相似也，何獨至於人而疑

nature is good. Does this mean that all the others are mistaken?'

'As far as what is genuinely in him is concerned, a man is capable of becoming good,' said Mencius. 'That is what I mean by good. As for his becoming bad, that is not the fault of his native endowment. The heart of compassion is possessed by all men alike; likewise the heart of shame, the heart of respect, and the heart of right and wrong. The heart of compassion pertains to benevolence, the heart of shame to dutifulness, the heart of respect to the observance of the rites, and the heart of right and wrong to wisdom.[4] Benevolence, dutifulness, observance of the rites, and wisdom do not give me a lustre from the outside, they are in me originally. Only this has never dawned on me. That is why it is said, "Seek and you will find it; let go and you will lose it."[5] There are cases where one man is twice, five times or countless times better than another man, but this is only because there are people who fail to make the best of their native endowment. The Odes say,

o It is only that we no longer heed Meng (Graham) 弗思耳矣

> Heaven produces the teeming masses,
> And where there is a thing there is a norm.
> If the people held on to their constant nature,
> They would be drawn to superior virtue.[6]

Confucius commented, "The author of this poem must have had knowledge of the Way." Thus where there is a thing there is a norm, and because the people hold on to their constant nature they are drawn to superior virtue.'

[3] According to the *Shi chi* (Records of the Historian), (1607) the Viscount of Wei was an elder brother of Tchou, and son of a concubine of low rank. For this reason, it has been pointed out that the description of having Tchou as nephew applies only to Pi Kan. Cf. the coupling of the name of Chi with that of Yü in IV. B. 29.

[4] Cf. II. A. 6.

[5] Cf. VII. A. 3.

[6] Ode 260.

7. Mencius said, 'In good years the young men are mostly lazy, while in bad years they are mostly violent. Heaven has not sent down men whose endowment differs so greatly. The difference is due to what ensnares their hearts. Take the barley for example. Sow the seeds and cover them with soil. The place is the same and

之？聖人，與我同類者。故龍子曰：'不知足而爲屨，我知其不爲蕢
也。'屨之相似，天下之足同也。口之於味，有同耆也；易牙先得我
口之所耆者也。如使口之於味也，其性與人殊，若犬馬之與我不同類
也，則天下何耆皆從易牙之於味也？至於味，天下期於易牙，是天下
之口相似也。惟耳亦然。至於聲，天下期於師曠，是天下之耳相似也。
惟目亦然。至於子都，天下莫不知其姣也。不知子都之姣者，無目者
也。故曰，口之於味也，有同耆焉；耳之於聲也，有同聽焉；目之於
色也，有同美焉。至於心，獨無所同然乎？心之所同然者何也？謂理
也，義也。聖人先得我心之所同然耳。故理義之悅我心，猶芻豢之悅
我口。"

8.　孟子曰："牛山之木嘗美矣，以其郊於大國也，斧斤伐之，可以
爲美乎？是其日夜之所息，雨露之所潤，非無萌蘗之生焉，牛羊又從
而牧之，是以若彼濯濯也。人見其濯濯也，以爲未嘗有材焉，此豈山
之性也哉？雖存乎人者，豈無仁義之心哉？其所以放其良心者，亦猶
斧斤之於木也，旦旦而伐之，可以爲美乎？其日夜之所息，平旦之氣，
其好惡與人相近也者幾希，則其旦晝之所爲，有梏亡之矣。梏之反覆，
則其夜氣不足以存；夜氣不足以存，則其違禽獸不遠矣。人見其禽獸
也，而以爲未嘗有才焉者，是豈人之情也哉？故苟得其養，無物不長；
苟失其養，無物不消。孔子曰：'操則存，舍則亡；出入無時，莫知
其鄉。'惟心之謂與？"

the time of sowing is also the same. The plants shoot up and by the summer solstice they all ripen. If there is any unevenness, it is because the soil varies in richness and there is no uniformity in the benefit of rain and dew and the amount of human effort devoted to tending it. Now things of the same kind are all alike. Why should we have doubts when it comes to man? The sage and I are of the same kind. Thus Lung Tzu said, "When someone makes a shoe for a foot he has not seen, I am sure he will not produce a basket." All shoes are alike because all feet are alike. All palates show the same preferences in taste. Yi Ya was simply the man first to discover what would be pleasing to my palate. Were the nature of taste to vary from man to man in the same way as horses and hounds differ from me in kind, then how does it come about that all palates in the world follow the preferences of Yi Ya? The fact that in taste the whole world looks to Yi Ya shows that all palates are alike. It is the same also with the ear. The fact that in sound the whole world looks to Shih K'uang shows that all ears are alike. It is the same also with the eye. The whole world appreciates the good looks of Tzu-tu; whoever does not is blind. Hence it is said: all palates have the same preference in taste; all ears in sound; all eyes in beauty. Should hearts prove to be an exception by possessing nothing in common? What is it, then, that is common to all hearts? Reason and rightness. The sage is simply the man first to discover this common element in my heart. Thus reason and rightness please my heart in the same way as meat pleases my palate.'

8. Mencius said, 'There was a time when the trees were luxuriant on the Ox Mountain, but as it is on the outskirts of a great metropolis, the trees are constantly lopped by axes. Is it any wonder that they are no longer fine? With the respite they get in the day and in the night, and the moistening by the rain and dew, there is certainly no lack of new shoots coming out, but then the cattle and sheep come to graze upon the mountain. That is why it is as bald as it is. People, seeing only its baldness, tend to think that it never had any trees. But can this possibly be the nature of a mountain? Can what is in man be completely lacking in moral inclinations? A man's letting go of his true heart is like the case of the trees and the axes. When the trees are lopped day after day, is

9.　孟子曰：“無或乎王之不智也。雖有天下易生之物也，一日暴之，十日寒之，未有能生者也。吾見亦罕矣，吾退而寒之者至矣，吾如有萌焉何哉？今夫弈之爲數，小數也；不專心致志，則不得也。弈秋，通國之善弈者也。使弈秋誨二人弈，其一人專心致志，惟弈秋之爲聽。一人雖聽之，一心以爲有鴻鵠將至，思援弓繳而射之，雖與之俱學，弗若之矣。爲是其智弗若與？曰：非然也。”

10.　孟子曰：“魚，我所欲也，熊掌亦我所欲也；二者不可得兼，舍魚而取熊掌者也。生亦我所欲也，義亦我所欲也；二者不可得兼，舍

it any wonder that they are no longer fine? If, in spite of the respite a man gets in the day and in the night and of the effect of the morning air on him, scarcely any of his likes and dislikes resembles those of other men, it is because what he does in the course of the day once again dissipates what he has gained. If this dissipation happens repeatedly, then the influence of the air in the night will no longer be able to preserve what was originally in him, and when that happens, the man is not far removed from an animal. Others, seeing his resemblance to an animal, will be led to think that he never had any native endowment. But can that be what a man is genuinely like? Hence, given the right nourishment there is nothing that will not grow, while deprived of it there is nothing that will not wither away. Confucius said, "Hold on to it and it will remain; let go of it and it will disappear. One never knows the time it comes or goes, neither does one know the direction." It is perhaps to the heart this refers.'

9. Mencius said, 'Do not be puzzled by the King's lack of wisdom. Even a plant that grows most readily will not survive if it is placed in the sun for one day and exposed to the cold for ten. It is very rarely that I have an opportunity of seeing the King, and as soon as I leave, those who expose him to the cold arrive on the scene. What can I do with the few new shoots that come out? Now take *yi*,[7] which is only an art of little consequence. Yet if one does not give one's whole mind to it, one will never master it. Yi Ch'iu is the best player in the whole country. Get him to teach two people to play, one of whom concentrates his mind on the game and listens only to what Yi Ch'iu has to say, while the other, though he listens, dreams of an approaching swan and wants to take up his bow and corded arrow to shoot at it. Now even though this man shares the lessons with the first, he will never be as good. Is this because he is less clever? The answer is, "No." '

[7]The ancient name for the game of *wei ch'i*, better known in the West by the name *go* which is simply the Japanese pronunciation of the Chinese word *ch'i*. This game is also mentioned in IV. B. 30.

10. Mencius said, 'Fish is what I want; bear's palm is also what I want. If I cannot have both, I would rather take bear's palm than

生而取義者也。生亦我所欲，所欲有甚於生者，故不爲苟得也；死亦
我所惡，所惡有甚於死者，故患有所不辟也。如使人之所欲莫甚於生，
則凡可以得生者，何不用也？使人之所惡莫甚於死者，則凡可以辟患
者，何不爲也？由是則生而有不用也，由是則可以辟患而有不爲也，
是故所欲有甚於生者，所惡有甚於死者。非獨賢者有是心也，人皆有
之，賢者能勿喪耳。一簞食，一豆羹，得之則生，弗得則死，嘑爾而
與之，行道之人弗受；蹴爾而與之，乞人不屑也；萬鍾則不辯禮義而
受之。萬鍾於我何加焉？爲宮室之美、妻妾之奉、所識窮乏者得我與？
鄉爲身死而不受，今爲宮室之美爲之；鄉爲身死而不受，今爲妻妾之
奉爲之；鄉爲身死而不受，今爲所識窮乏者得我而爲之，是亦不可以
已乎？此之謂失其本心。”

11.[1] 孟子曰：“仁，人心也；義，人路也。舍其路而弗由，放其心
而不知求，哀哉！人有雞犬放，則知求之；有放心而不知求。學問之
道無他，求其放心而已矣。”

fish. Life is what I want; dutifulness is also what I want. If I cannot *choice* have both, I would rather take dutifulness than life. On the one hand, though life is what I want, there is something I want more than life. That is why I do not cling to life at all costs. On the other hand, though death is what I loathe, there is something I loathe more than death. That is why there are troubles I do not avoid. If there is nothing a man wants more than life, then why should he have scruples about any means, so long as it will serve to keep him alive? If there is nothing a man loathes more than death, then why should he have scruples about any means, so long as it helps him to avoid trouble? Yet there are ways of remaining alive and ways of avoiding death to which a man will not resort. In other words, there are things a man wants more than life and there are also things he loathes more than death. This is an attitude not confined to the moral man but common to all men. The moral man simply never loses it.

'Here is a basketful of rice and a bowlful of soup. Getting them will mean life; not getting them will mean death. When these are given with abuse, even a wayfarer would not accept them; when these are given after being trampled upon, even a beggar would not accept them. Yet when it comes to ten thousand bushels of grain *gift* one is supposed to accept without asking if it is in accordance with the rites or if it is right to do so. What benefit are ten thousand bushels of grain to me? [Do I accept them] for the sake of beautiful houses, the enjoyment of wives and concubines, or for the sake of the gratitude my needy acquaintances will show me? What I would not accept in the first instance when it was a matter of life and death I now accept for the sake of beautiful houses; what I would not accept when it was a matter of life and death I now accept for the enjoyment of wives and concubines; what I would not accept when it was a matter of life and death I now accept for the sake of the gratitude my needy acquaintances will show me. Is there no way of putting a stop to this? This way of thinking is known as losing one's original heart.'

11. Mencius said, 'Benevolence is the heart of man, and rightness his road. Sad it is indeed when a man gives up the right road instead of following it and allows his heart to stray without enough sense

[1]《韓詩外傳》（卷四頁十五）引此章云：'孟子曰：仁，人心也；義，人路也。舍
其路弗由，放其心而弗求。人有雞犬放，則知求之；有放心而不知求；其於心爲
不若雞犬哉！不知類之甚矣！悲夫！終亦必亡而已矣。故學問之道無他焉，求其放
心而已。' 多 '其於心爲不若雞犬哉！不知類之甚矣！悲夫！終亦必亡而已矣，'
與下章 '此之謂不知類' 及十章 '終亦必亡而已矣，' 十八章 '亦終亦必亡而已矣'
文例相同，疑今本《孟子》誤脫。

12. 孟子曰："今有無名之指屈而不信，非疾痛害事也，如有能信之
者，則不遠秦楚之路，爲指之不若人也。指不若人，則知惡之；心不
若人，則不知惡，此之謂不知類也。"

13. 孟子曰："拱把之桐梓，人苟欲生之，皆知所以養之者。至於身，
而不知所以養之者，豈愛身不若桐梓哉？弗思甚也。"

14. 孟子曰："人之於身也，兼所愛。兼所愛，則兼所養也。無尺寸
之膚不愛焉，則無尺寸之膚不養也。所以考其善不善者，豈有他哉？
於己取之而已矣。體有貴賤，有大小。無以小害大，無以賤害貴。養
其小者爲小人，養其大者爲大人。今有場師，舍其梧檟，養其樲棘，
則爲賤場師焉。養其一指而失其肩背，而不知也，則爲狼疾人也。飲
食之人，則人賤之矣，爲其養小以失大也。飲食之人無有失也，則口
腹豈適爲尺寸之膚哉？"

to go after it. When his chickens and dogs stray, he has sense enough to go after them, but not when his heart strays.[8] The sole concern of learning is to go after this strayed heart. That is all.'

[8] As quoted in the *Han shih wai chuan* 4/27, this goes on as follows: 'Does he think less of his heart than of his chickens and dogs? This is an extreme case of a lack of knowledge of priorities. How sad! In the end such a man is sure only to perish.' This further passage must have dropped out of the present text by accident.

12. Mencius said, 'Now if one's third finger is bent and cannot stretch straight, though this neither causes any pain nor impairs the use of the hand, one would think nothing of the distance between Ch'in and Ch'u if someone able to straighten it could be found. This is because one's finger is inferior to other people's. When one's finger is inferior to other people's, one has sense enough to resent it, but not when one's heart is inferior. This is what is called a lack of knowledge of priorities.'

13. Mencius said, 'Even with a *t'ung* or a *tzu* tree one or two spans thick, anyone wishing to keep it alive will know how it should be tended, yet when it comes to one's own person, one does not know how to tend it. Surely one does not love one's person any less than the *t'ung* or the *tzu*? This is unthinking to the highest degree.'

14. Mencius said, 'A man loves all parts of his person without discrimination. As he loves them all without discrimination, he nurtures them all without discrimination. If there is not one foot or one inch of his skin that he does not love, then there is not one foot or one inch that he does not nurture. Is there any other way of telling whether what a man does is good or bad than by the choice he makes? The parts of the person differ in value and importance. Never harm the parts of greater importance for the sake of those of smaller importance, or the more valuable for the sake of the less valuable. He who nurtures the parts of smaller importance is a small man; he who nurtures the parts of greater importance is a great man. Now consider a gardener. If he tends the common trees, while neglecting the valuable ones, then he is a

15. 公都子問曰：“鈞是人也，或爲大人，或爲小人，何也？”
　　孟子曰：“從其大體爲大人，從其小體爲小人。”
　　曰：“鈞是人也，或從其大體，或從其小體，何也？”
　　曰：“耳目之官不思，而蔽於物。物交物，則引之而已矣。心之官則思，思則得之，不思則不得也。此天之所與我者。先立乎其大者，則其小者不能奪也。此爲大人而已矣。”

16. 孟子曰：“有天爵者，有人爵者。仁義忠信，樂善不倦，此天爵也；公卿大夫，此人爵也。古之人脩其天爵，而人爵從之。今之人脩其天爵，以要人爵；既得人爵，而棄其天爵，則惑之甚者也，終亦必亡而已矣。”

bad gardener. A man who takes care of one finger to the detriment of his shoulder and back without realizing his mistake is a muddled man. A man who cares only about food and drink is despised by others because he takes care of the parts of smaller importance to the detriment of the parts of greater importance. If a man who cares about food and drink can do so without neglecting any other part of his person, then his mouth and belly are much more than just a foot or an inch of his skin.'

15. Kung-tu Tzu asked, 'Though equally human, why are some men greater than others?'

'He who is guided by the interests of the parts of his person that are of greater importance is a great man; he who is guided by the interests of the parts of his person that are of smaller importance is a small man.'

'Though equally human, why are some men guided one way and others guided another way?'

'The organs of hearing and sight are unable to think and can be misled by external things. When one thing acts on another, all it does is to attract it. The organ of the heart can think. But it will find the answer only if it does think; otherwise, it will not find the answer. This is what Heaven has given me. If one makes one's stand on what is of greater importance in the first instance, what is of smaller importance cannot displace it. In this way, one cannot but be a great man.'

16. Mencius said, 'There are honours bestowed by Heaven, and there are honours bestowed by man. Benevolence, dutifulness, conscientiousness, truthfulness to one's word, unflagging delight in what is good,—these are honours bestowed by Heaven. The position of a Ducal Minister, a Minister, or a Counsellor is an honour bestowed by man. Men of antiquity bent their efforts towards acquiring honours bestowed by Heaven, and honours bestowed by man followed as a matter of course. Men of today bend their efforts towards acquiring honours bestowed by Heaven in order to win honours bestowed by man, and once the latter is won they discard the former. Such men are deluded to the extreme, and in the end are sure only to perish.'

17. 孟子曰：“欲貴者，人之同心也。人人有貴於己者，弗思耳矣。人之所貴者，非良貴也。趙孟之所貴，趙孟能賤之。詩云：‘既醉以酒，既飽以德。’言飽乎仁義也，所以不願人之膏粱之味也；令聞廣譽施於身，所以不願人之文繡也。”

18. 孟子曰：“仁之勝不仁也，猶水之勝火。今之爲仁者，猶以一杯水救一車薪之火也；不熄，則謂之水不勝火，此又與於不仁之甚者也，亦終必亡而已矣。”

19. 孟子曰：“五穀者，種之美者也；苟爲不熟，不如荑稗。夫仁，亦在乎熟之而已矣。”

20. 孟子曰：“羿之敎人射，必志於彀；學者亦必志於彀。大匠誨人必以規矩，學者亦必以規矩。”

17. Mencius said, 'All men share the same desire to be exalted. But as a matter of fact, every man has in him that which is exalted. The fact simply never dawned on him. What man exalts is not truly exalted. Those Chao Meng exalts, Chao Meng can also humble. The *Ode* says,

> Having filled us with drink,
> Having filled us with virtue, . . .[9]

The point is that, being filled with moral virtue, one does not envy other people's enjoyment of fine food and, enjoying a fine and extensive reputation, one does not envy other people's fineries.'

[9] Ode 247.

18. Mencius said, 'Benevolence overcomes cruelty just as water overcomes fire. Those who practise benevolence today are comparable to someone trying to put out a cartload of burning firewood with a cupful of water. When they fail to succeed, they say water cannot overcome fire. For a man to do this is for him to place himself on the side of those who are cruel to the extreme, and in the end he is sure only to perish.'

19. Mencius said, 'The five types of grain are the best of plants, yet if they are not ripe they are worse than the wild varieties. With benevolence the point, too, lies in seeing to its being ripe.'

20. Mencius said, 'In teaching others archery, Yi naturally aims at drawing the bow to the full, and the student naturally also aims at drawing the bow to the full. In teaching others, the master carpenter naturally does so by means of compasses and square, and the student naturally also learns by means of compasses and square.'

告子章句下

1.　任人有問屋廬子曰：“禮與食孰重？”

　　曰：“禮重。”

　　“色與禮孰重？”

　　曰：“禮重。”

　　曰：“以禮食，則飢而死；不以禮食，則得食，必以禮乎？親迎，則不得妻；不親迎，則得妻，必親迎乎？”

　　屋廬子不能對，明日之鄒以告孟子。

　　孟子曰：“於答是也，何有？不揣其本，而齊其末，方寸之木可使高於岑樓。金重於羽者，豈謂一鉤金與一輿羽之謂哉？取食之重者與禮之輕者而比之，奚翅食重？取色之重者與禮之輕者而比之，奚翅色重？往應之曰：‘紾兄之臂而奪之食，則得食；不紾，則不得食，則將紾之乎？踰東家牆而摟其處子，則得妻；不摟，則不得妻；則將摟之乎？’”

2.　曹交問曰：“人皆可以爲堯舜，有諸？”

　　孟子曰：“然。”

BOOK VI · PART B

1. A man from Jen asked Wu-lu Tzu, 'Which is more important, the rites or food?'

'The rites.'

'Which is more important, the rites or sex?'

'The rites.'

'Suppose you would starve to death if you insisted on the observance of the rites, but would manage to get something to eat if you did not. Would you still insist on their observance? Again, suppose you would not get a wife if you insisted on the observance of *ch'in ying*,[1] but would get one if you did not. Would you still insist on its observance?'

Wu-lu Tzu was unable to answer. The following day he went to Tsou and gave an account of the discussion to Mencius.

'What difficulty is there,' said Mencius, 'in answering this? If you bring the tips to the same level without measuring the difference in the bases, you can make a piece of wood an inch long reach a greater height than a tall building. In saying that gold is heavier than feather, surely one is not referring to the amount of gold in a clasp and a whole cartload of feathers? If you compare a case where food is important with a case where the rite is inconsequential, then the greater importance of food is not the only absurd conclusion you can draw. Similarly with sex. Go and reply to the questioner in this way, "Suppose you would manage to get something to eat if you took the food from your elder brother by twisting his arm, but would not get it if you did not. Would you twist his arm? Again, suppose you would get a wife if you climbed over the wall of your neighbour on the east side and dragged away the daughter of the house by force, but would not if you did not. Would you drag her away by force?" '

[1] This is the part of the marriage rites where the groom goes to the home of the bride to fetch her.

2. Ts'ao Chiao asked, 'Is it true that all men are capable of becoming a Yao or a Shun?'

'Yes,' said Mencius.

　　"交聞文王十尺，湯九尺，今交九尺四寸以長，食粟而已，如何則可？"

　　曰："奚有於是？亦爲之而已矣。有人於此，力不能勝一匹雛，則爲無力人矣；今曰舉百鈞，則爲有力人矣。然則舉烏獲之任，是亦爲烏獲而已矣。夫人豈以不勝爲患哉？弗爲耳。徐行後長者謂之弟，疾行先長者謂之不弟。夫徐行者，豈人所不能哉？所不爲也。堯舜之道，孝悌而已矣。子服堯之服，誦堯之言，行堯之行，是堯而已矣。子服桀之服，誦桀之言，行桀之行，是桀而已矣。"

　　曰："交得見於鄒君，可以假館，願留而受業於門。"

　　曰："夫道若大路然，豈難知哉？人病不求耳。子歸而求之，有餘師。"

3.　　公孫丑問曰："高子曰：小弁，小人之詩也。"

　　孟子曰："何以言之？"

　　曰："怨。"

　　曰："固哉，高叟之爲詩也！有人於此，越人關弓而射之，則己談笑而道之；無他，疏之也。其兄關弓而射之，則己垂涕泣而道之；無他，戚之也。小弁之怨，親親也。親親，仁也。固矣夫高叟之爲詩也！"

'I heard that King Wen was ten foot[2] tall, while T'ang was nine. Now I am a little more than nine foot four inches, yet all I can do is to eat rice. What should I do?'

'What difficulty is there? All you have to do is to make an effort. Here is a man who cannot lift a chicken. He is, indeed, a weak man. Now if he were to lift a ton, then he would, indeed, be a strong man. In other words, whoever can lift the same weight as Wu Huo[3] is himself a Wu Huo. The trouble with a man is surely not his lack of sufficient strength, but his refusal to make the effort. One who walks slowly, keeping behind his elders, is considered a well-mannered younger brother. One who walks quickly, overtaking his elders, is considered an ill-mannered younger brother. Walking slowly is surely not beyond the ability of any man. It is simply a matter of his not making the effort. The way of Yao and Shun is simply to be a good son and a good younger brother. If you wear the clothes of Yao, speak the words of Yao and behave the way Yao behaved, then you *are* a Yao. On the other hand, if you wear the clothes of Chieh, speak the words of Chieh and behave the way Chieh behaved, then you *are* a Chieh. That is all.'

'If the ruler of Tsou receives me and I am given a place to lodge, then I should like to stay and be a disciple of yours.'

'The Way is like a wide road. It is not at all difficult to find. The trouble with people is simply that they do not look for it. You go home and look for it and there will be teachers enough for you.'

[2] The Chinese foot in this period was, needless to say, much shorter than the English foot.
[3] A byword for a strong man.

3. Kung-sun Ch'ou said, 'According to Kau Tzu, the *Hsiao p'an*[4] is the ode of a petty man.'

'Why did he say so?'

'Because there is a plaintive note.'

'How rigid was old Master Kau in his interpretation of the *Odes*! Here is a man. If a man from Yüeh bends his bow to take a shot at him, one can recount the incident in a light-hearted manner. The reason is simply that one feels no concern for the man from Yüeh. If it had been one's own elder brother who did this, then one

曰：“凱風何以不怨？”

曰：“凱風，親之過小者也；小弁，親之過大者也。親之過大而不怨，是愈疏也；親之過小而怨，是不可磯也。愈疏，不孝也；不可磯，亦不孝也。孔子曰：‘舜其至孝矣，五十而慕。’”

4.　宋牼將之楚，孟子遇於石丘，曰：“先生將何之？”

曰：“吾聞秦楚構兵，我將見楚王說而罷之。楚王不悅，我將見秦王說而罷之。二王我將有所遇焉。”

曰：“軻也請無問其詳，願聞其指。說之將何如？”

曰：“我將言其不利也。”

曰：“先生之志則大矣，先生之號則不可。先生以利說秦楚之王，秦楚之王悅於利，以罷三軍之師，是三軍之士樂罷而悅於利也。為人臣者懷利以事其君，為人子者懷利以事其父，為人弟者懷利以事其兄，是君臣、父子、兄弟終去仁義，懷利以相接，然而不亡者，未之有也。先生以仁義說秦楚之王，秦楚之王悅於仁義，以罷三軍之師，是三軍之士樂罷而悅於仁義也。為人臣者懷仁義以事其君，為人子者懷仁義以事其父，為人弟者懷仁義以事其兄，是君臣、父子、兄弟去利，懷仁義以相接也，然而不王者，未之有也。何必曰利？”

would be in tears while recounting the incident. The reason for the difference is simply that one feels concern for one's brother. The plaintive note is due to the poet's feeling of intimate concern for his parent. To feel this is benevolence. How rigid was old Master Kau in his interpretation of poetry!'

'Why is there no plaintive note in the *K'ai feng*?'[5]

'The *K'ai feng* deals with a minor wrong committed by the parent while the *Hsiao p'an* deals with a major wrong. Not to complain about a major wrong committed by one's parent is to feel insufficient concern; on the other hand, to complain about a minor wrong is to react too violently. Insufficient concern and too violent a reaction are both actions of a bad son. Confucius said, "Shun was the highest example of a good son. At the age of fifty, he still yearned for his parents." '[6]

[4] Ode 197.
[5] Ode 32.
[6] Cf. V. A. 1.

4. Sung K'eng was on his way to Ch'u. Mencius, meeting him at Shih Ch'iu, asked him, 'Where are you going, sir?'

'I heard that hostilities had broken out between Ch'in and Ch'u. I am going to see the king of Ch'u and try to persuade him to bring an end to them. If I fail to find favour with the king of Ch'u I shall go to see the king of Ch'in and try to persuade him instead. I hope I shall have success with one or other of the two kings.'

'I do not wish to know the details, but may I ask about the gist of your argument? How are you going to persuade the kings?'

'I shall explain to them the unprofitability of war.'

'Your purpose is lofty indeed, but your slogan is wrong. If you place profit before the kings of Ch'in and Ch'u, and they call off their armies because they are drawn to profit, then it means that the soldiers in their armies retire because they are drawn to profit. If a subject, in serving his prince, cherished the profit motive, and a son, in serving his father, and a younger brother, in serving his elder brother, did likewise, then it would mean that in their mutual relations, prince and subject, father and son, elder brother and younger brother, all cherished the profit motive to the total exclusion of morality. The prince of such a state is sure to perish.

5. 孟子居鄒，季任爲任處守，以幣交，受之而不報。處於平陸，儲子爲相，以幣交，受之而不報。他日，由鄒之任，見季子；由平陸之齊，不見儲子。屋廬子喜曰：“連得間矣。”問曰：“夫子之任，見季子；之齊，不見儲子，爲其爲相與？”

曰：“非也；書曰：‘享多儀，儀不及物曰不享，惟不役志于享。’爲其不成享也。”

屋廬子悅。或問之。屋廬子曰：“季子不得之鄒，儲子得之平陸。”

6. 淳于髡曰：“先名實者，爲人也；後名實者，自爲也[1]。夫子在三卿之中，名實未加於上下而去之，仁者固如此乎？”

---

[1]《說苑》引此章作‘先名實者，爲人者也；後名實者，自爲者也。’（卷十八頁五上）‘爲人’‘自爲’下並有‘者’字，文義較完。

仁義

If, on the other hand, you placed morality before the kings of Ch'in and Ch'u and they called off their armies because they were drawn to morality, then it would mean that the soldiers in their armies retired because they were drawn to morality. If a subject, in serving his prince, cherished morality, and a son, in serving his elder brother, did likewise, then it would mean that in their mutual relations, prince and subject, father and son, elder brother and younger brother, all cherished morality to the exclusion of profit. The prince of such a state is sure to become a true King. What is the point of mentioning the word "profit"?'

5. When Mencius was staying in Tsou, Chi Jen, who was acting for the Lord of Jen, sought his friendship by sending a gift. Mencius accepted it without any gesture in return. When Mencius was in P'ing Lu, Ch'u Tzu, who was a minister of Ch'i, also sought his friendship by sending a gift. Mencius, again, accepted it without any gesture in return. Subsequently, when Mencius went to Jen from Tsou he went to see Chi Tzu, but when he went to Ch'i from P'ing Lu he did not go to see Ch'u Tzu. Wu-lu Tzu was overjoyed and said, 'At last I have found an opening.' He asked Mencius, 'Master, you went to see Chi Tzu when you went to Jen but did not go to see Ch'u Tzu when you went to Ch'i. Is this because the latter is only a minister?'

'No. The *Book of History* says,

> In a gift what counts is the politeness. If the thing outstrips the polite-
> ness, that is tantamount to not making the gift. This is because the gift
> fails to embody the good will of the giver.[7]

That is to say, there is something wanting in the gift.'

Wu-lu Tzu was pleased. Someone questioned him, and he replied, 'Chi Tzu was unable to go to Tsou, but Ch'u Tzu could have gone to P'ing Lu.'

[7] See *Shu ching*, 15. 19b.

6. Ch'un-yü K'un said, 'He who puts reputation and real achieve-ment first is a man who tries to benefit others; he who puts repu-tation and real achievement last is a man who tries to benefit himself. You are numbered among the three Ministers yet you fail

孟子曰："居下位，不以賢事不肖者，伯夷也；五就湯，五就桀者，伊尹也；不惡汙君，不辭小官者，柳下惠也。三子者不同道，其趣一也。一者何也？曰，仁也。君子亦仁而已矣，何必同？"

曰："魯繆公之時，公儀子為政，子柳子思為臣，魯之削也滋甚；若是乎，賢者之無益於國也！"

曰："虞不用百里奚而亡，秦繆公用之而霸。不用賢則亡，削何可得與？"

曰："昔者王豹處於淇，而河西善謳；緜駒處於高唐，而齊右善歌；華周杞梁之妻善哭其夫而變國俗。有諸內，必形諸外。為其事而無其功者，髡未嘗覩之也。是故無賢者也；有則髡必識之。"

曰："孔子為魯司寇，不用，從而祭，燔肉不至，不稅冕而行。不知者以為為肉也，其知者以為為無禮也。乃孔子則欲以微罪行，不欲為苟去。君子之所為，衆人固不識也。"

to make any reputation and real achievement either in your services to your prince or in your services to the people. Is that all that one can expect of a benevolent man?'

'Even when in a low position,' said Mencius, 'a man was not willing, as a good man, to serve a bad ruler. Such was Po Yi. Another went five times to T'ang and five times to Chieh. Such was Yi Yin. Yet another was not ashamed of a prince with a tarnished reputation, nor was he disdainful of a modest post.[8] Such was Liu Hsia Hui. These three followed different paths, but their goal was one. What is meant by "one"? The answer is, "Benevolence". All that is to be expected of a gentleman is benevolence. Why must he be exactly the same as other gentlemen?'

'In the time of Duke Mu of Lu, Kung-yi Tzu was in charge of affairs of state, and Tzu-liu and Tzu-ssu were in office, yet Lu dwindled in size even more rapidly than before. Are good and wise men of so little benefit to a state?'

'Yü was annexed for failing to employ Po-li Hsi, while Duke Mu of Ch'in, by employing him, became leader of the feudal lords.[9] A state which fails to employ good and wise men will end by suffering annexation. How can it hope to suffer no more than a reduction in size?'

'Formerly, when Wang Pao settled on the River Ch'i, the district to the west of the Yellow River came to be known for song; when Mien Chü settled in Kao T'ang, the right part of Ch'i likewise came to be known for song. The wives of Hua Chou and Ch'i Liang, being supreme in the way they wept for their husbands, transformed the practice of a whole state. When one has something within, it necessarily shows itself without. I have not seen anyone who devotes himself to any pursuit without some achievement to show for it. Hence there cannot be any good and wise men, otherwise I am bound to know of them.'

'Confucius was the police commissioner of Lu, but his advice was not followed. He took part in a sacrifice, but, afterwards, was not given a share of the meat of the sacrificial animal. He left the state without waiting to take off his ceremonial cap. Those who did not understand him thought he acted in this way because of the meat, but those who understood him realized that he left because Lu failed to observe the proper rites. For his part Confucius

7.　　孟子曰：“五霸者，三王之罪人也；今之諸侯，五霸之罪人也；今之大夫，今之諸侯之罪人也。天子適諸侯曰巡狩，諸侯朝於天子曰述職。春省耕而補不足，秋省歛而助不給。入其疆，土地辟，田野治，養老尊賢，俊傑在位，則有慶；慶以地。入其疆，土地荒蕪，遺老失賢，掊克在位，則有讓。一不朝，則貶其爵；再不朝，則削其地；三不朝，則六師移之。是故天子討而不伐，諸侯伐而不討。五霸者，摟諸侯以伐諸侯者也，故曰，五霸者，三王之罪人也。五霸，桓公爲盛。葵丘之會，諸侯束牲載書而不歃血。初命曰，誅不孝，無易樹子，無以妾爲妻。再命曰，尊賢育才，以彰有德。三命曰，敬老慈幼，無忘賓旅。四命曰，士無世官，官事無攝，取士必得，無專殺大夫。五命曰，無曲防，無遏糴，無有封而不告。曰，凡我同盟之人，既盟之後，言歸于好。今之諸侯皆犯此五禁，故曰，今之諸侯，五霸之罪人也。長君之惡其罪小，逢君之惡其罪大。今之大夫皆逢君之惡，故曰，今之大夫，今之諸侯之罪人也。”

preferred to be slightly at fault in thus leaving rather than to leave
with no reason at all. The doings of a gentleman are naturally
above the understanding of the multitude.'

[8] Cf. II. A. 9 and V. B. 1.
[9] Cf. V. A. 9.

7. Mencius said, 'The Five Leaders of the feudal lords were
offenders against the Three Kings; the feudal lords of today are
offenders against the Five Leaders of the feudal lords; the Counsellors of today are offenders against the feudal lords of today.

'When the Emperor goes to the feudal lords, this is known as
"a tour of inspection". When the feudal lords go to pay homage to
the Emperor, this is known as "a report on duties". In spring the
purpose is to inspect ploughing so that those who have not enough
for sowing may be given help; in autumn the purpose is to inspect
the harvesting so that those who are in need may be given aid.[10]
When the Emperor enters the domain of a feudal lord, if the land
is opened up and the fields are well cultivated, the old are cared
for and the good and wise honoured, and men of distinction are in
positions of authority, then that feudal lord is rewarded—rewards
taking the form of land. On the other hand, on entering the
domain of a feudal lord, if he finds the land is neglected, the old
are forgotten and the good and wise overlooked, and grasping men
are in positions of power, then there is reprimand.

'If a feudal lord fails to attend court, he suffers a loss in rank
for a first offence, and is deprived of part of his territory for a
second offence, and for a third offence the Six Armies will move
into his state.

'Hence the Emperor punishes but does not attack, while a
feudal lord attacks but does not punish. The Five Leaders of the
feudal lords intimidated feudal lords into joining them in their
attacks on other feudal lords. That is why I said, "The Five Leaders
of the feudal lords were offenders against the Three Kings."

'Of the Five Leaders, Duke Huan of Ch'i was the most illus-
trious. In the meeting of K'uei Ch'iu, the feudal lords bound the
animals, placed the text of the pledge on record, but did not sip
the blood of the animals. The first item of the pledge was, "Sons
who are not dutiful are to be punished; heirs should not be put

8.　魯欲使慎子爲將軍。孟子曰：“不敎民而用之，謂之殃民。殃民者，不容於堯舜之世。一戰勝齊，遂有南陽，然且不可——”

慎子勃然不悅曰：“此則滑釐所不識也。”

曰：“吾明告子。天子之地方千里；不千里，不足以待諸侯。諸侯之地方百里；不百里，不足以守宗廟之典籍。周公之封於魯，爲方百里也；地非不足，而儉於百里。太公之封於齊也，亦爲方百里也；地非不足也，而儉於百里。今魯方百里者五，子以爲有王者作，則魯在所損乎，在所益乎？徒取諸彼以與此，然且仁者不爲，況於殺人以求之乎？君子之事君也，務引其君以當道，志於仁而已。”

aside; concubines should not be elevated to the status of wives."
The second was, "Honour good and wise men and train the
talented so as to make known the virtuous." The third was,
"Respect the aged and be kind to the young; do not forget the
guest and the traveller." The fourth was, "Gentlemen should not
hold office by heredity; different offices should not be held con-
currently by the same man; the selection of Gentlemen should be
appropriate; a feudal lord should not exercise sole authority in the
execution of a Counsellor." The fifth was, "Dykes should not be
diverted; the sale of rice to other states should not be prohibited;
any fief given should be reported." The text went on to say, "All
those who have taken part in this pledge should, after the event,
come to an amicable understanding." The feudal lords of today all
violate these five injunctions. That is why I said, "The feudal lords
of today are offenders against the Five Leaders of the feudal lords."
   'The crime of encouraging a ruler in his evil deeds is small
compared to that of pandering to his unspoken evil desires. The
Counsellors of today all do wrong in order to please their prince.
That is why I said, "The Counsellors today are offenders against
the feudal lords of today." '

[10]Cf. I. B. 4.

8. Lu wanted to make Shen Tzu commander of the army. Mencius
said, 'To send the people to war before they are trained is to bring
disaster upon them. One who brings disaster upon the people
would not have been tolerated in the days of Yao and Shun. Even
if Ch'i could be defeated in one battle and Nan Yang annexed, it
would still not be permissible . . .'
   Shen Tzu, looking displeased, said, 'This is something I do not
understand.'
   'I shall tell you plainly. The domain of the Emperor is a thousand
li square, for anything less will not be sufficient to enable him to
receive the feudal lords. The domain of a feudal lord is a hundred
li square, for with anything less he will not be able to safeguard
the archives of the ancestral temple. When the Duke of Chou was
enfeoffed in Lu, his domain was a hundred li square. There was
no shortage of land, but the fief he was given did not exceed a

9. 孟子曰："今之事君者皆曰，'我能爲君辟土地，充府庫。'今之所謂良臣，古之所謂民賊也。君不鄉道，不志於仁，而求富之，是富桀也。'我能爲君約與國，戰必克。'今之所謂良臣，古之所謂民賊也。君不鄉道，不志於仁，而求爲之强戰，是輔桀也。由今之道，無變今之俗，雖與之天下，不能一朝居也。"

10. 白圭曰："吾欲二十而取一，何如？"

孟子曰："子之道，貉道也。萬室之國，一人陶，則可乎？"

曰："不可，器不足用也。"

曰："夫貉，五穀不生，惟黍生之；無城郭、宮室、宗廟、祭祀之禮，無諸侯幣帛饔飧，無百官有司，故二十取一而足也。今居中國，去人倫，無君子，如之何其可也？陶以寡，且不可以爲國，況無君子乎？欲輕之於堯舜之道者，大貉小貉也；欲重之於堯舜之道者，大桀小桀也。"

hundred *li*. When T'ai Kung was enfeoffed in Ch'i, his domain was a hundred *li* square. There was no shortage of land, but the fief he was given did not exceed a hundred *li*. Today Lu is five times a hundred *li* square. If a true King arises, do you think Lu will be one of the states he will enlarge or one of the states he will reduce? A benevolent man would not even take from one man to give to another, let alone seek territory at the cost of human lives. In serving his lord, a gentleman has only one aim and that is to put him on the right path and set his mind on benevolence.'

9. Mencius said, 'Those who are in the service of princes today all say, "I am able to extend the territory of my prince, and fill his coffers for him." The good subject of today would have been looked upon in antiquity as a pest on the people. To enrich a prince who is neither attracted to the Way nor bent upon benevolence is to enrich a Chieh.

'Again, they say, "I am able to gain allies and ensure victory in war for my prince." The good subject of today would have been looked upon in antiquity as a pest on the people. To try to make a prince strong in war who is neither attracted to the Way nor bent upon benevolence is to aid a Chieh.

'Following the practice of the present day, unless there is a change in the ways of the people, a man could not hold the Empire for the duration of one morning, even if it were given to him.'

10. Po Kuei said, 'I should like to fix the rate of taxation at one in twenty. What do you think of it?'

'Your way,' said Mencius, 'is that of the Northern barbarians. In a city of ten thousand households, would it be enough to have a single potter?'

'No. There will be a shortage of earthenware.'

'In the land of the Northern barbarians, the five grains do not grow. Millet is the only crop that grows. They are without city walls, houses, ancestral temples or the sacrificial rites. They do not have diplomacy with its attendant gifts and banquets, nor have they the numerous offices and officials. That is why they can manage on a tax of one in twenty. Now in the Central Kingdoms,

11.　白圭曰：“丹之治水也愈於禹。”

　　孟子曰：“子過矣。禹之治水，水之道也，是故禹以四海爲壑。今吾子以鄰國爲壑。水逆行謂之洚水——洚水者，洪水也——仁人之所惡也。吾子過矣。”

12.　孟子曰：“君子不亮，惡乎執？”

13.　魯欲使樂正子爲政。孟子曰：“吾聞之，喜而不寐。”

　　公孫丑曰：“樂正子强乎？”

　　曰：“否。”

　　“有知慮乎？”

　　曰：“否。”

　　“多聞識乎？”

　　曰：“否。”

　　“然則奚爲喜而不寐？”

　　曰：“其爲人也好善。”

　　“好善足乎？”

　　曰：“好善優於天下，而況魯國乎？夫苟好善，則四海之內皆將輕千里而來告之以善；夫苟不好善，則人將曰，‘訑訑，予旣已知之矣。’訑訑之聲音顏色距人於千里之外。士止於千里之外，則讒諂面諛之人至矣。與讒諂面諛之人居，國欲治，可得乎？”

how can human relationships and men in authority be abolished? The affairs of a city cannot be conducted when there is a shortage even of potters. How much more so if the shortage is of men in authority? Those who wish to reduce taxation to below the level laid down by Yao and Shun are all, to a greater or less degree, barbarians; while those who wish to increase it are all, to a greater or less degree, Chiehs.'

11. Po Kuei said, 'In dealing with water I am better than Yü.'

'You are mistaken,' said Mencius. 'In dealing with water, Yü followed the natural tendency of water. Hence he emptied the water into the Four Seas. Now you empty the water into the neighbouring states. When water goes counter to its course, it is described as a "deluge", in other words, a "flood", and floods are detested by the benevolent man. You are mistaken, my good sir.'

12. Mencius said, 'Other than adherence to his word, wherein can a gentleman be guilty of inflexibility?'[11]

[11]Cf. 'A great man need not keep his word nor does he necessarily see his action through to the end. He aims only at what is right.' (IV. B. 11)

13. Lu wished to entrust the government to Yüeh-cheng Tzu.

'When I heard this,' said Mencius, 'I was so happy that I could not sleep.'

'Has Yüeh-cheng Tzu,' asked Kung-sun Ch'ou, 'great strength of character?'

'No.'

'Is he a man of thought and foresight?'

'No.'

'Is he widely informed?'

'No.'

'Then why were you so happy that you could not sleep?'

'He is a man who is drawn to the good.'

'Is that enough?'

'To be drawn to the good is more than enough to cope with the Empire, let alone the state of Lu. If a man is truly drawn to the good, then, within the Four Seas, men will come, thinking

14. 陳子曰：“古之君子何如則仕？”

　　孟子曰：“所就三，所去三。迎之致敬以有禮；言將行其言也，則就之。禮貌未衰，言弗行也，則去之。其次，雖未行其言也，迎之致敬以有禮，則就之。禮貌衰，則去之。其下，朝不食，夕不食，飢餓不能出門戶，君聞之，曰，‘吾大者不能行其道，又不能從其言也，使飢餓於我土地，吾恥之。’周之，亦可受也，免死而已矣。”

15. 孟子曰：“舜發於畎畝之中，傅說舉於版築之間，膠鬲舉於魚鹽之中，管夷吾舉於士，孫叔敖舉於海，百里奚舉於市，故天將降大任於是人也，必先苦其心志，勞其筋骨，餓其體膚，空乏其身，行拂

nothing of the distance of a thousand *li*, to bring to his notice what is good. On the other hand, if he is not drawn to the good, then men will say of him, "He seems to say 'I know it all'." The way one says "I know it all" with its accompanying look of complacence will repel men a thousand *li* away. If Gentlemen stay a thousand *li* away, then the flatterers will arrive. Can one succeed in one's wish to govern a state properly when one is surrounded by flatterers?'

14. Ch'en Tzu said, 'Under what condition would a gentleman in antiquity take office?'

'There are three conditions,' said Mencius, 'under each of which he would take office; equally, there are three conditions under each of which he would relinquish it.

'First, when he was sent for with the greatest respect, in accordance with the proper rites, and told that his advice would be put into practice, he would go. But when his advice was not put into practice, he would leave, even though the courtesies were still observed.

'Second, when he was sent for with the greatest respect, in accordance with the proper rites, he would go, though his advice was not put into practice. But he would leave when the courtesies were no longer meticulously observed.

'Third, when he could no longer afford to eat either in the morning or in the evening, and was so weak from hunger that he could no longer go out of doors, then he could accept charity from the prince who, hearing of his plight, gave to him out of kindness, saying, "As I have failed, in the first instance, to put into practice the way he taught, and then failed to listen to his advice, it will be to my shame if he dies of hunger in my domain." But the purpose of this acceptance is merely to ward off starvation.'[12]

[12] Cf. V. B. 5 and V. B. 6.

15. Mencius said, 'Shun rose from the fields; Fu Yüeh was raised to office from amongst the builders; Chiao Ke from amidst the fish and salt; Kuan Chung from the hands of the prison officer; Sun Shu-ao from the sea and Po-li Hsi from the market. That is

亂其所爲，所以動心忍性，曾益其所不能。人恆過，然後能改；困於心，衡於慮而後作；徵於色，發於聲而後喻。入則無法家拂士，出則無敵國外患者，國恆亡。然後知生於憂患而死於安樂也。"

16. 孟子曰："教亦多術矣，予不屑之教誨也者，是亦教誨之而已矣。"

why Heaven, when it is about to place a great burden on a man, always first tests his resolution, exhausts his frame and makes him suffer starvation and hardship, frustrates his efforts so as to shake him from his mental lassitude, toughen his nature and make good his deficiencies. As a rule, a man can mend his ways only after he has made mistakes. It is only when a man is frustrated in mind and in his deliberations that he is able to innovate. It is only when his intentions become visible on his countenance and audible in his tone of voice that others can understand him. As a rule, a state without law-abiding families and reliable Gentlemen on the one hand, and, on the other, without the threat of foreign invasion, will perish. Only then do we learn the lesson that we survive in adversity and perish in ease and comfort.'

16. Mencius said, 'There are more ways than one of instructing others. My disdain to instruct a man is itself one way of instructing him.'

盡心章句上

1.　　孟子曰：“盡其心者，知其性也。知其性，則知天矣。存其心，養其性，所以事天也。殀壽不貳，脩身以俟之，所以立命也。”

2.　　孟子曰：“莫非命也，順受其正；是故知命者不立乎巖牆之下。盡其道而死者，正命也；桎梏死者，非正命也。”

3.　　孟子曰：“求則得之，舍則失之，是求有益於得也，求在我者也。求之有道，得之有命，是求無益於得也，求在外者也。”

4.　　孟子曰：“萬物皆備於我矣。反身而誠，樂莫大焉。強恕而行，求仁莫近焉。”

5.　　孟子曰：“行之而不著焉，習矣而不察焉，終身由之而不知其道者，衆也。”

6.　　孟子曰：“人不可以無恥，無恥之恥，無恥矣。”

BOOK VII · PART A

1. Mencius said, 'For a man to give full realization to his heart is for him to understand his own nature, and a man who knows his own nature will know Heaven. By retaining his heart and nurturing his nature he is serving Heaven. Whether he is going to die young or to live to a ripe old age makes no difference to his steadfastness of purpose. It is through awaiting whatever is to befall him with a perfected character that he stands firm on his proper Destiny.'

2. Mencius said, 'Though nothing happens that is not due to Destiny, one accepts willingly only what is one's proper Destiny. That is why he who understands Destiny does not stand under a wall on the verge of collapse. He who dies after having done his best in following the Way dies according to his proper Destiny. It is never anyone's proper Destiny to die in fetters.'

3. Mencius said, 'Seek and you will get it; let go and you will lose it. If this is the case, then seeking is of use to getting and what is sought is within yourself.[1] But if there is a proper way to seek it and whether you get it or not depends on Destiny, then seeking is of no use to getting and what is sought lies outside yourself.'[2]

[1] This refers to one's true heart. The opening sentence is also to be found in VI. A. 6.
[2] This refers to external possessions like wealth and position.

4. Mencius said, 'All the ten thousand things are there in me. There is no greater joy for me than to find, on self-examination, that I am true to myself. Try your best to treat others as you would wish to be treated yourself, and you will find that this is the shortest way to benevolence.'

5. Mencius said, 'The multitude can be said never to understand what they practise, to notice what they repeatedly do, or to be aware of the path they follow all their lives.'

6. Mencius said, 'A man must not be without shame, for the shame of being without shame is shamelessness indeed.'

7.　孟子曰：“恥之於人大矣，爲機變之巧者，無所用恥焉。不恥不若人，何若人有？”

8.　孟子曰：“古之賢王好善而忘勢；古之賢士何獨不然？樂其道而忘人之勢，故王公不致敬盡禮，則不得亟見之。見且由不得亟，而況得而臣之乎？”

9.　孟子謂宋句踐曰：“子好遊乎？吾語子遊。人知之，亦囂囂；人不知，亦囂囂。”

曰：“何如斯可以囂囂矣？”

曰：“尊德樂義，則可以囂囂矣。故士窮不失義，達不離道。窮不失義，故士得己焉；達不離道，故民不失望焉。古之人，得志，澤加於民；不得志，脩身見於世。窮則獨善其身，達則兼善天下。”

10.　孟子曰：“待文王而後興者，凡民也。若夫豪傑之士，雖無文王猶興。”

11.　孟子曰：“附之以韓魏之家，如其自視欿然，則過人遠矣。”

12.　孟子曰：“以佚道使民，雖勞不怨。以生道殺民，雖死不怨殺者。”

7. Mencius said, 'Great is the use of shame to man. He who indulges in craftiness has no use for shame. If a man is not ashamed of being inferior to other men, how will he ever become their equal?'

8. Mencius said, 'Wise kings in antiquity devoted themselves to goodness, forgetting their own exalted position. How should wise Gentlemen in antiquity be any different? They delighted in the Way, forgetting the exalted position of others. That is why kings and dukes could not get to see them often except by showing them due respect and observing due courtesy. If just to see them often was so difficult, how much more so to induce them to take office.'

9. Mencius said to Sung Kou-chien, 'You are fond of travelling from state to state, offering advice. I shall tell you how this should be done. You should be content whether your worth is recognized by others or not.'

'What must a man be before he can be content?'

'If he reveres virtue and delights in rightness, he can be content. Hence a Gentleman never abandons rightness in adversity, nor does he depart from the Way in success. By not abandoning rightness in adversity, he finds delight in himself; by not departing from the Way in success, he remains an example the people can look up to. Men of antiquity made the people feel the effect of their bounty when they realized their ambition, and, when they failed to realize their ambition, were at least able to show the world an exemplary character. In obscurity a man makes perfect his own person, but in prominence he makes perfect the whole Empire as well.'

10. Mencius said, 'Those who make the effort only when there is a King Wen are ordinary men. Outstanding men make the effort even without a King Wen.'

11. Mencius said, 'To look upon oneself as deficient even though the possessions of the families of Han and Wei be added to one's own is to surpass other men by a long way.'

12. Mencius said, 'If the services of the common people were used

13. 孟子曰：“霸者之民驩虞如也，王者之民皥皥如也。殺之而不怨，利之而不庸，民日遷善而不知爲之者。夫君子所過者化，所存者神，上下與天地同流，豈曰小補之哉？”

14. 孟子曰：“仁言不如仁聲之入人深也，善政不如善教之得民也。善政，民畏之；善教，民愛之。善政得民財，善教得民心。”

15. 孟子曰：“人之所不學而能者，其良能也；所不慮而知者，其良知也。孩提之童無不知愛其親者，及其長也，無不知敬其兄也。親親，仁也；敬長，義也；無他，達之天下也。”

16. 孟子曰：“舜之居深山之中，與木石居，與鹿豕遊，其所以異於深山之野人者幾希；及其聞一善言，見一善行，若決江河，沛然莫之能禦也。”

17. 孟子曰：“無爲其所不爲，無欲其所不欲，如此而已矣。”

with a view to sparing them hardship, they would not complain even when hard driven. If the common people were put to death in pursuance of a policy to keep them alive, they would die bearing no ill-will towards the man who put them to death.'

13. Mencius said, 'The people under a leader of the feudal lords are happy; those under a true King are expansive and content. They bear no ill-will when put to death, neither do they feel any gratitude when profited. They move daily towards goodness without realizing who it is that brings this about. A gentleman transforms where he passes, and works wonders where he abides. He is in the same stream as Heaven above and Earth below. Can he be said to bring but small benefit?'

14. Mencius said, 'Benevolent words do not have as profound an effect on the people as benevolent music. Good government does not win the people as does good education. He who practises good government is feared by the people; he who gives the people good education is loved by them. Good government wins the wealth of the people; good education wins their hearts.'

15. Mencius said, 'What a man is able to do without having to learn it is what he can truly do; what he knows without having to reflect on it is what he truly knows. There are no young children who do not know loving their parents, and none of them when they grow up will not know respecting their elder brothers. Loving one's parents is benevolence; respecting one's elders is rightness. What is left to be done is simply the extension of these to the whole Empire.'

16. Mencius said, 'When Shun lived in the depth of the mountains, he lived amongst trees and stones, and had as friends deer and pigs. The difference between him and the uncultivated man of the mountains then was slight. But when he heard a single good word, witnessed a single good deed, it was like water causing a breach in the dykes of the Yangtse or the Yellow River. Nothing could withstand it.'

17. Mencius said, 'Do not do what you would not do; do not

18.　孟子曰：“人之有德慧術知者，恆存乎疢疾。獨孤臣孽子，其操心也危，其慮患也深，故達。”

19.　孟子曰：“有事君人者，事是君則爲容悅者也；有安社稷臣者，以安社稷爲悅者也；有天民者，達可行於天下而後行之者也；有大人者，正己而物正者也。”

20.　孟子曰：“君子有三樂，而王天下不與存焉。父母俱存，兄弟無故，一樂也；仰不愧於天，俯不怍於人，二樂也；得天下英才而教育之，三樂也。君子有三樂，而王天下不與存焉。”

21.　孟子曰：“廣土衆民，君子欲之，所樂不存焉；中天下而立，定四海之民，君子樂之，所性不存焉。君子所性，雖大行不加焉，雖窮居不損焉，分定故也。君子所性，仁義禮智根於心，其生色也，睟然見於面，盎於背，施於四體。四體不言而喻。”

desire what you would not desire. That is all.'

18. Mencius said, 'It is often through adversity that men acquire virtue, wisdom, skill and cleverness. The estranged subject or the son of a concubine, because he conducts himself with the greatest of caution and is constantly on the watch out for possible disasters, succeeds where others would have failed.'

19. Mencius said, 'There are men whose purpose is to serve a prince. They will try to please whatever prince they are serving. There are men whose aim is to bring peace to the state. They achieve satisfaction through bringing this about. There are the subjects of Heaven. They practise only what could be extended to the whole Empire. There are the great men. They can rectify others by rectifying themselves.'

20. Mencius said, 'There are three things a gentleman delights in, and being ruler over the Empire is not amongst them. His parents are alive and his brothers are well. This is the first delight. Above, he is not ashamed to face Heaven; below, he is not ashamed to face man. This is the second delight. He has the good fortune of having the most talented pupils in the Empire. This is the third delight. There are three things a gentleman delights in and being ruler over the Empire is not amongst them.'

21. Mencius said, 'An extensive territory and a huge population are things a gentleman desires, but what he delights in lies elsewhere. To stand in the centre of the Empire and bring peace to the people within the Four Seas is what a gentleman delights in, but that which he follows as his nature lies elsewhere. That which a gentleman follows as his nature is not added to when he holds sway over the Empire, nor is it detracted from when he is reduced to straitened circumstances. This is because he knows his allotted station. That which a gentleman follows as his nature, that is to say, benevolence, rightness, the rites and wisdom, is rooted in his heart, and manifests itself in his face, giving it a sleek appearance. It also shows in his back and extends to his limbs, rendering their message intelligible without words.'

22. 孟子曰："伯夷辟紂，居北海之濱，聞文王作，興曰：'盍歸乎
來，吾聞西伯善養老者。'太公辟紂，居東海之濱，聞文王作，興曰：
'盍歸乎來，吾聞西伯善養老者。' 天下有善養老，則仁人以爲己歸
矣。五畝之宅，樹牆下以桑，匹婦蠶之，則老者足以衣帛矣。五母雞，
二母彘，無失其時，老者足以無失肉矣。百畝之田，匹夫耕之，八口
之家足以無飢矣。所謂西伯善養老者，制其田里，教之樹畜，導其妻
子使養其老。五十非帛不煖，七十非肉不飽。不煖不飽，謂之凍餒。
文王之民無凍餒之老者，此之謂也。"

23. 孟子曰："易其田疇，薄其稅斂，民可使富也。食之以時，用之
以禮，財不可勝用也。民非水火不生活，昏暮叩人之門戶求水火，無
弗與者，至足矣。聖人治天下，使有菽粟如水火。菽粟如水火，而民
焉有不仁者乎？"

22. Mencius said, 'Po Yi fled from Tchou and settled on the edge of the North Sea. When he heard of the rise of King Wen he stirred and said, "Why not go back? I hear that Hsi Po³ takes good care of the aged." T'ai Kung fled from Tchou and settled on the edge of the East Sea. When he heard of the rise of King Wen he stirred and said, "Why not go back? I hear that Hsi Po takes good care of the aged."⁴ When there is someone in the Empire who takes good care of the aged, benevolent men will look upon him as their refuge.

'If the mulberry is planted at the foot of the walls in every homestead of five *mu* of land and the woman of the house keeps silkworms, then the aged can wear silk. If there are five hens and two sows, and these do not miss their breeding season, then the aged will not be deprived of meat. If a man tills a hundred *mu* of land, there will be enough for his family of eight mouths not to go hungry.⁵

'When Hsi Po was said to "take good care of the aged", what was meant is this. He laid down the pattern for the distribution of land, taught the men the way to plant trees and keep animals, and showed their womenfolk the way to care for the aged. A man needs silk for warmth at fifty and meat for sustenance at seventy. To have neither warm clothes nor a full belly is to be cold and hungry. The people under King Wen had no old folk who were cold and hungry.'

³i.e. King Wen.
⁴Cf. IV. A. 13.
⁵Cf. I. A. 3 and I. A. 7. The wording, however, is slightly different in the present passage.

23. Mencius said, 'Put in order the fields of the people, lighten their taxes, and the people can be made affluent. If one's consumption of food is confined to what is in season and one's use of other commodities is in accordance with the rites, then one's resources will be more than sufficient. The common people cannot live without water and fire, yet one never meets with a refusal when knocking on another's door in the evening to beg for water or fire. This is because these are in such abundance. In governing the Empire, the sage tries to make food as plentiful as water and

24. 孟子曰："孔子登東山而小魯，登太山而小天下，故觀於海者難
爲水，遊於聖人之門者難爲言。觀水有術，必觀其瀾。日月有明，容
光必照焉。流水之爲物也，不盈科不行；君子之志於道也，不成章不
達。"

25. 孟子曰："雞鳴而起，孳孳爲善者，舜之徒也；雞鳴而起，孳孳
爲利者，蹠之徒也。欲知舜與蹠之分，無他，利與善之間也。"

26. 孟子曰："楊子取爲我，拔一毛而利天下，不爲也。墨子兼愛，
摩頂放踵利天下，爲之。子莫執中。執中爲近之。執中無權，猶執一
也。所惡執一者，爲其賊道也，舉一而廢百也。"

fire. When that happens, how can there be any amongst his people who are not benevolent?'

24. Mencius said, 'When he ascended the Eastern Mount, Confucius felt that Lu was small, and when he ascended Mount T'ai, he felt that the Empire was small. Likewise it is difficult for water to come up to the expectation of someone who has seen the Sea, and it is difficult for words to come up to the expectation of someone who has studied under a sage. There is a way to judge water. Watch for its ripples. When the sun and moon shine, the light shows up the least crack that will admit it. Flowing water is such that it does not go further forward until it has filled all the hollows.[6] A gentleman, in his pursuit of the Way, does not get there unless he achieves a beautiful pattern.'

[6] Cf. IV. B. 18.

25. Mencius said, 'He who gets up with the crowing of the cock and never tires of doing good is the same kind of man as Shun; he who gets up with the crowing of the cock and never tires of working for profit is the same kind of man as Chih.[7] If you wish to understand the difference between Shun and Chih, you need look no further than the gap separating the good and the profitable.'

[7] A byword for robbers.

26. Mencius said, 'Yang Tzu chooses egoism. Even if he could benefit the Empire by pulling out one hair he would not do it.[8] Mo Tzu advocates love without discrimination. If by shaving his head and showing his heels he could benefit the Empire, he would do it. Tzu-mo holds on to the middle, half way between the two extremes. Holding on to the middle is closer to being right, but to do this without the proper measure is no different from holding to one extreme. The reason for disliking those who hold to one extreme is that they cripple the Way. One thing is singled out to the neglect of a hundred others.'

[8] This is almost certain to be a distortion of Yang Chu's doctrine. What he taught was rather that one should not give a hair on one's body in exchange for the enjoyment of the Empire.

27. 孟子曰：“飢者甘食，渴者甘飲，是未得飲食之正也，飢渴害之也。豈惟口腹有飢渴之害？人心亦皆有害。人能無以飢渴之害爲心害，則不及人不爲憂矣。”

28. 孟子曰：“柳下惠不以三公易其介。”

29. 孟子曰：“有爲者辟若掘井，掘井九軔而不及泉，猶爲棄井也。”

30. 孟子曰：“堯舜，性之也；湯武，身之也；五霸，假之也。久假而不歸，惡知其非有也。”

31. 公孫丑曰：“伊尹曰：‘予不狎于不順，’放太甲于桐，民大悅。太甲賢，又反之，民大悅。賢者之爲人臣也，其君不賢，則固可放與？”
　　孟子曰：“有伊尹之志，則可；無伊尹之志，則篡也。”

32. 公孫丑曰：“詩曰：‘不素餐兮’。君子之不耕而食，何也？”
　　孟子曰：“君子居是國也，其君用之，則安富尊榮；其子弟從之，則孝悌忠信。‘不素餐兮’，孰大於是？”

27. Mencius said, 'A hungry man finds his food delectable; a thirsty man finds his drink delicious. Both lack the proper measure of food and drink because hunger and thirst interfere with his judgement. The palate is not the only thing which is open to interference by hunger and thirst. The human heart, too, is open to the same interference. If a man can prevent hunger and thirst from interfering with his heart, then he does not need to worry about being inferior to other men.'

28. Mencius said, 'Liu Hsia Hui would not have compromised on his integrity for the sake of the three ducal offices.'

29. Mencius said, 'To try to achieve anything is like digging a well. You can dig a hole nine fathoms deep, but if you fail to reach the source of water, it is just an abandoned well.'

30. Mencius said, 'Yao and Shun had it as their nature. T'ang and King Wu embodied it.[9] The Five Leaders of the feudal lords borrowed it.[10] But if a man borrows a thing and keeps it long enough, how can one be sure that it will not become truly his?'

[9] Cf. VII. B. 33.
[10] Cf. II. A. 3. The 'it' here would seem to refer to benevolence.

31. Kung-sun Ch'ou said, 'Yi Yin banished T'ai Chia to T'ung, saying, "I do not wish to be close to one who is intractable", and the people were greatly pleased. When T'ai Chia became good, Yi Yin restored him to the throne, and the people, once again, were pleased. When a prince is not good, is it permissible for a good and wise man who is his subject to banish him?'

'It is permissible,' said Mencius, 'only if he had the motive of a Yi Yin; otherwise, it would be usurpation.'

32. Kung-sun Ch'ou said, 'The *Odes* say,

> [A gentleman] enjoys only food he has earned.

Why, then, does a gentleman eat food when he does not share in the work of tilling the land?'

'When a gentleman stays in a state,' said Mencius, 'if he is

33.　王子墊問曰：“士何事？”

　　孟子曰：“尚志。”

　　曰：“何謂尚志？”

　　曰：“仁義而已矣。殺一無罪非仁也，非其有而取之非義也。居惡在？仁是也；路惡在？義是也。居仁由義，大人之事備矣。”

34.　孟子曰：“仲子，不義與之齊國而弗受，人皆信之，是舍簞食豆羹之義也。人莫大焉亡親戚君臣上下。以其小者信其大者，奚可哉？”

35.　桃應問曰：“舜爲天子，皋陶爲士，瞽瞍殺人，則如之何？”

　　孟子曰：“執之而已矣。”

　　“然則舜不禁與？”

　　曰：“夫舜惡得而禁之？夫有所受之也。”

　　“然則舜如之何？”

　　曰：“舜視棄天下猶棄敝蹝也。竊負而逃，遵海濱而處，終身訢然，樂而忘天下。”

employed he can make the prince secure, rich and honoured, and, if the young men come under his influence, he can make them dutiful to their parents and elders, conscientious in their work and faithful to their word. Is there a truer case of "enjoying only food he has earned"?'

33. Prince Tien asked, 'What is the business of a Gentleman?'
'To set his mind on high principles.'
'What do you mean by this?'
'To be moral. That is all. It is contrary to benevolence to kill one innocent man; it is contrary to rightness to take what one is not entitled to. Where is one's dwelling? In benevolence. Where is one's road? In rightness. To dwell in benevolence and to follow rightness constitute the sum total of the business of a great man.'

34. Mencius said, 'Everyone believes that Ch'en Chung would refuse the state of Ch'i were it offered to him against the principles of rightness. But what he calls rightness is merely the rightness which refuses a basketful of rice and a bowlful of soup.[11] No one surpasses him in the neglect of parents and the denial of relationships between prince and subject and between superior and inferior.[12] How, then, can we take on trust his conduct on important issues simply on the strength of his conduct in minor matters?'

[11] For Ch'en Chung see III. B. 10, and for the refusal of a basketful of rice and a bowlful of soup see VI. A. 10.
[12] This sentence is exceedingly obscure and the translation is, therefore, tentative.

35. T'ao Ying asked, 'When Shun was Emperor and Kao Yao was the judge, if the Blind Man killed a man, what was to be done?'
'The only thing to do was to apprehend him.'
'In that case, would Shun not try to stop it?'
'How could Shun stop it? Kao Yao had authority for what he did.'
'Then what would Shun have done?'
'Shun looked upon casting aside the Empire as no more than discarding a worn shoe. He would have secretly carried the old man on his back and fled to the edge of the Sea and lived there

36. 孟子自范之齊，望見齊王之子，喟然嘆曰：“居移氣，養移體，大哉居乎！夫非盡人之子與？”

　　孟子曰：“王子宮室、車馬、衣服多與人同，而王子若彼者，其居使之然也；況居天下之廣居者乎？魯君之宋，呼於垤澤之門。守者曰：‘此非吾君也，何其聲之似我君也？’此無他，居相似也。”

37. 孟子曰：“食而弗愛，豕交之也；愛而不敬，獸畜之也。恭敬者，幣之未將者也。恭敬而無實，君子不可虛拘。”

38. 孟子曰：“形色，天性也；惟聖人然後可以踐形。”

39. 齊宣王欲短喪。公孫丑曰：“為朞之喪，猶愈於已乎？”

　　孟子曰：“是猶或紾其兄之臂，子謂之姑徐徐云爾，亦敎之孝悌而已矣。”

　　王子有其母死者，其傅為之請數月之喪。公孫丑曰：“若此者何如也？”

happily, never giving a thought to the Empire.'

36. Mencius went to Ch'i from Fan. When he saw the son of the King of Ch'i from a distance, he sighed and said, 'A man's surroundings transform his air just as the food he eats changes his body. Great indeed are a man's surroundings. Otherwise, are we not all the son of some man or another?[13]'

He added, 'The house, carriage, horses and dress of the prince are not so different from those of other people, yet the prince is so different. This is because of the surroundings. How much more if one were to live in the loftiest of dwellings[14] in the Empire.

'The lord of Lu went to Sung, and called in front of the Tieh Tse Gate. The keeper said, "This is not my lord, yet how like is the voice to that of my lord." The reason is simply that both princes came from similar surroundings.'

[13] Chao Ch'i takes this as a chapter, separate from what follows. Seeing that the word *chü* (surroundings) appear in both parts, the separation into two chapters does not seem justified.
[14] i.e. benevolence. Cf. VII. A. 33; also IV. A. II. The term is also found in III. B. 2.

37. Mencius said, 'To feed a man without showing him love is to treat him like a pig; to love him without showing him respect is to keep him like a domestic animal. Respect is but a gift that is not yet presented. Respect that is without reality will not take a gentleman in merely by its empty show.'

38. Mencius said, 'Our body and complexion are given to us by Heaven. Only a sage can give his body complete fulfilment.'

39. King Hsüan of Ch'i wanted to cut short the period of mourning. Kung-sun Ch'ou commented, 'Is it not better to observe a year's mourning than not to observe any mourning at all?'

'This is the same,' said Mencius, 'as saying to someone who is twisting his elder brother's arm, "Do it gently". What you ought to do is simply to teach him the duties of a son and a younger brother.'

There was a prince whose mother died. His tutor requested, on his behalf, permission to observe mourning for a number of

曰：“是欲終之而不可得也。雖加一日愈於已，謂夫莫為者也。”

40. 孟子曰：“君子之所以教者五：有如時雨化之者，有成德者，有達財者，有荅問者，有私淑艾者。此五者，君子之所以教也。”

41. 公孫丑曰：“道則高矣，美矣，宜若登天然，似不可及也；何不使彼為可幾及而日孳孳也？”

孟子曰：“大匠不為拙工改廢繩墨，羿不為拙射變其彀率。君子引而不發，躍如也。中道而立，能者從之。”

42. 孟子曰：“天下有道，以道殉身；天下無道，以身殉道；未聞以道殉乎人者也。”

43. 公都子曰：“滕更之在門也，若在所禮，而不荅，何也？”

孟子曰：“挾貴而問，挾賢而問，挾長而問，挾有勳勞而問，挾故而問，皆所不荅也。滕更有二焉。”

months. Kung-sun Ch'ou asked, 'How about this?'

'This is a case where the man has no hope of realizing his wish to observe the full period of mourning. Under such circumstances, even to prolong the period by a single day is better than not to prolong it at all. What I said the other day referred to those who failed to act even when there were no obstacles.'

40. Mencius said, 'A gentleman teaches in five ways. The first is by a transforming influence like that of timely rain. The second is by helping the student to realize his virtue to the full. The third is by helping him to develop his talent. The fourth is by answering his questions. And the fifth is by setting an example others not in contact with him can emulate. These five are the ways in which a gentleman teaches.'

41. Kung-sun Ch'ou said, 'The Way is indeed lofty and beautiful, but to attempt it is like trying to climb up to Heaven which seems beyond one's reach. Why not substitute for it something which men have some hopes of attaining so as to encourage them constantly to make the effort?'

'A great craftsman,' said Mencius, 'does not put aside the plumb-line for the benefit of the clumsy carpenter. Yi did not compromise on his standards of drawing the bow for the sake of the clumsy archer.[15] A gentleman is full of eagerness when he has drawn his bow, but before he lets fly the arrow, he stands in the middle of the path, and those who are able to do so follow him.'

[15]Cf. VI. A. 20.

42. Mencius said, 'When the Way prevails in the Empire, it goes where one's person goes; when the Way is eclipsed, one's person goes where the Way has gone. I have never heard of making the Way go where other people are going.'

43. Kung-tu Tzu said, 'When T'eng Keng was studying under you, he appeared to deserve your courtesy; yet you never answered his questions. Why was that?'

'I never answer any questioner,' said Mencius, 'who relies on

44. 孟子曰：「於不可已而已者，無所不已。於所厚者薄，無所不薄也。其進銳者，其退速。」

45. 孟子曰：「君子之於物也，愛之而弗仁；於民也，仁之而弗親。親親而仁民，仁民而愛物。」

46. 孟子曰：「知者無不知也，當務之爲急；仁者無不愛也，急[1]親賢之爲務。堯舜之知而不徧物，急先務也；堯舜之仁不徧愛人，急親賢也。不能三年之喪，而緦、小功之察；放飯流歠，而問無齒決，是之謂不知務。」

[1] '親賢之爲務' 與 '當務之爲急' 相對成文，'急' 字蓋蒙下文 '急親賢' 而衍。

the advantage he possesses of position, capability, age,[16] merit or status as an old friend. T'eng Keng was guilty on two of these counts.'

[16]Cf. V. B. 3.

44. Mencius said, 'He who stops where he ought not to will always stop wherever he may be. He who treats badly those he ought to treat well will always treat other people badly whoever they may be. He who advances sharply falls back rapidly.'

45. Mencius said, 'A gentleman is sparing with living creatures but shows no benevolence towards them; he shows benevolence towards the people but is not attached to them. He is attached to his parents but is merely benevolent towards the people; he is benevolent towards the people but is merely sparing[17] with living creatures.'

[17]Throughout this passage Mencius is exploiting the fact that the word *ai* means both 'to love' and 'to be sparing, to be frugal'.

46. Mencius said, 'A wise man knows everything, but he considers urgent only that which demands attention. A benevolent man loves everyone, but he devotes himself to the close association with good and wise men. Even Yao and Shun did not use their wisdom on all things alike; this is because they put first things first. Nor did they use their benevolence to love everyone; this is because they considered urgent the close association with good and wise men. For a man to observe meticulously three or five months' mourning while failing to observe three years' mourning or for him to ask whether he is guilty of breaking the food with his teeth while bolting down his food and drink is for him to show an ignorance of priorities.'

盡心章句下

1.　孟子曰：“不仁哉梁惠王也！仁者以其所愛及其所不愛，不仁者
以其所不愛及其所愛。”

　　公孫丑問曰：“何謂也？”

　　“梁惠王以土地之故，糜爛其民而戰之，大敗，將復之，恐不能
勝，故驅其所愛子弟以殉之，是之謂以其所不愛及其所愛也。”

2.　孟子曰：“春秋無義戰。彼善於此，則有之矣。征者，上伐下也，
敵國不相征也。”

3.　孟子曰：“盡信書，則不如無書。吾於武成，取二三策而已矣。
仁人無敵於天下，以至仁伐至不仁，而何[1] 其血之流杵也？”

> [1]《論衡‧語增篇》引此文‘而何’作‘如何’（卷七頁十六），‘而’蓋讀作‘如。’

4.　孟子曰：“有人曰，‘我善爲陳，我善爲戰。’大罪也。國君好
仁，天下無敵焉。’南面而征，北夷怨；東面而征，西夷怨，曰：“奚
爲後我？”’武王之伐殷也，革車三百兩，虎賁三千人。王曰：‘無畏！
寧爾也，非敵百姓也。’若崩厥角稽首。征之爲言正也，各欲正己也，
焉用戰？”

BOOK VII · PART B

1. Mencius said, 'How ruthless was King Hui of Liang! A benevolent man extends his love from those he loves to those he does not love. A ruthless man extends his ruthlessness from those he does not love to those he loves.'

'What do you mean?' asked Kung-sun Ch'ou.

'King Hui of Liang sent his people to war, making pulp of them, for the sake of gaining further territory. He suffered a grave defeat and when he wanted to go to war a second time he was afraid he would not be able to win, so he herded the young men he loved to their death as well. This is what I meant when I said he extended his ruthlessness from those he did not love to those he loved.'

2. Mencius said, 'The *Spring and Autumn Annals* acknowledges no just wars. There are only cases of one war not being quite as bad as another. A punitive expedition is a war waged by one in authority against his subordinates. It is not for peers to punish one another by war.'

3. Mencius said, 'If one believed everything in the *Book of History*, it would have been better for the *Book* not to have existed at all. In the *Wu ch'eng* chapter[1] I accept only two or three strips.[2] A benevolent man has no match in the Empire. How could it be that "the blood spilled was enough to carry staves along with it", when the most benevolent waged war against the most cruel?'[3]

[1] One of the lost chapters of the *Book of History*. The chapter by the same name in the present text of the *Book of History* is spurious.
[2] In ancient China books were written on narrow bamboo strips which were bound together by leather thongs or cords so that they could be rolled up when not in use.
[3] The *Wu ch'eng* gives an account of the war waged by King Wu against the tyrant Tchou.

4. Mencius said, 'There are people who say, "I am expert at military formations; I am expert at waging war." This is a grave crime. If the ruler of a state is drawn to benevolence he will have no match in the Empire. "When he marched on the south, the northern barbarians complained; when he marched on the east, the western

5.　孟子曰：“梓匠輪輿能與人規矩，不能使人巧。”

6.　孟子曰：“舜之飯糗茹草也，若將終身焉；及其爲天子也，被袗衣，鼓琴，二女果，若固有之。”

7.　孟子曰：“吾今而後知殺人親之重也：殺人之父，人亦殺其父；殺人之兄，人亦殺其兄。然則非自殺之也，一間耳。”

8.　孟子曰：“古之爲關也，將以禦暴；今之爲關也，將以爲暴。”

9.　孟子曰：“身不行道，不行於妻子；使人不以道，不能行於妻子。”

10.　孟子曰：“周于利者凶年不能殺，周于德者邪世不能亂。”

barbarians complained. They all said, 'Why does he not come to us first?' "[4]

'When King Wu marched on Yin, he had three hundred war chariots and three thousand brave warriors. He said, "Do not be afraid. I come to bring you peace, not to wage war on the people." And the sound of the people knocking their heads on the ground was like the toppling of a mountain. To wage a punitive war is to rectify.[5] There is no one who does not wish himself rectified. What need is there for war?'

[4] For this quotation see I. B. 11.
[5] The two verbs in Chinese are cognate.

5. Mencius said, 'A carpenter or a carriage-maker can pass on to another the rules of his craft, but he cannot make him skilful.'

6. Mencius said, 'When Shun lived on dried rice and wild vegetables, it was as though he was going to do this for the rest of his life. But when he became Emperor, clad in precious robes, playing on his lute, with the two daughters [of Yao] in attendance, it was as though this was what he had been used to all his life.'

7. Mencius said, 'Only now do I realize how serious it is to kill a member of the family of another man. If you killed his father, he would kill your father; if you killed his elder brother, he would kill your elder brother. This being the case, though you may not have killed your father and brother with your own hands, it is but one step removed.'

8. Mencius said, 'In antiquity, a border station was set up as a precaution against violence. Today it is set up to perpetrate violence.'

9. Mencius said, 'If you do not practise the Way yourself, you will not have your way even with your own wife and children. If you do not impose work on others in accordance with the Way, you cannot have your way even with your own wife and children.

10. Mencius said, 'He who never misses a chance for profit cannot

11. 孟子曰：“好名之人能讓千乘之國，苟非其人，簞食豆羹見於色。”

12. 孟子曰：“不信仁賢，則國空虛；無禮義，則上下亂；無政事，則財用不足。”

13. 孟子曰：“不仁而得國者，有之矣；不仁而得天下者，未之有也。”

14. 孟子曰：“民為貴，社稷次之，君為輕。是故得乎丘民而為天子，得乎天子為諸侯，得乎諸侯為大夫。諸侯危社稷，則變置。犧牲既成，粢盛既絜，祭祀以時，然而旱乾水溢，則變置社稷。”

15. 孟子曰：“聖人，百世之師也，伯夷、柳下惠是也。故聞伯夷之風者，頑夫廉，懦夫有立志；聞柳下惠之風者，薄夫敦，鄙夫寬。奮乎百世之上，百世之下，聞者莫不興起也。非聖人而能若是乎？──而況於親炙之者乎？”

be killed by a bad year; he who is equipped with every virtue cannot be led astray by a wicked world.'

11. Mencius said, 'A man who is out to make a name for himself will be able to give away a state of a thousand chariots, but reluctance would be written all over his face if he had to give away a basketful of rice and a bowlful of soup when no such purpose was served.'

12. Mencius said, 'If the benevolent and the good and wise are not trusted, the state will only be a shell; if the rites and rightness are absent, the distinction between superior and inferior will not be observed; if government is not properly regulated, the state will not have enough resources to meet expenditure.'

13. Mencius said, 'There are cases of a ruthless man gaining possession of a state, but it has never happened that such a man gained possession of the Empire.'

14. Mencius said, 'The people are of supreme importance; the altars to the gods of earth and grain come next; last comes the ruler. That is why he who gains the confidence of the multitudinous people will be Emperor; he who gains the confidence of the Emperor will be a feudal lord; he who gains the confidence of a feudal lord will be a Counsellor. When a feudal lord endangers the altars to the gods of earth and grain[6] he should be replaced. When the sacrificial animals are sleek, the offerings are clean and the sacrifices are observed at due times, and yet floods and droughts come, then the altars should be replaced.'

[6] The symbol of independence of the state.

15. Mencius said, 'The sage is teacher to a hundred generations. Such were Po Yi and Liu Hsia Hui. Hence hearing of the way of Po Yi, a covetous man will be purged of his covetousness and a weak man will become resolute; hearing of the way of Liu Hsia Hui, a mean man will become generous and a narrow-minded man tolerant.[7] Can these two, if they were not sages, have inspired by

16. 孟子曰：「仁也者，人也。合而言之，道也。」

17. 孟子曰：「孔子之去魯，曰，'遲遲吾行也，去父母國之道也。'去齊，接淅而行。去他國之道也。」

18. 孟子曰：「君子之戹於陳蔡之間，無上下之交也。」

19. 貉稽曰：「稽大不理於口。」
    孟子曰：「無傷也。士憎茲多口。詩云：'憂心悄悄，慍于羣小。'孔子也。'肆不殄厥慍，亦不殞厥問。' 文王也。」

20. 孟子曰：「賢者以其昭昭使人昭昭，今以其昏昏使人昭昭。」

their example all those who come a hundred generations after them? How much more inspiring they must have been to those who were fortunate enough to have known them personally!'

[7]Cf. V. B. 1.

16. Mencius said, ' "Benevolence" means "man".[8] When these two are conjoined, the result is "the Way".'

[8]This is not a simple phonetic gloss based on identical pronunciations, as the two words are in fact cognate.

17. Mencius said, 'When he left Lu, Confucius said, "I proceed as slowly as possible." This is the way to leave the state of one's father and mother. When he left Ch'i he started after emptying the rice from the steamer.[9] This is the way to leave a foreign state.'

[9]Cf. V. B. 1.

18. Mencius said, 'That the gentleman[10] was in difficulties in the region of Ch'en and Ts'ai was because he had no friends at court.'

[10]i.e. Confucius.

19. Mo Chi said, 'I am not much of a speaker.'
'There is no harm in that,' said Mencius. 'A Gentleman dislikes those who speak too much. The *Odes* say,

> I am sad and silent,
> For I am hated by the small men.[11]

Such a one was Confucius.

> He neither dispelled the dislike of others
> Nor did he lose his own reputation.[12]

Such a one was King Wen.'

[11]Ode 26.
[12]Ode 237.

20. Mencius said, 'A good and wise man helps others to understand clearly by his own clear understanding. Nowadays, men try to help others understand by their own benighted ignorance.'

21. 孟子謂高子曰：“山徑之蹊，間介然用之而成路；爲間不用，則茅塞之矣。今茅塞子之心矣。”

22. 高子曰：“禹之聲尙文王之聲。”
孟子言：“何以言之？”
曰：“以追蠡。”
曰：“是奚足哉？城門之軌，兩馬之力與？”

23. 齊饑。陳臻曰：“國人皆以夫子將復爲發棠，殆不可復。”
孟子曰：“是爲馮婦也。晉人有馮婦者，善搏虎，卒爲善士。則之野，有衆逐虎。虎負嵎，莫之敢攖。望見馮婦，趨而迎之。馮婦攘臂下車。衆皆悅之，其爲士者笑之。”

24. 孟子曰：“口之於味也，目之於色也，耳之於聲也，鼻之於臭也，四肢之於安佚也，性也，有命焉，君子不謂性也。仁之於父子也，義之於君臣也，禮之於賓主也，知之於賢者也，聖人[1] 之於天道也，命也，有性焉，君子不謂命也。”

[1] 龐朴根據馬王堆《老子甲本》卷後古佚書認爲 ‘“聖人之於天道也”一句中的 “人”字，是衍文，應予削去。’（《帛書五行篇研究》頁20）但作 ‘聖之於天道也’ 與上文句例不一致，意義亦不明白，只能聊備一說。

25. 浩生不害問曰：“樂正子何人也？”

21. Mencius said to Kau Tzu, 'A trail through the mountains, if used, becomes a path in a short time, but, if unused, becomes blocked by grass in an equally short time. Now your heart is blocked by grass.'

22. Kau Tzu said, 'The music of Yü surpassed that of King Wen.'
'What makes you say that?' said Mencius.
'It is the bell-rope. It is almost worn through.'
'That is not sufficient as evidence. Do you imagine that the rut through the city gates was made by a single pair of horses?'

23. There was a famine in Ch'i. Ch'en Chen said, 'The people all thought that you, Master, were going to bring about another distribution of grain from the T'ang granary. I suppose there is no hope of that happening?'
'To do this,' said Mencius, 'is to do a "Feng Fu". There was a man in Chin by the name of Feng Fu. He was an expert at seizing tigers with his bare hands, but in the end he became a good Gentleman. It happened that he went to the outskirts of the city, and there was a crowd pursuing a tiger. The tiger turned at bay and no one dared go near it. On seeing Feng Fu, the people hastened to meet him. Feng Fu rolled up his sleeves and got off his carriage. The crowd was delighted, but those who were Gentlemen laughed at him.'

24. Mencius said, 'The way the mouth is disposed towards tastes, the eye towards colours, the ear towards sounds, the nose towards smells, and the four limbs towards ease is human nature, yet therein also lies the Decree. That is why the gentleman does not describe it as nature. The way benevolence pertains to the relation between father and son, duty to the relation between prince and subject, the rites to the relation between guest and host, wisdom to the good and wise man, the sage to the way of Heaven, is the Decree, but therein also lies human nature. That is why the gentleman does not describe it as Decree.'

25. Hao-sheng Pu-hai asked, 'What sort of a man is Yüeh-cheng Tzu?'

孟子曰：“善人也，信人也。”

“何謂善？何謂信？”

曰：“可欲之謂善，有諸己之謂信，充實之謂美，充實而有光輝之謂大，大而化之之謂聖，聖而不可知之之謂神。樂正子，二之中、四之下也。”

26. 孟子曰：“逃墨必歸於楊，逃楊必歸於儒。歸，斯受之而已矣。今之與楊、墨辯者，如追放豚，既入其苙，又從而招之。”

27. 孟子曰：“有布縷之征，粟米之征，力役之征。君子用其一，緩其二。用其二而民有殍，用其三而父子離。”

28. 孟子曰：“諸侯之寶三；土地、人民、政事。寶珠玉者，殃必及身。”

29. 盆成括仕於齊，孟子曰：“死矣盆成括！”

盆成括見殺，門人問曰：“夫子何以知其將見殺？”

曰：“其爲人也小有才，未聞君子之大道也，則足以殺其軀而已矣。”

30. 孟子之滕，館於上宮。有業屨於牖上，館人求之弗得。或問之曰：“若是乎從者之廋也？”

'A good man,' said Mencius. 'A true man.'

'What do you mean by "good" and "true"?'

'The desirable is called "good". To have it in oneself is called "true". To possess it fully in oneself is called "beautiful", but to shine forth with this full possession is called "great". To be great and be transformed by this greatness is called "sage"; to be sage and to transcend the understanding is called "divine". Yüeh-cheng Tzu has something of the first two qualities but has not quite reached the last four.'

26. Mencius said, 'Those who desert the Mohist school are sure to turn to that of Yang; those who desert the Yang school are sure to turn to the Confucianist. When they turn to us we simply accept them. Nowadays, those who debate with the followers of Yang and Mo behave as if they were chasing strayed pigs. They are not content to return the pigs to the sty, but go on to tie their feet up.'

27. Mencius said, 'There is taxation levied in cloth, in grain, and in labour. A gentleman employs one to the full while relaxing the other two. If two are employed to the full, there would be death from starvation amongst the people, and if all three are so employed, father will be separated from son.'

28. Mencius said, 'The feudal lords have three treasures: land, people and government. Those who treasure pearls and jade are sure to suffer the consequences in their own lifetime.'

29. P'en-ch'eng K'uo took office in Ch'i. Mencius said, 'He is going to meet his death.'

P'en-ch'eng K'uo was killed and Mencius' disciples asked, 'How did you, Master, know that he was going to be killed?'

'He was a man with limited talent who had never been taught the great way of the gentleman. That was just enough to cost him his life.'

30. Mencius went to T'eng and put up at the Shang Kung. There was a pair of unfinished sandals on the window-sill. The men in the hostelry looked for them in vain. Someone asked Mencius,

曰：“子以是爲竊屨來與？”

曰：“殆非也。”

“夫予之設科也，往者不追，來者不拒。苟以是心至，斯受之而已矣。”

31. 孟子曰：“人皆有所不忍，達之於其所忍，仁也；人皆有所不爲，達之於其所爲，義也。人能充無欲害人之心，而仁不可勝用也；人能充無穿踰之心，而義不可勝用也；人能充無受爾汝之實，無所往而不爲義也。士未可以言而言，是以言餂之也；可以言而不言，是以不言餂之也，是皆穿踰之類也。”

32. 孟子曰：“言近而指遠者，善言也；守約而施博者，善道也。君子之言也，不下帶而道存焉；君子之守，脩其身而天下平。人病舍其田而芸人之田——所求於人者重，而所以自任者輕。”

'Are your followers so deceitful in appearance?'

'Do you think that they have come with the express purpose of stealing the sandals?'

'Is that not so?'

'In setting myself up as a teacher, I do not go after anyone who leaves, nor do I refuse anyone who comes. So long as he comes with the right attitude of mind, I accept him. That is all.'[13]

[13] Mencius' attitude towards those who came to study under him is reminiscent of the attitude of Confucius. Cf. the *Analects of Confucius*, VII. 29.

31. Mencius said, 'For every man there are things he cannot bear. To extend this to what he can bear is benevolence.[14] For every man there are things he is not willing to do. To extend this to what he is willing to do is rightness. If a man can extend to the full his natural aversion to harming others, then there will be an over-abundance of benevolence. If a man can extend his dislike for boring holes and climbing over walls,[15] then there will be an over-abundance of rightness. If a man can extend his unwillingness to suffer the actual humiliation of being addressed as "thou" and "thee", then wherever he goes he will not do anything that is not right.

'To speak to a Gentleman who cannot be spoken to is to use speech as a bait; on the other hand, not to speak to one who could be spoken to is to use silence as a bait.[16] In either case, the action is of the same kind as that of boring holes and climbing over walls.'

[14] Cf. VII. B. 1.

[15] Cf. 'those who bore holes in the wall to peep at one another, and climb over it to meet illicitly' (III. B. 3).

[16] Cf. the *Analects of Confucius*, XV. 8.

32. Mencius said, 'Words near at hand but with far-reaching import are good words. The way of holding on to the essential while giving it wide application is a good way. The words of a gentleman never go as far as below the sash, yet in them is to be found the Way. What the gentleman holds on to is the cultivation of his own character, yet this brings order to the Empire. The trouble with people is that they leave their own fields to weed the fields of others. They are exacting towards others but indulgent towards themselves.'

33. 孟子曰：“堯舜，性者也；湯武，反之也。動容周旋中禮者，盛德之至也。哭死而哀，非爲生者也。經德不回，非以干祿也。言語必信，非以正行也。君子行法，以俟命而已矣。”

34. 孟子曰：“說大人，則藐之，勿視其巍巍然。堂高數仞，榱題數尺，我得志，弗爲也。食前方丈，侍妾數百人，我得志，弗爲也。般樂飲酒，驅騁田獵，後車千乘，我得志，弗爲也。在彼者，皆我所不爲也；在我者，皆古之制也，吾何畏彼哉？”

35. 孟子曰：“養心莫善於寡欲。其爲人也寡欲，雖有不存焉者，寡矣；其爲人也多欲，雖有存焉者，寡矣。”

36. 曾晳嗜羊棗，而曾子不忍食羊棗。公孫丑問曰：“膾炙與羊棗孰美？”

　　孟子曰：“膾炙哉！”

33. Mencius said, 'Yao and Shun had it as their nature; T'ang and King Wu returned to it.[17] To be in accord with the rites in every movement is the highest of virtue. When one mourns sorrowfully over the dead it is not to impress the living. When one follows unswervingly the path of virtue it is not to win advancement. When one invariably keeps one's word it is not to establish the rectitude of one's actions. A gentleman merely follows the norm and awaits his destiny.'[18]

[17]Cf. VII. A. 30. The 'it' here must also be referring to benevolence.
[18]Cf. VII. A. 1.

34. Mencius said, 'When speaking to men of consequence it is necessary to look on them with contempt and not be impressed by their lofty position. Their hall is tens of feet high; the capitals are several feet broad. Were I to meet with success, I would not indulge in such things. Their tables, laden with food, measure ten feet across, and their female attendants are counted in the hundreds. Were I to meet with success, I would not indulge in such things. They have a great time drinking, driving and hunting, with a retinue of a thousand chariots. Were I to meet with success I would not indulge in such things. All the things they do I would not do, and everything I do is in accordance with ancient institutions. Why, then, should I cower before them?'

35. Mencius said, 'There is nothing better for the nurturing of the heart than to reduce the number of one's desires. When a man has but few desires, even if there is anything he fails to retain in himself, it cannot be much; but when he has a great many desires, then even if there is anything he manages to retain in himself, it cannot be much.'[19]

[19]Cf. IV. B. 28, 'A gentleman differs from other men in that he retains his heart. A gentleman retains his heart by means of benevolence and the rites.'

36. Because Tseng Hsi[20] was fond of eating jujubes, Tseng Tzu could not bring himself to eat them. Kung-sun Ch'ou asked, 'Which is more tasty, mince and roast or jujubes?'
'Mince and roast, of course,' said Mencius.

公孫丑曰：“然則曾子何爲食膾炙而不食羊棗？”

曰：“膾炙所同也，羊棗所獨也。諱名不諱姓，姓所同也，名所獨也。”

37. 萬章問曰：“孔子在陳曰：‘盍歸乎來！吾黨之小子狂簡，進取，不忘其初。’孔子在陳，何思魯之狂士？”

孟子曰：“孔子‘不得中道而與之，必也狂狷乎！狂者進取，狷者有所不爲也’。孔子豈不欲中道哉？不可必得，故思其次也。”

“敢問何如斯可謂狂矣？”

曰：“如琴張、曾晳、牧皮者，孔子之所謂狂矣。”

“何以謂之狂也？”

曰：“其志嘐嘐然，曰，‘古之人，古之人。’夷考其行，而不掩焉者也。狂者又不可得，欲得不屑不絜之士而與之，是獧也，是又其次也。孔子曰：‘過我門而不入我室，我不憾焉者，其惟鄉原乎！鄉原，德之賊也。’”

曰：“何如斯可謂之鄉原矣？”

曰：“‘何以是嘐嘐也？言不顧行，行不顧言，則曰，古之人，古之人。行何爲踽踽涼涼？生斯世也，爲斯世也，善斯可矣。’閹然媚於世也者，是鄉原也。”

'In that case why did Tseng Tzu eat mince and roast, but not jujubes?'

'Mince and roast were a taste shared by others, but not jujubes. A personal name is tabooed but not a surname, because a surname is shared while a personal name is not.'

[20]Tseng Tzu's father.

37. Wan Chang asked, 'When Confucius was in Ch'en, he exclaimed, "Let us go home. The young men of my school are wild and unconventional, rushing forward while not forgetting their origins."[21] As Confucius was in Ch'en, what made him think of the wild Gentlemen of Lu?'

Mencius answered, 'Confucius [said], "If one fails to find those who follow the middle way as associates, one can only fall back on the wild and the squeamish. The wild rush forward, while the squeamish find certain things beneath them."[22] Of course Confucius wanted those who followed the middle way, but he could not be sure of finding such men. Hence he thought of the second best.'

'May I ask what sort of a person will be described as "wild"?'

'Men like Ch'in Chang, Tseng Hsi and Mu P'i were what Confucius described as "wild".'

'Why were they called "wild"?'

'They had great ambition and were always saying "The ancients! The ancients!" and yet, when one examines their conduct, it did not always fall within prescribed limits. When even the "wild" could not be found, Confucius wished to find for associates Gentlemen who were aloof. These are the squeamish, and they are one step further down. Confucius said, "The only people who pass my house by without causing me regret are perhaps the village honest men. The village honest man is the enemy of virtue." '[23]

'What sort of a man will be described as a "village honest man"?'

'[The man who says] "What is the point of having such great ambition? Their words and deeds take no notice of each other, and yet they keep on saying, 'The ancients! The ancients!' Why must they walk along in such solitary fashion? Being in this world, one must behave in a manner pleasing to this world. So long as one

萬子曰：“一鄉皆稱原人焉，無所往而不爲原人，孔子以爲德之賊，何哉？”

曰：“非之無舉也，刺之無刺也，同乎流俗，合乎汙世，居之似忠信，行之似廉絜，衆皆悅之，自以爲是，而不可與入堯舜之道，故曰‘德之賊’也。孔子曰：惡似而非者：惡莠，恐其亂苗也；惡佞，恐其亂義也；惡利口，恐其亂信也，惡鄭聲，恐其亂樂也；惡紫，恐其亂朱也；惡鄉原，恐其亂德也。君子反經而已矣。經正，則庶民興；庶民興，斯無邪慝矣。”

38. 孟子曰：“由堯舜至於湯，五百有餘歲；若禹、皋陶，則見而知之；若湯，則聞而知之。由湯至於文王，五百有餘歲，若伊尹、萊朱，則見而知之；若文王，則聞而知之。由文王至於孔子，五百有餘歲，若太公望、散宜生，則見而知之；若孔子，則聞而知之。由孔子而來至於今，百有餘歲，去聖人之世若此其未遠也，近聖人之居若此其甚也，然而無有乎爾，則亦無有乎爾。”

is good, it is all right." He tries in this way cringingly to please the world. Such is the village honest man.'

'If a man is praised for his honesty in his village,' said Wan Tzu, 'then he is an honest man wherever he goes. Why did Confucius consider such a man an enemy of virtue?'

'If you want to censure him, you cannot find anything; if you want to find fault with him, you cannot find anything either. He shares with others the practices of the day and is in harmony with the sordid world. He pursues such a policy and appears to be conscientious and faithful, and to show integrity in his conduct. He is liked by the multitude and is self-righteous. It is impossible to embark on the way of Yao and Shun with such a man. Hence the name "enemy of virtue". Confucius said, "I dislike what is specious. I dislike the foxtail in case it should pass for seedlings; I dislike flattery in case it should pass for what is right; I dislike glibness in case it should pass for the truthful; I dislike the music of Cheng in case it should pass for proper music; I dislike purple in case it should pass for vermilion; I dislike the village honest man in case he should pass for the virtuous."[24] A gentleman goes back to the norm. That is all. When the norm is properly set then the common people will be stirred; when the common people are stirred then heresy and aberration will disappear.'

[21] Cf. the *Analects of Confucius*, V. 2.
[22] Cf. ibid., XIII. 21.
[23] Cf. ibid., XVII. 13.
[24] Cf. ibid., XVII. 18.

38. Mencius said, 'From Yao and Shun to T'ang it was over five hundred years. Men like Yü and Kao Yao knew Yao and Shun personally, while those like T'ang knew them only by reputation. From T'ang to King Wen it was over five hundred years. Men like Yi Yin and Lai Chu knew T'ang personally, while those like King Wen knew him only by reputation. From King Wen to Confucius it was over five hundred years. Men such as T'ai Kung Wang and San-yi Sheng knew King Wen personally, while those like Confucius knew him only by reputation. From Confucius to the present it is over a hundred years. In time we are so near to the age of the sage while in place we are so close to his home,

yet if there is no one who has anything of the sage, well then, there is no one who has anything of the sage.'

Appendix 1

THE DATING OF EVENTS IN
THE LIFE OF MENCIUS

The earliest account of the life of Mencius is to be found in the *Shih chi* (*Records of the Historian*), the earliest general history of China, written at the beginning of the first century B.C. by Ssu-ma Ch'ien:

> Meng K'e (Mencius) was a man from the state of Tsou. He studied under a disciple of Tzu Ssu,[1] and when he had mastered the Way he travelled to Ch'i where he took office at the court of King Hsüan who, however, was unable to entrust him with affairs of state. He then went to Liang. King Hui of Liang found Mencius' views, before he had fully listened to them, to be impracticable and remote from actuality.
>
> At that time, Ch'in had put Lord Shang into power, greatly enhancing the wealth and military power of the state; Ch'u and Wei in turn entrusted Wu Ch'i with the government of the state and were able to be victorious in war, weakening their enemies; while King Wei and King Hsüan of Ch'i made the feudal lords turn east and pay homage to Ch'i by employing Sun Tzu, T'ien Chi and others. When the Empire, busily engaged now in vertical, and now in horizontal, alliances, valued only military prowess, Meng K'e preached the virtuous tradition of T'ang, Yü and the Three Dynasties. For this reason he never secured a sympathetic hearing no matter where he went. He then retired and, together with Wan Chang and others, wrote the *Mencius* in seven books, giving an exposition of the *Odes* and the *History* and developing the ideas of Confucius. (*Shih chi*, chüan 74)

This account differs on one important point from the *Mencius*. Here Mencius is said to have visited Ch'i before he went to Liang whereas in the *Mencius* he visited Liang first. Now the chronology of the Warring States period in the *Shih chi* is inaccurate in many places. Where Mencius is concerned the mistakes in the dates of King Hui of Liang and King Hsüan of Ch'i are particularly important. According to the *Shih chi*, the reign periods of the Liang kings from 370 to 296 B.C. are as follows: King Hui 370-335; King Hsiang 334-319; King Ai 318-296. But the correct dates established with the help of the *Bamboo Annals*[2] are as follows: King Hui 370-319; King Hsiang 318-296.

---

[1] Grandson of Confucius.

[2] The *Bamboo Annals* were discovered in 281 A.D. and were still extant in T'ang times. They were then lost and the present work bearing that title is a reconstitution and, as such, not altogether reliable. But there are numerous quotations from it in early sources and these have proved invaluable for rectifying the mistakes in the *Shih chi* chronology of the Warring States period. It is interesting that the *Bamboo Annals* were,

There are circumstances which render the mistakes in the *Shih chi* understandable. King Hui was originally Ying, the Marquis of Wei, but in 334, he and King Wei of Ch'i had a meeting at Hsü Chou where they agreed to recognize each other as king. To mark this event, King Hui initiated a new reign period. Ssu-ma Ch'ien mistook this as marking the beginning of the reign of his successor, King Hsiang. Having done this, it is natural for him to make the further mistake of treating the death of King Hui in 319 as the death of King Hsiang. He was then left with the period 318-296 without a king and King Ai was invented to fill the gap. But even this invention is not altogether without foundation in fact. It is very likely that King Hsiang's full title was King Ai Hsiang, though he was generally known only as King Hsiang. This is, to a certain extent, supported by the fact that there was also a King Ai Hsiang in Han. What Ssu-ma Ch'ien did was to make two kings out of one.

The reign periods of the Ch'i kings from 378 to 284 B.C. are given in the *Shih chi* as follows: King Wei 378-343; King Hsüan 342-324; King Min 323-284. The correct dates, again established with the help of the *Bamboo Annals*, are as follows: King Wei 357-320; King Hsüan 319-301; King Min 300-284.[3]

To go back to the difference between the *Shih chi* and the *Mencius* on the order of the visits to Liang and Ch'i. One may easily think that the putting of the visit to Ch'i before the visit to Liang in the *Shih chi* is due to the mistakes in the chronology, but this is not so. For though King Hui is made to die sixteen years earlier in 335, so, too, is King Hsüan made to succeed his father twenty-three years earlier in 342, and as Ssu-ma Ch'ien, knowing that Mencius visited Liang a year before King Hui's death, placed Mencius' visit to Liang in 336 (when it should, of course, have been in 320), it would still have been possible for him to place Mencius' visit to Liang before his visit to Ch'i. Thus the mistaken chronology is not really responsible for Ssu-ma Ch'ien's mistake. While this is true, nevertheless, if he had got his chronology right he would have seen that it was impossible for Mencius to have visited Ch'i in 319, stayed for several years and then to visit Liang before the death of King Hui.

Now the correct dates of King Hui of Liang were well known to scholars for a very long time. The *Tzu chih t'ung chien*, the monumental chronological history of China covering the period from 403 B.C. to 959 A.D., completed in 1085 by Ssu-ma Kuang, already gave the correct dates. But the correct dates of King Hsüan of Ch'i were less well known. The *Mencius* mentions

---

in fact, the annals of Wei (or Liang) and recorded events up to the time of King Hsiang who is referred to as 'the present ruler'.

[3] For detailed discussions of these problems see Ch'ien Mu, *Hsien Ch'in chu tzu hsi nien*, revised and enlarged edition, Hong Kong, 1956, and Yang K'uan, *Chan kuo shih*, Shanghai, 1955.

more than once in the invasion of Yen by Ch'i. In I. B. 10 and I. B. 11, King Hsüan is mentioned by name, while in II. B. 8 and II. B. 9 the text only says 'the King of Ch'i', but in II. B. 8 Tzu-k'uai and Tzu-chih are mentioned. Now the abdication of Tzu-k'uai in favour of Tzu-chih, we know, from a number of sources, took place in 315 or 314. For those who accepted the dates of King Hsüan of Ch'i as given in the *Shih chi*, there is the problem of reconciling the fact that the invasion of Yen after Tzu-k'uai's abdication was known to have taken place in 314.[4] Two solutions have been proposed, neither of which is satisfactory. According to the first, since King Hsüan died before the invasion which took place in 314 but is mentioned in connexion with an invasion in Book I, there must have been two invasions. The invasion referred to in Book I took place in 333 while the one mentioned in Book II in connexion with Tzu-k'uai's abdication indeed took place in 314, but the unnamed king involved was King Min and not King Hsüan.[5] This solution has at least the merit of respecting the text of the *Mencius*. The second solution is nothing if not drastic. According to this, the only king in Ch'i Mencius ever saw was King Min. The numerous places in the present text where the name of King Hsüan is to be found are all due to the tampering with the text by editors.[6]

But from the eighteenth century onwards, there has been no lack of scholars who saw that the problem was due to a mistake in the chronology of the Ch'i kings in the *Shih chi*. Ts'ui Shu (1740-1816) pointed out that the difficulty arose because Ssu-ma Ch'ien moved the reigns of King Wei and King Hsüan back twenty years as a result of having left out two earlier rulers.[7] Apart from Ts'ui Shu, Lin Ch'un-p'u (1775-1861)[8] and Wei Yuan (1794-1856)[9] both arrived at the same conclusion.[10]

There are two other rulers mentioned in the *Mencius* whose dates are given incorrectly in the *Shih chi*. The first is Duke P'ing of Lu, the dates of whose

[4] The *Tzu chih t'ung chien* (72, 90) arbitrarily moved the reign of King Hsüan forward ten years to 332-314 simply to bring the invasion of Yen just within his lifetime.

[5] This suggestion is recorded by Huang Chen in his *Huang shih jih ch'ao*, quoted by Lin Ch'un-p'u, *Meng tzu shih shih nien piao huo shuo* (*Chu po shan fang shih wu chung* edition), 1816, pp. 4b-6a.

[6] This theory is quoted with approval by no less an authority than Ch'ien Ta-hsin (1728-1804). See his *Shih chia chai yang hsin lu* (Basic Sinological Series edition), 1935, pp. 54-5.

[7] Ts'ui Shu, *Meng tzu shih shih lu* (*K'ao hsin lu, Wan yu wen k'u* edition), 1937, p. 672.

[8] Lin Ch'un-p'u, loc. cit.

[9] Wei Yuan, *Meng tzu nien piao*, 2.25 (*Ku wei t'ang nei wai chi* edition, 1878).

[10] Amongst Western scholars Henri Maspero was the first to write on the problem of the chronology of the Ch'i kings. See his *La chronologie des rois de Ts'i au IVe siècle avant notre ère* (*T'oung Pao*, Vol. XXV, 1928, pp. 367-86).

reign are given as 314-297 when they should be 322-303. The second is Yen, King of Sung (posthumous name King K'ang) the dates of whose reign are given as 328-286 when they should be 337-286. The year 328 was the year he assumed the title of king and not the date of his accession as Ssu-ma Ch'ien took it to be.[11]

We have seen that there is no reason to doubt the order of events implicit in Book I of the *Mencius* and where the *Shih chi* disagrees with the *Mencius* it is the *Shih chi* that is at fault. But there still remains one question concerning the dating of the events in Mencius' life. Book I covers the period from 320 to some time after the end of the invasion of Yen by Ch'i begun in 314. The question is: are there any events recorded in the *Mencius* which can be shown definitely to date from before the year 320? There are a number of events which, some scholars have argued, must have taken place before 320. It is then further argued from this that Mencius must have made another visit to Ch'i before the time of King Hsüan and this earlier visit must have been in the time of King Wei. It is, therefore, worthwhile examining the evidence to see if it is, in fact, sound.

(1) There are two related passages which we shall take together. According to II. B. 7, while in Ch'i Mencius made a visit to Lu for the burial of his mother. In I. B. 16, Duke P'ing of Lu was dissuaded by Tsang Ts'ang, a favourite of his, from going to see Mencius on the grounds that he gave a more splendid funeral to his mother than to his father who died earlier. There are two questions concerning these two passages. The first is, was it before 319 that Mencius returned to Lu from Ch'i to bury his mother? The second is, did the incident with Duke P'ing occur during Mencius' return to Lu to bury his mother? Mr. Ch'ien Mu, for instance, answers both questions in the affirmative. He starts from the assumption that the position of Mencius throughout his stay in Ch'i from 319 was that of a Minister (*ch'ing*). He, then, goes on to make two points. First, at the time of the burial, Mencius' official position was that of a Counsellor (*ta fu*) as was stated by Yüeh-cheng Tzu. Since his position in Ch'i in the time of King Hsüan was that of a Minister, his return to Lu must have been during a previous visit in the time of King Wei. Second, Tsang Ts'ang referred to Mencius as 'a common fellow'. This would be inconceivable if Mencius was in fact a Minister. Hence the incident involving Duke P'ing must also date from before 319.[12] It seems to me that Mr. Ch'ien's process of reasoning is rather odd, to say the least. Let us take his second point first. That Mencius' position was that of a Counsellor at the time of the burial is not in dispute. If Tsang Ts'ang's remark was made soon afterwards,

[11] See Ch'ien Mu, op. cit., p. 339 and p. 274.
[12] op. cit., pp. 349-50.

he was calling him 'a common fellow' in spite of the fact that he was a Counsellor. Why, then, should he not have done so even if Mencius had been a Minister? If it is seriously suggested that Tsang Ts'ang could have called Mencius 'a common fellow' only if he was without any official rank, then this would, in fact, be an argument in favour of this having been done when Mencius visited Lu after his final departure from Ch'i some time after 314, for he would then be indeed without official position of any kind, whereas he would have been a Counsellor if the remark was made during his return to bury his mother. But I do not think that the remark 'a common fellow' can be used as serious evidence at all. It was simply a term of abuse and nothing more. Now the argument that Mencius must have returned to Lu from Ch'i to bury his mother before 319 rests solely on the assumption that from 319 onwards Mencius was a Minister. But there is no firm evidence that this was the case. True, in II. B. 6 and VI. B. 6, it is said that Mencius was a Minister in Ch'i, but as his whole stay lasted at least five or six years, all we can be sure of is that *at some stage* he was made a Minister. We cannot rule out the possibility that he was only a Counsellor in the initial period of his stay. There seems, therefore, no reason why we should not place Mencius' return to Lu after 319. As to the incident with Duke P'ing, the fact that the section is placed at the end of Book I Part B seems to imply that it was after Mencius' final departure from Ch'i.

(2) There are the three passages which refer to Sung. In II. B. 3, we find Ch'en Chen questioning Mencius on why he accepted in Sung a gift of gold, having refused previously a gift in Ch'i. This clearly shows that Mencius visited Sung after he had been in Ch'i. The question is, does this refer to his visit to Ch'i in 319? In III. B. 6, we find Mencius talking to Tai Pu-sheng who, it is clear from the context, was an official at the court of the king of Sung. In III. B. 5, Wan Chang asked Mencius, 'If Sung, a small state, were to practise Kingly government and be attacked by Ch'i and Ch'u for doing so, what could be done about it?' Now there is no doubt that the king of Sung during this period was Yen, because, as we have seen, he reigned from 337-286. But as Yen assumed the title of king in 328, Mr Ch'ien Mu argues that it must be soon after he assumed the title of king that he wished to practise Kingly government. It is concluded from this that Mencius' visit to Sung must be in 328 or shortly after, and the visit to Ch'i which preceded this must have been before 319 in the time of King Wei.[13] This again seems to me hardly convincing as an argument. Though Yen assumed the title of king in 328, as he reigned for over forty years, one can hardly insist that it must have been shortly after he assumed the title of king that he decided to practise Kingly

---

[13] op. cit., p. 314.

government. Moreover, Wan Chang's question is, on my interpretation, couched in a hypothetical form and has no actual reference to any particular period of his reign. Finally, even if he started practising Kingly government in 328, this was likely to have gone on for a good many years and there is no reason to think that Mencius must have arrived on the scene shortly after 328. Once again, there is no evidence to show that the visit to Sung could not have taken place after Mencius' final departure from Ch'i.

(3) There is Mencius' friendship with K'uang Chang. In IV. B. 30, when questioned why he not only befriended K'uang Chang but treated him with courtesy, Mencius answered that K'uang Chang had none of the failings commonly regarded as undutiful in a son. He went on to describe what happened in his case between him and his father:

> In his case father and son are at odds through taxing each other over a moral issue. It is for friends to demand goodness from each other. For father and son to do so seriously undermines the love between them. Do you think that Chang Tzu does not want to be with his wife and sons? Because of his offence, he is not allowed near his father. Therefore, he sent his wife and sons away and refused to allow them to look after him. To his way of thinking, unless he acted in this way, his offence would be the greater. That is Chang Tzu for you.'

It is rather tantalizing that Mencius does not tell us what the moral issue is between K'uang Chang and his father. In an effort to throw some light on this obscure topic, some commentators relate this passage of the *Mencius* to a passage in the *Chan kuo ts'e*. This gives an account of King Wei of Ch'i sending a man called Chang Tzu to lead the army against the invading forces from Ch'in. When some one reported that Chang Tzu had gone over to the enemy, King Wei expressed his firm faith in Chang Tzu by saying:

> Ch'i, the mother of Chang Tzu, offended his father and he killed her and had her buried beneath the stables. In giving the command to Chang Tzu, I said to him, by way of encouragement, 'If with your prowess you bring the troops safely home, I promise you I shall have your mother re-buried.' He answered, 'It is not that I am unable to re-bury her. Ch'i, my mother, offended my father and my father died without leaving instructions. If I should re-bury my mother in spite of the fact that my father left no instructions, this is taking advantage of my father because he is dead. That is why I have not dared do so.' If a man would not, as a son, take advantage of his dead father, is he likely, as a subject, to take advantage of his living prince? (*Ch'i ts'e*, 1/13)

This account, it is believed, explains why K'uang Chang was dubbed an undutiful son by the whole country. It is then further argued that as King Wei must have had Chang Tzu's mother re-buried after the campaign, he would no longer be dubbed an undutiful son, so Mencius' remarks must have been made before this happened. As the campaign took place in the time of King Wei, it follows that Mencius must have visited Ch'i in the time of King Wei when he befriended K'uang Chang.[14] There seems to me to be a major flaw in this argument. The justification for relating the *Chan kuo ts'e* passage to the *Mencius* passage is that it throws light on the latter. But there is, in fact, no point of contact between the two passages. In the *Mencius*, K'uang Chang was dubbed an undutiful son because he was at odds with his father, and although we do not know the nature of the issue between them we do know that this happened during the lifetime of his father, and that he was not allowed near his father. In the *Chan kuo ts'e*, Chang Tzu is said not to be able to re-bury his mother because his father died without leaving instructions. This concerns his relationship with his dead father and there is no mention of any dispute between him and his father when his father was alive. Thus this throws no light on the *Mencius* passage at all. This being the case, it is not unreasonable to question whether the Chang Tzu in the *Chan kuo ts'e* is the same as the K'uang Chang in the *Mencius*. While it is true that Mencius referred to K'uang Chang as Chang Tzu, it does not follow that anyone referred to as Chang Tzu must be K'uang Chang. Again, the *Chan kuo ts'e* is not always reliable as history, and this invasion of Ch'i by Ch'in has never been definitely identified and supported by other sources. We cannot be sure even of the correctness of the reference to King Wei. Once more, we see that there is no real evidence to show that Mencius must have visited Ch'i before 319.

Although the results we have arrived at in our examination of the purported evidence for events in the *Mencius* having taken place before 320 are negative, this at least shows that there is no real evidence against the apparent chronological order in which the sections of Book I of the *Mencius* are arranged, neither is there any event in the whole work which can be shown to date definitely from a date before the year 320 B.C.

---

[14] Ch'ien Mu, op. cit., p. 316.

Appendix 2

EARLY TRADITIONS ABOUT MENCIUS

There are certain traditions about Mencius to be found in two works of the Western Han, the *Han shih wai chuan* of the second century B.C. and the *Lieh nü chuan* just over a century later. It is difficult to know how much credence is to be given to these traditions but they are of some interest in their own right because of the wide currency they attained as cautionary tales.

(A) HAN SHIH WAI CHUAN

1. When Mencius was a boy, he was repeating his lessons while his mother was weaving. He stopped abruptly and then went on again. His mother knew that he could not remember the text. She called him to her and asked, 'Why did you stop?' He answered, 'I lost the thread, but I picked it up again.' His mother drew a knife and cut what she had woven, to drive home the lesson that he must not repeat his mistake again. From then on, Mencius never again forgot his lessons.

When Mencius was a boy, the neighbour on the east side once slaughtered a piglet. He asked his mother, 'Why does our neighbour on the east side slaughter a piglet?' 'Why, in order to offer you some pork to eat, of course,' answered his mother. She then regretted what she had said. 'When I was carrying this boy, I would not sit when the mat was not in position;[1] nor would I eat when the meat was not cut in regular shapes,' said she to herself. 'This is because it was the way of pre-natal education. Now he has just reached the age of understanding and I have told him an untruth. This is to teach him to be dishonest.' So she bought some pork from the neighbour and gave it to Mencius to eat, to show that she had not been dishonest with him.

The *Odes* say,

It is only to be expected that your sons and grandsons should be prudent,[2]

meaning that a good and wise mother will make her son good and wise as well. (9/1)

2. Mencius' wife was alone and she was sitting with her knees up, Mencius

[1] Read *cheng* for *chih*.
[2] Ode 5.

entered the room, stared at her and went to tell his mother. 'My wife is lacking in manners. Please send her away.' 'What has happened?' asked his mother. 'She is sitting with her knees up.' 'How did you know?' 'I saw her with my own eyes.' 'It is not your wife but you who are lacking in manners. Do the *Rites* not prescribe,

On entering the gate of the house,
Ask which members of the family are still alive;[3]
On ascending the hall,
Raise your voice;
On entering the door of a room,
Lower your eyes.

This is to avoid catching people unawares. Now you went to her private chamber and failed to raise your voice on entering so that you found her sitting with her knees up and you stared at her. It is not your wife but you who are lacking in manners.'

Thereupon Mencius blamed himself and dared not send his wife away.

The *Odes* say,

When gathering turnips
Pay no heed to the roots.[4] (9/15)

(B) LIEH NÜ CHUAN

1. The mother of Meng K'e of Tsou was known as Mother Meng. Her house was near a graveyard, and the boy Mencius played at grave-digging and was most energetic at building and interring. 'This is no place for my child,' said Mother Meng, so she moved to live next to the market. Mencius played he was a hawker hawking his goods. Once more Mother Meng said, 'This is no place for my child.' Once again she moved to live near a school. Mencius played at sacrificial and ceremonial rituals. 'This is truly a place for my son,' said Mother Meng and she settled there. When Mencius became a man, he studied the six arts and became known as a great Confucianist.

In the opinion of the gentleman, Mother Meng knew the method of gradual transformation. The *Odes* say,

That docile boy,
What should one give him?[5]

This is a case in point.

[3] This line has been inserted on the authority of the parallel in the *Lieh nü chuan* passage. See below.
[4] Ode 35.
[5] Ode 53.

2. When Mencius was a boy, he came home one day from school. Mother Meng who was weaving asked him, 'Where have you got to in your lessons?' 'The same place as I got to before,' answered Mencius. With her knife Mother Meng cut what she had woven. This frightened Mencius and he asked why she had done it. 'Your neglecting your lessons is just like my cutting this fabric. Now a gentleman studies in order to make a name and to make his knowledge extensive. For this reason, when he stays at home he will be safe and when he is abroad no harm will come near him. Now you neglect your lessons. This means that you will escape neither servitude nor disaster. What difference is there between this and abandoning half way one's weaving and spinning on which one's livelihood depends? How can one clothe one's husband and avoid shortage of food for long? A woman who gives up her means of livelihood or a man who is indolent in the cultivation of his virtue will either become a thief or a slave.' This frightened Mencius. He studied with industry incessantly day and night and became a disciple of Tzu-ssu. In the end he became a Confucianist known throughout the Empire.

In the opinion of the gentleman, Mother Meng knew how to be a mother. The *Odes* say,

> That docile boy,
> What should one tell him?[6]

This is a case in point.

3. After Mencius was married, one day when he was just about to enter his private chamber, he found his wife scantily clad, Mencius was displeased and left without entering. His wife took leave of Mother Meng and asked to be allowed to go. 'I have heard', she said, 'that ceremony between husband and wife does not extend to the private chamber. Just now I was relaxing in my room and my husband, seeing me, showed anger in his face. This is treating me as a visitor. It is not right for a woman to stay overnight as a visitor. I beg to be allowed to return to my parents.' So Mother Meng summoned Mencius and told him, 'According to the *Rites*,

> On entering the gate of a house,
> Ask which members of the family are still alive.

This is in order to pay one's respects.

> On ascending the hall,
> Raise your voice.

This is in order to give warning.

---

[6]loc. cit.

> On entering the door of a room,
> Lower your eyes.

This is for fear of seeing others at fault.

'Now you expect others to conform to the *Rites* while failing yourself to see their import. Is this not wide of the mark?'

Mencius apologized and kept his wife. In the opinion of the gentleman, Mother Meng understood the *Rites* and knew how to be a mother-in-law.

4. When Mencius was in Ch'i, he looked worried. On seeing this, Mother Meng said, 'You seem to be worried. What is the matter?' 'Nothing,' said Mencius.

On another day, when he was not doing anything, Mencius put his arms round a pillar and sighed. On seeing this, Mother Meng said, 'Some time ago, I saw you looking worried, but you said, "Nothing". Now you put your arms round a pillar and sigh. What is the matter?' 'I have heard,' answered Mencius, 'that a gentleman takes a position that is commensurate with his person. He does not accept a reward he does not deserve; nor does he covet honour and wealth. When a feudal lord does not listen to his views, he will not allow his name to be placed before the authorities. When a feudal lord listens to his views but will not have them put into practice, he will not set foot in his court. Now as the Way is not put into practice in Ch'i, I wish to leave, but you, mother, are advanced in years. That is what is worrying me.' 'Now according to the *Rites*, all a woman has to do is to be good at the five kinds of cooked rice, to cover up the drinks with a cloth, to minister to the needs of the father and mother of her husband, and to sew. Hence she should be concerned with the orderly running of the household and not with affairs beyond the boundary.

'The *Book of Changes* says,

> It lies in feeding the family.
> There is no taking upon herself of affairs.[7]

The *Odes* say,

> Neither wrong nor right
> But only wine and food are her concern.[8]

In other words, it is not for a woman to take on herself the making of decisions; her guiding principle is the "three submissions". In youth, she submits to her parents; after marriage, to her husband; after the death of her husband, to her son. This is in accordance with the rites. Now you are a

[7] Hexagram 37.
[8] Ode 189.

grown man and I am old. You do what is right for you and I act according to the rites which apply to me.'

In the opinion of the gentleman, Mother Meng understood the way of a woman. The *Odes* say,

> Gentle and smiling,
> Neither angry nor eager to correct.[9]

Mother Meng is a case in point (chüan 1).

---

[9] Ode 299. There is a difference in the last line between the quotation and the present text of the Mao school which reads, 'Correcting without being angry.'

Appendix 3

THE TEXT OF THE *MENCIUS*

There are two theories concerning the composition of *Mencius*. The first is that the work was written by Mencius himself. The second is that it was produced by some of his disciples or, perhaps, by the disciples of his disciples. There are certain arguments in favour of the second theory. The feudal lords who appear in the work are referred to by their posthumous titles, but some of these must have survived Mencius and their posthumous titles could not have been known to him. Hence the *Mencius* must have, at least, undergone some editing after the death of Mencius. Again, most of the disciples of Mencius are referred to as *tzu* with the exception of Wan Chang and Kung-sun Ch'ou. If Mencius had written the work himself, it would be strange for him to show them the deference implicit in this appellation, and even more strange, if he decided to do so, to make an exception of Wan Chang and Kung-sun Ch'ou. Again, this seems obviously the work of some editor and what appears to be strange will become quite natural if Wan Chang and Kung-sun Ch'ou were two of the editors. If this were so, can we assume that the editors compiled the *Mencius* out of the notes taken by a number of disciples rather than just out of their own notes of the sayings and conversations of the Master? There is one feature of the work which may have some bearing on this point. In the *Mencius* there are a dozen or so cases of the same passage appearing in more than one section. This in itself is nothing surprising. Thinkers of the Warring States period were in the habit of having a ready stock of illustrations and homilies to be used on appropriate occasions, and Mencius was no exception. But there are two or three cases which do not seem to fall within this category. For instance, I. B. 13 and I. B. 14, taken together, seem just to be a variant version of I. B. 15. Again, V. B. 1, apart from the final comment, consists solely of passages to be found elsewhere in the work, and VII. B. 17 is simply a duplication of one of these passages without even affording a fresh context. If Mencius actually wrote the *Mencius*, it would be odd that he should have left such repetitions in. On the other hand, if the *Mencius* was compiled by an editor from notes taken down by Mencius' disciples, then it is not surprising that some repetitions should have escaped the editing. In this connexion, a passage quoting the words of Yi Yin which is found both in V. B. 1 and V. A. 7 is particularly interesting. The text is identical in the two sections except for the use of the two particles *ssu* and *tz'u*—both meaning 'this'; where V. B. 1 has *ssu* V. A. 7 has *tz'u* and vice versa. This is not difficult to understand if the two versions of the same passages represent notes taken down by two disciples.

If we accept the hypothesis that the *Mencius* was compiled from notes taken by his disciples, does this detract from its authoritativeness? The answer is, No. The notes must have been verbatim notes for there is rarely any divergence in the text where the same passage is found more than once. The words of the Master were, as is to be expected, sacrosanct in the eyes of the disciples, and the greatest care must have been taken to preserve them as they were spoken by him. Thus the question whether Mencius actually wrote the *Mencius* becomes one of little significance. While Mencius may not have composed the work, the words contained in it are his very words, or as near to being his very words as to make little difference, and carry with them the same authority as if he had written them himself.

The text of the *Mencius* as we have it has come down to us through Chao Ch'i (d. A.D. 201). Not only was Chao Ch'i one of the earliest commentators on the *Mencius* but his commentary is the only early commentary to have come down to us and, as such, is of considerable value to the understanding of the text. Chao Ch'i mentions that, apart from the seven inner books, there were four outer books which he decided to expunge because 'these books, lacking in width and depth, bear no resemblance to the inner books and are likely to be the spurious work of a later age rather than the authentic work of Mencius.' The question naturally arises: was Chao Ch'i right in expunging the outer books? To this one can only return a tentative answer, as the outer books are lost to us—the extant work bearing the title *The Outer Books of Mencius* being a late forgery. There are quotations from the *Mencius* in various works which are not to be found in the present text, and these taken together have some relevance to our question. Fortunately for us, there are two collections of such quotations. The first was by Li T'iao-yüan (1734-1803) and the second by Ma Kuo-han (1794-1857).[1] The first has eighteen items while the second has thirty-two, with a certain amount of overlapping. If we confine ourselves to works before Chao Ch'i's time or contemporary with him, the number of such quotations is no more than a dozen. None of these quotations are significant in content. Again, if we should take the *T'ai p'ing yü lan*, the famous encyclopaedia compiled between A.D. 977 and 984 and based on earlier encyclopaedias, there are only four out of more than 180 quotations from the *Mencius* that are not to be found in the present text. We do not know, of course, whether these quotations which are not found in the present text come from the outer books or from the inner books. Even if, for

---

[1] See Li T'iao-yüan, *Yi Meng tzu* (*Han hai*, t'ao 25) and Ma Kuo-han, *Yi Meng tzu* (*Yü han shan fang chi yi shu, Mu keng t'ieh hsü pu, Ching pien, Meng tzu lei*).

argument's sake, we were to assume that they all came from the outer books, it would only show that there was little worth quoting in them. On the other hand, if we assumed that the quotations came from the inner books we can see that, as the quotations are so few in number, our present text is pretty sound. In fact considering that works from the Warring States period tend to abound in textual corruptions, one's impression of the *Mencius* is that the text is extraordinarily well preserved. Here and there there is a possibility of textual corruption,[2] but these are few and far between. There are, of course, variant readings, but again there are few that are significant. It is no exaggeration to say that in the *Mencius* we have one of the best preserved texts from the Warring State period. In this we are, indeed, fortunate, for Mencius, besides being one of the greatest thinkers, happens to be one of the greatest stylists in the whole history of Chinese literature.

[2] See V. B. 1 and VI. A. 11.

Appendix 4

ANCIENT HISTORY AS UNDERSTOOD
BY MENCIUS

Chinese thinkers were in the habit of appealing to examples in history, and each' school had its own favourites amongst the ancient kings. For the Confucianists these were Yao and Shun, Yü, T'ang, King Wen and King Wu. Mencius, for instance, frequently cites the authority of Yao and Shun, but ancient history was for Mencius something more than an authority for occasional citation. Its significance is twofold. First, ancient personages were made concrete embodiments of moral qualities. On the one hand, Yao was the embodiment of kingly virtue, and Shun, besides being a sage king, was also the embodiment of filial virtue. On the other, Chieh and Tchou were bywords for wickedness in a ruler. Second, these idealized personages are envisaged in actual situations and these are discussed in detail and in all earnestness. For instance, after Shun became Emperor, what would he have done if his recalcitrant father, the Blind Man, were to commit murder? This serves the same purpose as the artificially contrived examples some Western philosophers use. Such as whether one should return a lethal weapon to a mad man. It is to give concrete shape to abstract moral problems. The example cited above raises the problem of the conflict between the duty of a good son and the duty of a good Emperor.

Thus we can see that a knowledge of ancient history is not only necessary as a general background to the *Mencius* but is in fact something without which a good deal of the work would be unintelligible. The reader who has the patience can piece together a good deal of ancient history from passages scattered in the *Mencius*, but this is a tedious task. To save him this trouble, in what follows passages in the *Mencius* concerning ancient history are collected together and arranged in chronological order, supplemented where necessary from other sources. It is fortunate for us that the Confucianist version of ancient history is based on the *Shu ching* (*Book of History*) and the account in the *Shih chi* (*Records of the Historian*) also follows this tradition and thus can be used to supplement the accounts found in the *Mencius*.

It is, perhaps, not out of place to emphasize that the Confucianist version was only one version of ancient history and that there were other traditions. For instance, according to the Confucianist version, Yao abdicated in favour of Shun while Ch'i, the son of Yü, succeeded his father as Emperor because the common people turned to him instead of to Yi. But according to the *Bamboo Annals*, Shun imprisoned Yao and Ch'i put Yi to death. Again, according to the Confucianist version, Yi Yin banished T'ai Chia because he upset the laws of T'ang but restored him to the throne when he reformed (V. A. 6). But according to the *Bamboo Annals*, Yi Yin banished T'ai Chia and usurped the throne, only to be killed by T'ai Chia who returned secretly. It is futile to try to decide which is the true version as we cannot even be sure whether Yao and Shun existed or not. The reader should, therefore, take the account of ancient history that follows simply as an aid to the understanding of the *Mencius*.

(A) THE FIVE EMPERORS

Traditionally there were Emperors earlier than the Five Emperors. One of these, Shen Nung, is, indeed, mentioned in the *Mencius*, but he is only mentioned in connexion with a man called Hsü Hsing who preached his doctrines, and has no significance for Mencius. There are also various ways of counting the Five Emperors, but the way they differ does not concern us either, as only the last two, Yao and Shu, appear in the *Mencius*.

Yao was the Emperor whose dynasty is known as T'ang. Of his early life nothing is said in the *Mencius*. It is in connexion with the Flood that Yao is first mentioned:

> In the time of Yao, the Empire was not yet settled. The Flood still raged unchecked, inundating the Empire; plants grew thickly; birds and beasts multiplied; the five grains did not ripen; birds and beasts encroached upon men, and their trail criss-crossed even the Central Kingdoms. The lot fell on Yao to worry about this situation. (III. A. 4)

Kun was recommended to Yao as capable of dealing with the Flood. After nine years he met with no success. Then after seventy years as Emperor, Yao wanted a successor and Shun was recommended to him. Yao gave Shun his two daughters as wives (V. A. 1, V. B. 6, VII. B. 6). Though Shun was still a Commoner, Yao treated him as equal:

> Shun went to see the Emperor, who placed his son-in-law in a separate mansion. He entertained Shun but also allowed himself to be entertained in return. This is an example of an Emperor making friends with a common man. (V. B. 3)

Then Shun was raised to a position of authority (V. B. 6), and after a number of years he was made regent (V. A. 4).

During his regency Shun punished the four most wicked men in the Empire. He 'banished Kung Kung to Yu Chou and Huan Tou to Mount Ch'ung; he banished San Miao to San Wei and killed Kun [presumably for his failure to deal successfully with the Flood] on Mount Yü' (V. A. 3).

On Yao's death the *Yao tien* has this to say:

> After twenty-eight years, Fang Hsün died. It was as if the people had
> lost their fathers and mothers. For three years all musical instruments
> were silenced. (V. A. 4)

Shun succeeded Yao as Emperor because, as Mencius puts it, 'Yao recommended Shun to Heaven and Heaven accepted him; he presented him to the
people and the people accepted him.'

> Yao died, and after the mourning period of three years, Shun withdrew
> to the south of Nan Ho, leaving Yao's son in possession of the field, yet
> the feudal lords of the Empire coming to pay homage and those who
> were engaged in litigation went to Shun, not to Yao's son, and ballad
> singers sang the praises of Shun, not of Yao's son. . . . Only then did
> Shun go to the Central Kingdoms and ascend the Imperial throne.
> (V. A. 5)

Shun was said to be an Eastern barbarian who was born in Chu Feng,
moved to Fu Hsia and died in Ming T'iao (IV. B. 1). He came from very
humble circumstances. According to Mencius, 'he rose from the fields'
(VI. B. 15), and had also been a fisherman, and a potter (II. A. 8).

Shun's father, known as the Blind Man, was a most perverse man, his
mother was stupid, and his younger brother Hsiang took after his father.
When Yao wanted to give his two daughters to Shun as wives, he had to do so
without letting the Blind Man know or he would have prevented the marriage
(V. A. 2, IV. A. 26). Even after Shun married the daughters of the Emperor,
the Blind Man and Hsiang were constantly plotting against his life:

> Shun's parents sent him to repair the barn. Then they removed the
> ladder and the Blind Man set fire to the barn. They sent Shun to dredge
> the well, and then set out after him and blocked up the well over him.
> (V. A. 2)

It is said that Shun escaped on the first occasion by flying down from the
barn, using two bamboo hats as wings, and on the second by getting out
through some hidden opening. After the attempt on Shun's life when he
thought Shun dead,

> Hsiang said, 'The credit for plotting against the life of Shun goes to me.
> The cattle and sheep go to you, father and mother, and the granaries as
> well. But the spears go to me, and the lute and the *ti* bow as well. His
> two wives should also be made to look after my quarters.' Hsiang went
> into Shun's house and there Shun was, seated on the bed playing on the
> lute. Hsiang looking awkward said, 'I was thinking of you.' Shun said,
> 'I am thinking of my subjects. You can help me in the task of govern-
> ment.' (loc. cit.)

While he was regent, 'Shun put Yi in charge of fire. Yi ringed off the mountains and valleys and set them alight, and the birds and beasts went into hiding.' Shun gave Yü the task of controlling the Flood, and Ch'i that of teaching the people cultivation of the five grains, and made Hsieh the Minister of Education (III. A. 4), and Kao Yao the judge (VII. A. 35).

When Shun became Emperor the dynasty was known as Yü. Even as Emperor he continued to behave towards his father in a manner befitting a son (V. A. 4). He also enfeoffed Hsiang in Yu Pi (V. A. 3). For Mencius, Shun was the symbol of a perfectly good son. After years of striving, he was able in the end to please his father. 'Once the Blind Man was pleased, the pattern for the relationship between father and son in the Empire was set' (IV. A. 28). In the eyes of Mencius, Shun also furnished incontrovertible evidence of the goodness of human nature. He was an ordinary man in whom the incipient moral tendencies were strong.

> When Shun lived in the depth of the mountains, he lived amongst trees and stones, and had as friends deer and pigs. The difference between him and the uncultivated man of the mountains was slight. But when he heard a single good word, witnessed a single good deed, it was like water causing a breach in the dykes of the Yangtse or the Yellow River. Nothing could withstand it. (VII. A. 16)

Yü helped Shun to govern the Empire for seventeen years before Shun died.

> When the mourning period of three years was over Yü withdrew to Yang Ch'eng, leaving Shun's son in possession of the field, yet the people of the Empire followed him just as, after Yao's death, the people followed Shun instead of Yao's son. (V. A. 6)

(B) THE THREE DYNASTIES

Yü became the first Emperor of the Hsia Dynasty which, according to tradition, ended after 471 years when Chieh was overthrown by T'ang. Yü is known in history for his success in controlling the Flood. There are two accounts of this in the *Mencius*. In III. A. 4, we have:

> Yü dredged the Nine Rivers, cleared the courses of the Chi and the T'a to channel the water into the Sea, deepened the beds of the Ju and the Han, and raised the dykes of the Huai and the Ssu to empty them into the River. Only then were the people of the Central Kingdoms able to find food for themselves. During this time Yü spent eight years abroad and passed the door of his own house three times without entering.

In III. B. 9, we have:

> In the time of Yao, the water reversed its natural course, flooding the

central regions, and the reptiles made their homes there, depriving the people of a settled life. In low-lying regions, people lived in nests; in high regions, they lived in caves. . . . Yü was entrusted with the task of controlling it. He led the flood water into the seas by cutting channels for it in the ground, and drove the reptiles into grassy marshes. The water, flowing through the channels, formed the Yangtse, the Huai, the Yellow River and the Han. Obstacles receded and the birds and beasts harmful to men were annihilated. Only then were the people able to level the ground and live on it.

In controlling the Flood, Yü is said to have worked until there was no hair left on his thighs and shins (*Han fei tzu*, ch. 49). It is perhaps for this reason that Yü acquired the reputation of an ascetic. In the *Analects of Confucius*, he is said to spend little on clothes, food and houses, but lavishly on sacrifices to the gods and on drainage (VIII. 21), while Mencius also says that he 'disliked delicious wine but was fond of good advice' (IV. B. 20), so much so that 'when he heard a fine saying, Yü bowed low before the speaker' (II. A. 8).

Yü recommended Yi to Heaven as his successor. When he died seven years later, after

the mourning period of three years was over, Yi withdrew to the northern slope of Mount Ch'i, leaving Yü's son in possession of the field. Those who came to pay homage and those who were engaged in litigation went to Ch'i [Yü's son] instead of Yi, saying, 'This is the son of our prince.' Ballad singers sang the praises of Ch'i instead of Yi, saying 'This is the son of our prince.' (V. A. 6)

The question why Yü was succeeded by his son while he himself and Shun before him came to the throne through abdication of their predecessors is an important one for Mencius. Was it, as Wan Chang put it, because virtue declined with Yü? Mencius' answer was, No. There were two reasons for the difference. First, Yi assisted Yü for only seven years, while Shun assisted Yao for twenty-eight, and Yü assisted Shun for seventeen. Second, Ch'i, Yü's son, was a good man while Tan Chu, the son of Yao, and the son of Shun were both depraved.

The last Emperor of the Hsia was Chieh. Although he became for posterity a byword for depravity, even in the *Shih chi* none of his depraved deeds are recorded. His rule was intolerable for the common people, but he was so sure of the immutability of the Mandate of Heaven that he said, 'My possession of the Empire is like there being a sun in Heaven. Is there a time when the sun will perish? If the sun perishes, then I shall perish' (*Han shih wai chuan* 2/22). Mencius quotes the *T'ang Shih* as saying,

O Sun, when wilt thou perish?
We care not if we have to die with thee. (I. A. 2)

It is in the *Han shih wai chuan* that accounts of his depravity are to be found, and it is perhaps ironical that a descendant of Yü who disliked delicious wine should be said to have made a lake of wine big enough for boats and for three thousand people to drink from it like cattle (4/2).

When T'ang was in Po he began punitive campaigns against the feudal lords, and the first to be punished was the Earl of Ke. There are two accounts of this in the *Mencius* (I. B. 11, III. B. 5). The account in III. B. 5 is more detailed,

When T'ang was in Po his territory adjoined the state of Ke. The Earl of Ke was a wilful man who neglected his sacrificial duties. T'ang sent someone to ask, 'Why do you not offer sacrifices?' 'We have no suitable animals.' T'ang had gifts of oxen and sheep sent to the Earl of Ke, but he used them for food and continued to neglect his sacrificial duties. T'ang once again sent someone to ask, 'Why do you not offer sacrifices?' 'We have no suitable grain.' T'ang sent the people of Po to help in the ploughing and also sent the aged and young with gifts of food. The Earl of Ke led his people out and waylaid those who were bringing wine, food, millet and rice, trying to take these things from them by force. Those who resisted were killed. A boy bearing millet and meat was killed and the food taken. The *Book of History* says,

The Earl of Ke treated those who brought food as enemies.

That is the incident to which this refers. When an army was sent to punish Ke for killing the boy, the whole Empire said, 'This is not coveting the Empire but avenging common men and women.'

T'ang began his punitive expeditions with Ke.

In eleven expeditions he became matchless in the Empire. When he marched on the east, the western barbarians complained, and when he marched on the south, the northern barbarians complained. They all said, 'Why does he not come to us first?' The people longed for his coming as they longed for rain in time of severe drought. Those who were going to market did not stop; those who were weeding went on weeding. He punished the rulers and comforted the people, like a fall of timely rain, and the people rejoiced greatly. The *Book of History* says,

We await our lord. When he comes we will suffer no more.

In the end T'ang attacked Chieh who fled to Ming T'iao and died in exile. Thus T'ang became the first Emperor of the Shang or Yin Dynasty which was said to have lasted for over six hundred years.

The man who was a key figure in the overthrow of Chieh was Yi Yin. Yi Yin is mentioned a number of times in the *Mencius*. As we shall see Yi Yin is particularly important for Mencius as an example of a good minister banishing a ruler who was bad.

There was a tradition that Yi Yin attracted the attention of T'ang by his culinary abilities. This is included in the *Shih chi* as, at least, one of the traditions. Mencius repudiates this as false and gives his own account of the matter:

Yi Yin worked in the fields in the outskirts of Yu Hsin, and delighted in the way of Yao and Shun. If it was contrary to what was right or to the Way, were he given the Empire he would have ignored it, and were he given a thousand teams of horses he would not have looked at them. If it was contrary to what was right or to the Way, he would neither give away a mite nor accept it. When T'ang sent a messenger with presents to invite him to court, he calmly said, 'What do I want T'ang's presents for? I much prefer working in the fields, delighting in the way of Yao and Shun.' Only after T'ang sent a messenger for the third time did he change his mind and say, 'Is it not better for me to make this prince a Yao or a Shun than to remain in the fields, delighting in the way of Yao and Shun? Is it not better for me to make the people subjects of a Yao or a Shun? Is it not better for me to see this with my own eyes? Heaven, in producing the people, has given to those who first attain under-standing the duty of awakening those who are slow to understand; and to those who are the first to awaken, the duty of awakening those who are slow to awaken. I am amongst the first of Heaven's people to awaken. I shall awaken this people by means of this Way. If I do not awaken them, who will do so?' When he saw a common man or woman who did not enjoy the benefit of the rule of Yao and Shun, Yi Yin felt as if he had pushed him or her into the gutter. This is the extent to which he considered the Empire his responsibility. So he went to T'ang and persuaded him to embark upon a punitive expedition against the Hsia to succour the people. (V. A. 7)

Mencius, however, did not seem to be consistent, for in another passage he said that Yi Yin 'went five times to T'ang and five times to Chieh' (VI. B. 6). This would seem to describe a man who was anxious to take office, rather than the man content to live in retirement depicted in the previous passage.

After Yi Yin went to T'ang, he was first treated as a teacher and only afterwards treated as a minister. It was for this reason, said Mencius, that T'ang was able to become a true King without much effort (II. B. 2). Yi Yin was, for Mencius, above all 'the sage who accepted responsibility' (V. B. 1).

When T'ang died, his eldest son T'ai Ting did not succeed to the throne as he, too, died soon afterwards. T'ai Ting's younger brother Wai Ping ruled for two years, and Wai Ping's younger brother, Chung Jen, ruled for four. T'ai Chia, the son of T'ai Ting, was then put on the throne by Yi Yin. According to Mencius,

T'ai Chia upset the laws of T'ang, and Yi Yin banished him to T'ung. After three years, T'ai Chia repented and reproached himself, and, while in T'ung, reformed and became a good and dutiful man. After another three years, since he heeded the instruction of Yi Yin, he was allowed to return to Po. (V. A. 6)

Mencius was asked by Kung-sun Ch'ou whether it was permissible for Yi Yin, a subject, to banish his Emperor, and his answer was that it was permissible only if he had the motive of a Yi Yin, otherwise it would have been usurpation (VII. A. 31).

Between T'ang and Tchou the only Emperor of the Yin to be mentioned in the *Mencius* is Wu Ting (II. B. 1). His minister, Fu Yüeh, who appeared to him in a dream, is also mentioned as having been raised from amongst the builders (VI. B. 15).

The name of Tchou, the last Emperor of the Yin, is always coupled with that of Chieh. His wicked deeds are, however, recorded in some detail in the *Shih chi*. He is said to have indulged excessively in drink and music. He, too, made a lake of wine and a forest of meat, and had all-night orgies in which men and women chased one another in the nude. He burned people over a charcoal grill. He killed Chiu Hou and E Hou, two of his three ducal ministers and imprisoned the third, Hsi Po (known to posterity as King Wen) who was only released when he made gifts of beautiful women, fine horses and rare objects to the tyrant.

Mencius mentions a number of good and wise men who assisted Tchou (II. A. 1). Of these, Ch'i, Viscount of Wei, an elder brother of Tchou, was the son of a concubine. He left after Tchou refused to listen to his advice on numerous occasions. Of Wei Chung, the younger brother of Ch'i, nothing is known. Prince Pi Kan angered Tchou by his insistent advice. Tchou had heard that sages had hearts with seven apertures, so he killed Prince Pi Kan to see if that was so. The Viscount of Chi was filled with fear, feigned madness and became a slave. Even then he was put in prison by Tchou. According to the *Kuo yü*, Chiao Ke went over to the Chou when Tchou showed excessive favour to Ta Chi, one of his concubines (7/2). It was during the time of Tchou that Po Yi fled to the edge of the North Sea and T'ai Kung to the edge of the East Sea (IV. A. 13, VII. A. 22). T'ai Kung subsequently played a very important part in helping King Wen towards winning the Empire.

The Chou were said to have been descended from Ch'i who, as we have seen, was given the task by Shun of teaching the people the cultivation of the five grains. Kung Liu, who is mentioned by Mencius for his fondness for money (I. B. 5), marked the beginning of the rise to power of the Chou, but the first important Chou king was Ku Kung Tan Fu, the grandfather of King Wen. He is known to posterity as T'ai Wang. That he was a benevolent ruler is evident from the fact that he would rather abandon the territory he had than to cause misery to his people by fighting the barbarians. This incident is mentioned three times in the *Mencius*. In I. B. 3, his serving of the Hsün Yü was given as an example of a small state serving a large one. The most complete account is, however, given in I. B. 15:

> In antiquity, when T'ai Wang was in Pin, the Ti tribes invaded the place.
> He tried to buy them off with skins and silks; he tried to buy them off

with horses and hounds; he tried to buy them off with pearls and jade; but all to no avail. Then he assembled the elders and announced to them, 'What the Ti tribes want is our land. I have heard that a man in authority never turns what is meant for the sustenance of men into a source of harm to them. It will not be difficult for you, my friends, to find another lord. I am leaving.' And he left Pin, crossed the Liang Mountains and built a city at the foot of Mount Ch'i and settled there. The men of Pin said, 'This is a benevolent man. We must not lose him.' They flocked after him as if to market.

In I. B. 14 Mencius again mentions this and comments, 'If a man does good deeds, then amongst his descendants in future generations there will rise one who will become a true King.' In other words, the eventual success of King Wu in winning the Empire was due, to no small extent, to the good that T'ai Wang did.

When King Wen succeeded to the throne, he was benevolent towards his people, treating them 'as if he were tending invalids' (IV. B. 20). The people, for their part, loved him so much that they named the terrace and pond they had built for him by their own sweat and toil as the 'Sacred Terrace' and the 'Sacred Pond' (I. A. 2). King Wen also showed great deference to good and wise men and they came flocking to him. Po Yi and T'ai Kung who had fled from Tchou to the edge of the sea came to him (IV. A. 13).

King Wen is said to have submitted to the K'un tribes whose state was smaller than his own, but he is also said to have shown his valour in stopping an invasion of Chü (I. B. 3).

In spite of his virtue, King Wen did not succeed in winning the Empire in his lifetime because, according to Mencius, 'the Empire was for long content to be ruled by the Yin', and what had gone on for long was difficult to change (II. A. 1).

After the death of King Wen, King Wu, aided by the Duke of Chou, made war on Tchou. According to the *Mencius*,

When King Wu marched on Yin, he had three hundred war chariots and three thousand brave warriors. He said, 'Do not be afraid. I come to bring you peace, not to wage war on the people.' And the sound of the people knocking their heads on the ground was like the toppling of a mountain. (VII. B. 4)

According to the *Wu ch'eng* chapter of the *Book of History*, however, in this war 'the blood spilled was enough to carry staves along with it'. Mencius expressed incredulity at this, for how could this happen when the most benevolent waged war on the most cruel? (VII. B. 3).

The Duke of Chou was the younger brother of King Wu. He assisted King Wu in overthrowing Tchou. Then he made Kuan Shu overlord of Yin and Kuan Shu used Yin as a base to stage a rebellion against King Ch'eng, the son

of King Wu. Ch'en Chia asked Mencius whether the Duke of Chou knew this
was going to happen. Mencius answered that as the Duke of Chou was the
younger brother of Kuan Shu it was only natural for him to have made such a
mistake.

The Duke of Chou, according to Mencius, tried to combine the achieve-
ments of the Three Dynasties and the administrations of the Four Kings, i.e.,
Yü, T'ang, King Wen and King Wu.

> Whenever there was anything he could not quite understand, he would
> tilt his head back and reflect, if need be through the night as well as the
> day. If he was fortunate enough to find the answer, he would sit up to
> await the dawn. (IV. B. 20)

The Duke of Chou and, before him, Yi and Yi Yin were all sages, and the
question arises why they never became Emperor. Mencius' answer to this is
that 'he who inherits the Empire is only put aside by Heaven if he is like
Chieh and Tchou' (V. A. 6). It was perhaps the misfortune of the Empire that
these sages did not live in the time of wicked tyrants.

Appendix 5

ON MENCIUS' USE OF THE METHOD
OF ANALOGY IN ARGUMENT

Reprinted from Asia Major, *N.S., Vol. X (1963) with the kind permission of the Editor. As this was written some years ago, the translation given in it of passages from the* Mencius *differs occasionally from the present translation, but I have decided, in the main, to leave it as it is. I have, however, corrected one or two minor errors.*

It is not unusual for a reader of the *Mencius* to be left with the impression that in argument with his opponents Mencius was a sophist with little respect for logic. Not the least contributory factor to this impression is the type of argument which centres round an analogy. Yet it is difficult to believe that a thinker of Mencius' calibre and reputation could have indulged consistently in what appears to be pointless argument or that his opponents were always effectively silenced by *non sequiturs*. The fault, we suspect, must lie with us. We must have somehow failed to understand these arguments. There are extenuating circumstances. In every case the bare bones of the argument alone are recorded, the background necessary to its understanding being tacitly assumed. There is no doubt that a good deal could be assumed to be familiar to the readers of Mencius' day, including assumptions accepted alike by Mencius and his opponents as well as the philosophical views peculiar to each side and also, of course, the method of analogy as used in argument. But for the modern reader, however, at least some of these things may be un-familiar, and we can understand the difficulties he finds in these arguments. The purpose of this paper is to examine the passages containing such argu-ments afresh, making explicit as much of the available background as is useful, and then to see if we could gain a better understanding of the way the method of analogy works and judge whether, by the standards of the time, Mencius was not an honest and skilful exponent of the method. The passages we shall examine are chapters 1-5 of Part A of Book VI and chapter 17 of Book IV Part A.

Kao Tzu said, 'Human nature is like the willow. *Yi*[1] is like cups. To make

---

[1] I have deliberately left the word *yi* 義 untranslated in all these passages from the *Mencius*, because in some cases it is not possible to retain the continuity of the argument if the word is translated, as there is no one English equivalent which will do in all con-texts. The reader can substitute 'right' 'righteous', 'rightness', 'duty' or 'dutiful', according to the demands of English usage in each case.

morality[2] out of human nature is like making cups out of the willow.'

Mencius said, 'Can you make cups by following the nature of the willow? Or must you do violence to the willow before you can make it into cups? If the latter is the case, must you, then, also do violence to a man before you can make him moral? It is these words of yours that will lead men in this world in bringing disaster upon morality.' (VI.A.1)

Kao Tzu said, 'Human nature is like whirling water. Give it an outlet in the east and it will flow east; give it an outlet in the west and it will flow west. That human nature shows no preference for either becoming good or becoming bad is like water showing no preference for either flowing east or flowing west.'

Mencius said, 'It is certainly the case that water shows no preference for either flowing east or flowing west, but does it show the same indifference to flowing upwards and flowing downwards? Human nature being good is like water seeking low ground. There is no man who is not good just as there is no water that does not flow downwards.

'Now with water, by splashing it one can make it shoot up higher than one's forehead, and by forcing it one can make it stay on a hill. But can that be said to be the nature of water? It is the special circumstances that make it behave so. That man can be made bad shows that his nature is open to similar treatment.' (VI. A. 2)

These two arguments are best taken together as they constitute different attempts on the part of Kao Tzu at elucidating, by means of different analogies, a basic thesis which is capable of varying interpretations. In VI. A. 6, Kung-tu Tzu quotes Kao Tzu as saying, 'There is in human nature neither good nor bad.' In our first passage, the analogy put forth by Kao Tzu is that human nature is like the willow and morality like cups, and that to make morality out of human nature is like making cups out of the willow. The point of the analogy is this. The willow is the raw material out of which cups can be made, but this possibility has no basis in the original nature of the willow. It is no part of the nature of the willow to be made into cups. Similarly, not only is morality not in original human nature, it is something alien to it. Thus to make man moral is as arbitrary and artificial as making the willow into cups. By means of his analogy, Kao Tzu is interpreting his thesis

[2]*Jen yi* has been translated as 'morality' and not as 'benevolence and *yi*' for two reasons. Firstly, by Mencius' time *jen yi* was almost always used as a single term meaning 'morality'. Secondly, in his opening statement Kao Tzu said only of *yi* that it was like cups; benevolence was not mentioned. In VI. A. 4, as we shall see, Kao Tzu was explicit on the point. 'Benevolence', he said, 'is internal, not external; *yi* is external, not internal.' This, as we shall also see, can only mean that in Kao Tzu's view benevolence was part of original human nature while *yi* was not. When he said that human nature was like the willow and that *yi* was like cups, he was making the same point. If in the next sentence, he were to say that making 'benevolence and *yi*' out of human nature was like making cups out of the willow, he would not only be inconsistent with what he had just said, but also contradicting what he said in VI. A. 4.

as meaning that man is naturally a-moral.

Mencius' basic objection to this is that human beings are in fact not a-moral. They have a natural tendency towards moral behaviour, though this tendency is weak and often submerged by the habit of egoistic behaviour. This is a point to which we shall return. For the time being, let us concentrate on Mencius' objection to the analogy itself. On the one hand, it is obvious that we cannot make cups out of the willow by following its nature and that we have to do violence to its nature in order to do so. On the other hand, were we to draw the parallel conclusion that we cannot make man moral except by doing violence to his nature this would have disastrous consequences for the authority and prestige of morality.

There are two points which Mencius does not state but which are implicit in his objection. It is perhaps legitimate to deal with them as if they had been made by Mencius. Firstly, when we say that it is necessary to do violence to man's nature in order to make him moral, we are in fact making a moral judgement. We are saying that it is bad to make man moral. But if man is by nature a-moral, moral judgements are artificial and unnatural things for him to make. Yet the paradox is that in stating this it is natural for us to make it in the form of a moral judgement. This would seem to show that the making of moral judgements is inescapable and so cannot be artificial and unnatural. Hence given a position like Kao Tzu's we have no right to say that it is bad to make man moral and yet this seems the natural thing for us to say.

Secondly, if man is by nature a-moral, it is as much a violation of his nature to make him immoral as to make him moral. Kao Tzu should have said that to make man immoral, no less than to make him moral, was like making cups out of the willow. As he omitted to do this, it is very easy for anyone hostile to morality to draw the one-sided and therefore wrong conclusion that it is only making man moral which involved doing violence to his nature. The next step would be to argue falsely that since it is unnatural for man to be moral it must be natural for him to be immoral. That is why Mencius said to Kao Tzu, 'It is these words of yours that will lead men in this world in bringing disaster upon morality.'

As no comment by Kao Tzu on Mencius' objection to his analogy is recorded and no linking passage between the two chapters is supplied, we can only conjecture that Kao Tzu must have accepted Mencius' objection as valid. He, then, puts forth a new analogy, viz., that human nature is like whirling water which will flow indifferently east or west as an outlet offers itself. In so doing Kao Tzu is giving up his earlier interpretation of his thesis that there is neither good nor bad in human nature, an interpretation capable of being misrepresented as meaning that morality runs counter to human nature, in other words, that man is naturally immoral. Instead, he accepts that morality is not alien to human nature, though he still wishes to maintain that man shows no preference for either the good or the bad. Man becomes good or bad as he happens to be guided one way or the other.

This analogy is worth more serious consideration because it represented more accurately Kao Tzu's true position. Perhaps Kao Tzu never meant his first analogy with the willow to be taken seriously. It was simply an opening gambit which allows him to give some concessions to his opponent without retreating beyond his real position. Whether this conjecture as to Kao Tzu's motive is justified or not, Mencius certainly takes the new analogy seriously and gets down to providing an alternative analogy which represents his own position and, in his view, better fits the facts of the case.

In VI. A. 6, apart from quoting Kao Tzu's view on human nature, Kung-tu Tzu attributes to an unnamed person the view that human nature can become either good or bad. Now this is a view which was likely to have been accepted by both Kao Tzu and Mencius, because it is no more than a description of the undeniable fact that human beings sometimes become good and sometimes become bad. But just as the fact itself admits of different interpretations, so does the description. The views of both Kao Tzu and Mencius can be looked upon as different interpretations of the fact and so also of the description. At any rate, the way Mencius criticized Kao Tzu's second analogy shows that he at least looked upon it as an elucidation of this ambiguous thesis of anonymous authorship. What Kao Tzu was doing was to interpret the statement that human nature can become either good or bad as meaning that human nature shows no preference for becoming good or bad and so as meaning that it is equally easy for it to become good or bad. And this is, presumably, also the meaning to be given to his own thesis that there is neither good nor bad in human nature. Whether the analogy with the indifference water shows to flowing east or west is acceptable or not depends on whether one accepts or rejects the view of human nature it is meant to illustrate.

Mencius rejects the analogy because, for him, to say that man can be made either good or bad does not imply either that it is equally difficult to make him good or bad, or that it is equally natural for him to become moral or immoral. For Kao Tzu's analogy he substitutes one of his own. It is true, human nature is like water, but it is, in its preference for the good, like water in its tendency to flow downwards. This, in Mencius' view, was a better analogy, because though water shows a definite preference for low ground, it is possible to make it go upwards—say by splashing or forcing it—and it is certainly not the case that it is as easy to make it go up as to make it go down. It is more natural for water to flow downwards, and this means that it is more difficult to make it go upwards. Far from its being the case that to make man moral is to go against his nature, as Kao Tzu's first analogy with the willow can be taken to imply, Mencius wanted to say that the contrary is the case. It is more natural for man to be moral and so easier to make him good. 'There is no man who is not good just as there is no water that does not flow downwards.' Though Mencius does not produce arguments in support of his view here, elsewhere he does try to produce evidence for the goodness of human nature. Briefly it is this. We all have the beginnings of morality in us. We all feel pity, spontaneously and without ulterior motive, at the sight of a baby creeping towards a well. We all have the *shih fei chih hsin* 是非之心 which distinguishes right from wrong and approves of the right, irrespective of what we in fact choose. If we happen to choose the wrong, we disapprove of our own action and feel a sense of shame.[3] In the argument under consideration Mencius is content to work Kao Tzu gradually round to his view. Firstly, he shows that the analogy with the willow is likely to be misrepresented as meaning that it is difficult to make man good because it is natural for him to be immoral and that this is unacceptable even to Kao Tzu and probably never intended by him. When Kao Tzu shifts his position to the analogy with whirling water, Mencius goes on to show that this is still not a satisfactory analogy because Kao Tzu was mistaken in thinking that this was based on the thesis that human nature can become either good or bad. The mistake lies in thinking that to say that man can become either good or bad implies that it is equally difficult or easy for him to become either. This is not the case. It is easier to make man good because it is, in a legitimate sense, more natural for him to be moral. What Mencius has done is, in fact, to turn Kao Tzu's first analogy upside down. It is making man immoral that is analogous to making cups out of the willow, because it is natural for man to become moral just as it is natural for water to flow downwards.

> Kao Tzu said, 'That which is inborn is what is meant by "nature".'[4]
> Mencius said, 'Is that the same as "white is what is meant by 'white' "?'
> 'Yes.'
> 'Is the whiteness of white feathers the same as the whiteness of white snow and the whiteness of white snow the same as the whiteness of white jade?'
> 'Yes.'

[3] For a fuller treatment of Mencius' theory that human nature is good, see my 'Theories of human nature in *Mencius* and *Shyuntzyy*' (*Bulletin of the School of Oriental and African Studies*, 1953, Vol. XV, pp. 541-65).

[4] Although the present text reads '*sheng chih wei hsing* 生之謂性', there is good reason to believe that originally 性 was simply written 生. (For a discussion of this point see Yü Yüeh 兪樾 *Ch'ün ching p'ing yi* 羣經平議, *Huang Ch'ing ching chieh hsü pien* 皇清經解續編 chüan 1394, pp. 16b-17a.) The two words, though cognate, were most probably slightly different in pronunciation, but the statement '*sheng chih wei hsing*' was at least tautologous in its written form and an exact parallel to '*pai chih wei pai*'.

'In that case is the nature of a dog the same as the nature of an ox and the nature of an ox the same as the nature of a man?' (VI. A. 3)

This is an interesting example of the use of analogy, because there are two features not met with in the examples we have seen. Firstly, it is not an analogy between two things but an analogy between two states of affairs which are described by statements of overtly identical form. 'That which is inborn is what is meant by "nature" ' and 'white is what is meant by "white" ' are both tautologous in form. The second feature is that the analogy was in fact suggested by Mencius in an attempt to elucidate Kao Tzu's initial statement. Kao Tzu accepted the suggestion, presumably not realizing that Mencius was going to show that the two statements were in fact not comparable. This meant that Kao Tzu was not, in the first instance, at all clear as to the implications of his own statement.

Mencius shows the difference between the two statements by saying that it follows that if white is what is meant by 'white' then the whiteness of white feathers is the same as the whiteness of white snow which in turn is the same as the whiteness of white jade. By the same token, it follows that if that which is inborn is what is meant by 'nature' then the nature of a dog is the same as the nature of an ox which in turn is the same as the nature of a man. But this was not acceptable, presumably even to Kao Tzu. What Kao Tzu's reaction was we are not told; neither are we given any explanation of why the analogy fails to hold. The former we can only conjecture, but towards making good the latter omission we can make some attempt.

The reason for the failure of the analogy is this. The term 'nature' is a formal, empty term. We cannot know, in specific terms, what precisely 'nature' is, unless the thing of which it is the nature is first specified. On the other hand, the term 'white' has a minimum specific content. We can know, up to a point, what white is without having to be told what it is the whiteness of. What is even more important is that when we specify the thing which is white—say, feathers or snow or jade—we may know more about its characteristics, but these must include the minimum specific content that we know from the term 'white' *per se*. If this condition is not fulfilled, then the thing is not really white. To put this whole point in another way. The 'nature' of a thing depends entirely on what the thing is, while whether a thing is 'white' or not depends on whether it includes the characteristic which we define as whiteness independently. In other words, in the expression 'the nature of x', the term 'nature' is a function of the term 'x', while in the expression 'the whiteness of white feathers', the term 'whiteness' is not a function of the term 'feathers' but has an independent value of its own.[5]

[5] There is also a formal difference between the two expressions which is a result of

It is not indicated how Kao Tzu made use of his thesis that 'that which is inborn is what is meant by "nature".' One suspects that this may well be connected with his view that appetite for food and sex is human nature (VI. A. 4). He might have argued that all living creatures are born with appetite for food and sex and that therefore this is 'nature' and so also 'human nature'. If he had argued thus, he would certainly have been helped by the practice, current by the time of Mencius, of using the word 'nature' to mean specifically 'human nature' when the context did not demand greater than usual precision. (When there was need for precision, the term 'the nature of man' was used, as we have seen in VI. A. 3 above.) If in meaning 'human nature' one says only 'nature', it is easy to assume that 'human nature' shares with the nature of other animals characteristics which go to make up the essence of 'nature' *sans phrase*.

Mencius' argument was designed to expose this unconscious assumption and to show that it was mistaken. He exposed it by explicitly asking the question, 'In that case is the nature of a dog the same as the nature of an ox and the nature of an ox the same as the nature of a man?' No one could return a positive answer who was not prepared to go all the way and say that the nature of all animals was identical in every respect. In this way, Mencius shows that what the nature of x is depends on what x is. That man shares with animals the appetite for food and sex is not sufficient grounds for equating this with the whole of 'nature', much less the whole of 'human nature'. There may be something else peculiar to human beings which is the essence of human nature, and in Mencius' view there is, and this is morality. Morality is peculiar to man, and distinguishes him from animals. It is worth mentioning that nowhere does Mencius deny that appetite for food and sex is human nature. All he asserts is that it is not the whole of human nature nor even the most important part, precisely because, being shared with all animals, it fails to mark him from the brutes. If we insist on saying that this constitutes the whole of human nature then we will have to accept the logical conclusion that the nature of a man is no different from that of a dog or an ox and this not even Kao Tzu was prepared to accept.

Ch'un-yü K'un said, 'Is it required by the rites that, in giving and receiving, man and woman should not touch each other?'
Mencius said, 'It is.'

---

this distinction. In the expression 'the whiteness of white feathers', the term 'white' is a constituent of the term 'white feathers'. This is because whiteness is not included in the essence of feathers but is an independent character which has to be explicitly mentioned if it is 'white feathers' and not simply 'feathers' that we wish to mean. The same is not true of the expression 'the nature of a dog'.

'When one's sister-in-law is drowning, does one stretch out a hand to help her?'

'Not to help a sister-in-law who is drowning is to be a brute. It is required by the rites that, in giving and receiving, man and woman should not touch each other, but to stretch out a hand to help the drowning sister-in-law is to use one's discretion (*ch'üan* 權).'

'Now the Empire is drowning, why do you not help it?'

'When the Empire is drowning, one helps it with the Way; when a sister-in-law is drowning one helps her with one's hand. Would you have me help the Empire with my hand?' (IV. A. 17)

This argument is puzzling at first sight. Mencius' final question seems totally irrelevant. Yet one cannot help feeling that there is more to it than meets the eye. When we examine the analogy in detail, we find that this feeling is fully justified, for the argument turns out to be of considerable complexity, and it is this complexity that hides the point from us on a casual reading.

The question raised by Ch'un-yü K'un concerns the salvation of an Empire in disorder. He draws an analogy between this and the rescue of a drowning woman. The point Ch'un-yü K'un makes is that just as one ought to use one's hand to rescue a sister-in-law who is drowning, though this involves a breach of the rule that man and woman should not, in giving and receiving, touch each other, so ought one to be prepared to make some concessions in one's attempt to save a drowning Empire. The means for rescuing a drowning person is the hand, while the means for saving the Empire is, as Mencius points out, the Way. In either case the end is not in question; what is in question is whether one is justified in using any means that involves a breach of the ethical code in order to realize the end. To understand this argument, it is therefore necessary to say something about the nature of the means mentioned in each case.

Let us first take the case of the rescue of the drowning woman by the use of one's hand. The hand is useful purely as an instrument to the realization of the end, but does not affect its nature. After the person is rescued, we would not know, unless we are told, by what means the rescue was effected, and what is more, it does not matter. We shall call this 'instrumental means'. If we turn to the salvation of the Empire, we find the case to be different. But first let us see how the salvation of an Empire in disorder was understood by Mencius and Ch'un-yü K'un. In their time, the common way of describing an Empire in disorder was to say that it lacked the Way (*wu tao* 無道). Hence to save the Empire is to provide it with the Way. When the Empire has attained order it would be in possession of the Way (*yu tao* 有道). We can see from this that the Way is a different kind of means. It becomes part of the end it helps to realize, and the end endures so long as the means remains a part of it. Remove the Way at any subsequent time, and the Empire will revert to disorder. We shall call this 'constitutive means'.[6]

There is another difference between the hand and the Way. The hand is only one of a number of possible means for rescuing a drowning person. One could equally use a stick or a rope. Furthermore, one's hand is as adequate a means for the purpose as any other. The Way, on the other hand, is a unique means for the realization of the desired end of saving the Empire. One could, of course, use a watered-down version of the Way instead, but then the end realized would be less perfect. This difference between the hand and the Way, though it does not follow from the distinction between them as instrumental and constitutive means, is not unconnected with it. The less any specific technique is required in the realization of an end, the less specific the instrumental means. For instance, few things other than a screw-driver will drive in a screw, but almost any blunt object can be used to hammer in a nail. The rescue of a drowning person involves no specific technique. Hence the variety of possible means. On the other hand, in a sense constitutive means are always unique. Vary the means and you vary the end as well. This is particularly true where the constitutive means furnishes the principle of organization. For instance, if one varies a mould slightly the resulting shape will, accordingly, be different. The Way is a regulative principle, and as such it is unique.

Now the use of the hand is in itself morally neutral. In the case under consideration this is wrong only because there is a rule against man and woman touching each other and because the drowning person happens to be a woman and the rescuer a man. All the same we are faced with a dilemma. On the one hand we have a duty to save life. On the other we also have a duty to observe accepted rules of conduct. The situation is such that there is no way of saving the life of the drowning woman except by the breach of a rule of conduct. We weigh up (*ch'üan*) the relative stringency of the conflicting claims and come to the conclusion that the duty to save life far outweighs the duty to observe rules of conduct. This weighing up is possible because we can appeal to basic moral principle. The Way, however, is not morally neutral. It *is* basic moral principle. It is therefore impossible for the use of the Way to be wrong in the manner the use of the hand can be wrong. And even if, for argument's sake, we were to grant that in using the Way we may be breaking some rule of conduct, we cannot see how this is to be justified: there is no moral principle more basic to which we can appeal for justification.

[6] I am aware that the distinction between instrumental and constitutive means is a crude one. Both form and matter would come under the latter term—and the Way is in fact form, as it furnishes the Empire with a regulative principle. I have not taken the discussion further, partly because this rough distinction is more or less adequate for my limited purpose of elucidating the argument we are considering, and partly because a more detailed discussion will take us too far afield.

We can now turn to the analogy. The main difficulty with this analogy is to see how it is meant to hold. For the moment let us leave aside the difference between instrumental and constitutive means and look upon both the Way and the hand simply as means. If we are to interpret the analogy exactly, we have to take it in the following way. Just as we have to use our hand to rescue our sister-in-law, though this involves the breach of a rule of conduct, so must we use the Way to save the Empire, though in so doing we err in a similar manner. This as we have just seen is both an impossibility and an absurdity. Moreover, this interpretation of the analogy renders it trivial, and was unlikely to have been what was intended by Ch'un-yü K'un.

A more likely interpretation is this. In using one's hand, when this involves the breach of a rule, one is resorting to a compromise. In saving the Empire, if need be, we should also be prepared to compromise. If the Way is too lofty for the ruler, we should offer him a watered-down version of it. This, as we have seen, is different in kind from the compromise in using one's hand, for in adopting the use of the hand we have chosen a means perfectly adequate to the realization of the end, while in adopting a watered-down version of the Way we are compromising on the end as well. To the extent the Way is watered-down, to that extent the end we realize will fall short of the perfection we aimed at in the first place. Furthermore, this is a double compromise. Firstly, one is compromising on the Way. Secondly, one is compromising on one's own standards. On our analogy, the compromise on the Way is to be justified, as we have seen, paradoxically by an appeal to the Way itself. Even leaving this aside, Mencius shows clearly that in his view there can be no justification for compromising on the Way at all. He thinks that as soon as one realizes that what one has been doing is wrong one should rectify the wrong immediately and completely. Difficulty cannot be used as a pretext for allowing an injustice to go on unredressed.

> Tai Ying-chih said, 'In the present year we are unable to change over to a tax of one in ten and to abolish custom and market duty. What do you think if we were to make some reductions and wait for next year before we put the change fully into effect?'
>
> Mencius said, 'Here is a man who appropriates one of his neighbour's chickens every day. Someone tells him, "This is not the way of the gentleman." He answers, "May I reduce this to one chicken a month and wait for next year before stopping altogether?"
>
> 'If one realizes that something is morally wrong, one should stop doing it as soon as possible. Why wait for next year?' (III. B. 8)

This shows clearly that Mencius would not approve of watering down the Way in face of difficulties. Mencius feels equally strongly about not compromising on one's own standards, because he thinks that a man who is willing to do so is not the man to put others right. He says, 'One who is willing to bend himself will never be able to straighten others' (III. B. 1), and again, 'I have never heard of anyone who can bend himself and rectify others' (V. A. 7).

If we take the compromise on the Way in this fashion, the analogy with the use of the hand is not an exact one. Firstly, in the case of the rescue of the drowning woman there is no constitutive means corresponding to the Way in the salvation of the Empire. Secondly, in deciding on the use of one's hand one is not accepting something less than the rescue of the drowning person. The hand is a perfectly adequate means for the realization of that end. But in using a watered-down version of the Way one is accepting as one's end something less than restoring the Empire to perfect order. If we wish to make the analogy more exact, we have to modify the facts of the situation concerning the rescue of the drowning person and to envisage something like this. We have no means of rescuing the drowning person outright and as a second best we decide to throw him a plank for him to hold on to for the time being. Even in this revised form the analogy does not hold completely. Whether we have the means to rescue a drowning person or not is a matter of fact, but whether we insist on the Way as means seems to be a matter of choice which depends more on our moral standards than on external circumstances.[7]

There is another way of revising the analogy to make it more exact, and that is by introducing the element of instrumental means into the case of the salvation of the Empire. In the time of Mencius, when philosophers travelled from one state to another, trying to gain a hearing, they had often to rely upon courtiers and favourites for access to princes. The temptation must have been at times great to enlist the help of those who were far from being men of honour. It is easy to argue that association with an unsavoury character was a cheap price to pay if in return a prince could be persuaded to adopt the Way in the government of his state. This would be parallel to the argument for using one's hand to rescue a drowning person though this involves the breach of a rule of conduct. We have seen that the general objection to this is that one can never hope to straighten others by first bending oneself, but Mencius has in fact something more specific to say about this problem. There were certain traditions about Confucius' behaviour in just such circumstances. In the *Analects of Confucius* there is an account of Confucius having an audience with Nan Tzu, the notorious wife of the Duke of Wei. Tzu-lu did

---

[7]Mencius thinks that a prince should not look upon himself as incapable of adopting the Way in his government. This can be seen from his remark to King Hui of Liang, 'For this reason, that Your Majesty fails to become a true King is a case of not doing so and not a case of not being able to do so' (I. A. 7). Of the subject who thinks of his prince as incapable of becoming a good ruler, Mencius has this to say, 'To say "My prince will never be able to do it" is to do him harm' (IV. A. 1).

not hide his displeasure and to placate him Confucius had to swear that there was nothing improper in what he did (VI. 28). There must have been other traditions concerning incidents of a similar nature, for we find Mencius expressing incredulity at these traditions which he took to be totally unfounded.

> Wan Chang asked, 'According to some, when he was in Wei Confucius had as host Yung Chü and in Ch'i he had the royal attendant Chi Huan. Is this true?
> Mencius said, 'No. That is not so. These were fabrications by busy-bodies. In Wei Confucius had as host Yen Ch'ou-yu. The wife of Mi Tzu was a sister of the wife of Tzu-lu. Mi Tzu said to Tzu-lu, "If Confucius would have me for a host, he can attain high office." Tzu-lu reported this to Confucius who said, "There is the Decree." Confucius advances in accordance with the rites and withdraws in accordance with *yi*, and in matters of success or failure says, "There is the Decree." If in spite of this he had had as hosts Yung Chü and the royal attendant Chi Huan, then he would be ignoring both *yi* and the Decree. . . .
> 'I have heard that one judges courtiers who are natives of the state by the people to whom they play host, and those who have come to court from abroad by the hosts they choose. If Confucius had had as hosts Yung Chü and the royal attendant Chi Huan he would not be Confucius.' (V. A. 8)

We can see from this passage that to Mencius the choice of one's associates is a vital matter. One may deceive oneself and think that association with influential but disreputable courtiers is only a means to a worthy end, but what is likely to happen is simply the degradation of one's own moral character to no purpose, as such people will never permit the Way to prevail for should such a thing happen they would be the first to suffer.

This last interpretation of the analogy is most likely to be the one that Mencius had in mind, and we can see that Mencius' final question 'Would you have me help the Empire with my hand?' was an expression of exasperation. Ch'un-yü K'un, in suggesting that Mencius should make a compromise in order to save the Empire, did not realize that the price for such a compromise was so high as to defeat its very purpose.

> Kao Tzu said, 'Appetite for food and sex is nature. Benevolence is internal, not external; *yi* is external, not internal.'
> Mencius said, 'Why do you say that benevolence is internal and *yi* is external?'
> 'He is old and I treat him as elder. He owes nothing of his elderliness to me, just as in treating him as white because he is white I only do so because of his whiteness which is external to me. That is why I call it external.'
> 'The case of *yi* is different from that of whiteness. The 'treating as

white' is the same whether one treats a horse as white[8] or a man as white. But I wonder if you would think that the "treating as old" is the same whether one is treating a horse as old or a man as elder? Furthermore, is it the one who is old that is *yi*, or is it the one who treats him as elder that is *yi*?'

'My brother I love, but the brother of a man from Ch'in I do not love. This means that the explanation lies in me. Hence I call it internal. Treating a man from Ch'u's elder as elder is no different from treating my own elder as elder. This means that the explanation[9] lies in their elderliness. Hence I call it external.'

'My relishing the roast provided by the man from Ch'in is no different from my relishing my own roast. Even with inanimate things, we can find cases similar to the one under discussion. Are we, then, to say that there is something external even in the relishing of roast?' (VI. A. 4)

Meng Chi Tzu asked Kung-tu Tzu, 'Why do you say that *yi* is internal?'

'It is the putting into practice of the respect that is in me. That is why I say it is internal.'

'If a man from your village is a year older than your eldest brother, which do you respect?'

'My brother.'

'In offering wine, which would you give precedence to?'

'The man from my village.'

'The one you respect is the former; the one you treat as elder is the latter. This shows that it is in fact external and not internal.'

Kung-tu Tzu was unable to find an answer to this and gave an account of the matter to Mencius.

Mencius said, '[Ask him,] . "Which do you respect, your uncle or your younger brother?" He will say, "My uncle." "When your younger brother is acting the part of an ancestor at a sacrifice, then which do you respect?" He will say, "My younger brother." You ask him, "What has happened to your respect for your uncle?" He will say, "It is because of the position my younger brother occupies." You can then

---

[8]Following Yü Yüeh I read 異於白白馬之白也 , repeating *pai*. See op. cit., pp. 17a-b. The same comment is also to be found in his *Ku shu yi yi chü li* 古書疑義舉例(*Ku shu yi yi chü li wu chung* 五種 , Shanghai, 1956, pp. 19-20).

[9]In translating *yüeh* 悅 in both instances as 'explanation', I am reading it as *shuo* 說 . In classical works the common form of the character was 說 , whether the meaning is 'to please' or 'to explain'. The *Mencius* is exceptional in that the distinction between the two forms is generally observed in it. But even in the *Mencius*, the character is not always written 悅, when it means 'to please'. It is, therefore, reasonable to suppose that the form used in any passage reflects no more than the reading adopted by some editor in the course of the transmission of the text. There is no reason why we should not depart from the existing reading when the sense of the text demands it, as in the present case. Dr. A. Waley has also expressed dissatisfaction with the reading. In his *Notes on Mencius*, he writes, 'The 悅 is unintelligible. The sense seems to be "make me the determining factor".' (*Asia Major*, New Series, Vol. I, p. 104). However, he made no suggestion as to the emendation of the reading of the character.

say, "[In the case of the man from my village] it is also because of the position he occupies. Normal respect is due to my elder brother; temporary respect is due to the man from my village." '

When Meng Chi Tzu heard this, he said, 'It is the same respect whether I am respecting my uncle or my younger brother. It is, as I have said, external and does not come from within.'

Kung-tu Tzu said, 'In winter one drinks hot water, in summer cold. Does that mean that even food and drink can be a matter of what is external?' (VI. A. 5)

As these two arguments deal with the same problem, whether *yi* is internal or external, they are best taken together. There are some preliminary points which must be made if we are to understand these arguments.

Firstly, Kao Tzu begins by saying that appetite for food and sex is nature, and although this is not discussed in the sequel it is of some importance. The fact that Kao Tzu states this before raising the problem about *yi* shows that Kao Tzu looks upon the problem as one concerning human nature as well. To say that *yi* is external though benevolence is internal is to say that benevolence is part of human nature but *yi* is not. This implies that to say something is internal is to say that it is part of human nature. That this implication is accepted by Mencius can be seen from one remark he made in VI. A. 6. Mencius says there, 'Benevolence, *yi*, observance of the rites and wisdom, do not give me a lustre *from the outside*. I had them from the very beginning. It is simply that I never reflected upon the matter.' Here Mencius implies that if something gives me a lustre from the outside, then it is not inherent in my nature. Conversely, whatever is inherent in my nature is internal and not external to me. Another point worth remembering is that with Kao Tzu's statement that appetite for food and sex is nature and that benevolence is internal Mencius has no quarrel. What Mencius objects to specifically is the position that *yi* is external. Mencius' view is that *yi*, no less than benevolence, is internal.

Secondly, neither Kao Tzu nor Mencius liked arguing in the abstract about benevolence and *yi*. They preferred to deal with concrete acts and situations which exemplify these abstract qualities. Mencius says elsewhere, 'The content of benevolence is the serving of one's parents; the content of *yi* is obedience to one's elder brothers' (IV. A. 27), and again, 'There is no child who does not know love for his parents, and, when he grows up, respect for his elder brothers. The love for one's parents is benevolence; the respect for one's elder brother is *yi*' (VII. A. 15). We can paraphrase Mencius' words by saying that to love one's parents is the typical benevolent act, while to show respect for one's elders is the act which is typically *yi*. We can, then, understand why Kao Tzu and Mencius should choose to conduct their arguments in terms of the concrete examples they used.

Thirdly, when the word *yi* is translated, the argument may seem forced and artificial, for in Chinese the same word *yi* can be applied to an act which is right as well as to the agent who does the right act, while in English if we use the word 'right' for the act, some other word like 'righteous' or 'dutiful' has to be used for the agent. The use of two different words in translating a single word in the original destroys the apparent continuity of the argument.

Furthermore, the dichotomy between 'internal' and 'external' is too simple for the statement or the solution of the problem. Kao Tzu and Mencius both start from the position that benevolence is internal and part of human nature, because benevolence is the outward manifestation of love which, without any doubt, is part of the original make-up of man. The question is whether *yi* is equally well-rooted in human nature. In the case of benevolence, we can decide whether an act is benevolent or not by referring to the motive. If it is motivated by love, then it is benevolent. But in the case of *yi*, the facts of the situation are more complicated. Whether an act is *yi* does not depend only on the motive, but also on whether it is fitting in the situation.[10] What makes the position worse is that the very existence of a specific motive for acts that are *yi* is, at times, challenged.

This problem, however muddled it may seem to us, must have appeared to be of crucial importance to Mencius. By Mencius' day the opposition between *hsing* 性 'human nature' and *ming* 命 'the Decree of Heaven' must have become acute. The sort of view that Mencius was trying to combat must have been something like this. In human nature there are simply appetites—for food and sex, for instance—and emotions like love, and it is unnatural for man to do anything for which his nature does not equip him with a motive. It is all very well to say that it is the Decree of Heaven that man should be moral, but if it is unnatural for him to be moral it would be unreasonable to expect him to obey the Decree. For this reason the question whether *yi* was internal or external was a vital one for Mencius and his contemporaries.

Let us now examine the first argument. The starting point is the act which is typically *yi*, viz.,

(1) the act of treating someone old as elder.

The analogy is then drawn by Kao Tzu between this and

(2) the act of treating someone white as white.

It is argued that in (2) I treat someone white as white solely because of his whiteness which is external to me. That is to say, whether I treat him as white

---

[10]In the *Chung yung* 中庸 (chapter 14), (*Li chi chu shu*, 52.18b) '*yi*' is defined as 'fitting' (義者宜也). This is more than just a meaning gloss by a near homophone, because the character was originally written 誼, thus showing that it was cognate with the character 宜.

or not depends solely on external circumstances. There is nothing in my nature which can have any bearing on my act. Similarly, whether I treat someone old as elder depends solely on his age which is external to me. There is nothing in my nature which can have any bearing on this act of mine either. Therefore *yi*, of which (1) is a typical example, is external.

Mencius answers by pointing out that the analogy fails to hold. This he does by producing two parallel statements, one about (2) and one about (1), and showing that though both are true one is positive and the other negative:

> (2.1) To treat a white horse as white is *no different* from treating a white man as white;
> (1.1) To treat an old horse as old *is different* from treating an old man as elder.

The failure of the analogy rests on two points of difference. In treating an old man as elder, respect is evinced, but not in treating an old horse as old. In (2.1), the question of internality does not arise in either of the two cases because respect does not come in, but in (1.1) it is not true that nothing except circumstances external to the agent is relevant. Respect is relevant and respect is internal to the agent. Furthermore, the term *yi* applies to the agent as well as to the act. (In this respect *yi* is like benevolence.) Kao Tzu's position is unsatisfactory on two counts. Firstly, it is based on *yi* only as applied to an act. Secondly, even there, he has failed to take into account the fact that an act which is *yi* involves respect which is a quality of the agent.

Having failed in his analogy between an act which is *yi* and an act which is indubitably external, i.e., between (1) and (2), Kao Tzu then tries to show that there are differences between an act which is *yi* and a benevolent act. For this purpose he brings in

> (3) the act of loving one's brother.

He makes two parallel statements, one about (3) and one about (1), and shows that though one is positive and the other negative both are true:

> (3.2) I love my brother but I do not love the brother of a man from Ch'in;
> (1.2) I treat the elder of a man from Ch'u as elder in the same way as I treat my own elder as elder.

Since (3) is agreed by both parties to be a typical benevolent act and benevolence is indubitably internal, this discrepancy between (1) and (3), in Kao Tzu's view, shows that *yi* is not internal. In fact, Kao Tzu goes on to say, it shows more. It shows positively that *yi* is external. Why do I love my brother and not the brother of a man from Ch'in? The explanation lies in his being *my* brother. In other words, I love him because of his relation to me. 'The explanation lies in me.' On the other hand, I treat the elder of a man from Ch'u as elder just as I treat an elder who is my own kith and kin as elder, because in either case my treatment is due to his age and this is a circumstance external to me. If my treatment of an elder as elder depends solely on external circumstances, then, it is concluded, *yi* is external.

Again, Mencius accepts what Kao Tzu has said about the facts as true but tries to show that it does not prove what Kao Tzu claims that it proves. In order to do this, Mencius brings in a fourth kind of act,

(4) the act of relishing roast.

Of this there can be no doubt as to its internality on the part of Kao Tzu, because he has said at the outset that appetite for food is nature. Yet of this one can make precisely the same statement as about (1), a statement which is supposed to prove that *yi* is external:

(4.2) I relish the roast provided by a man from Ch'in in the same way as I relish my own roast.

Thus Kao Tzu failed to establish the externality of *yi* either through the similarities (1) shows to (2) or through the dissimilarities (1) shows to (3). Mencius refuted the former by showing that there are dissimilarities between (1) and (2) overlooked by Kao Tzu, and the latter by showing that there are dissimilarities between (4) and (3) of the same kind as between (1) and (3), though there is no question of acts of relishing food being external.

The second argument opens with Kung-tu Tzu's statement that he considered *yi* to be internal because in performing acts which are *yi* he was putting into practice his respect. However, it consists mainly of Meng Chi Tzu's attempt to establish the externality of *yi*. Meng Chi Tzu's argument is as follows. There is a man from my village who is a year senior to my eldest brother. Although under normal circumstances I respect my brother, in offering wine I give precedence to the man from my village. My treatment of the latter is determined by external circumstances. As this is an act which is *yi*, *yi* is external. Apart from this, there is a further point which Meng Chi Tzu seems to be making by implication. By his careful wording he seems to imply that there is a distinction between showing respect and treating as elder: 'The one you *respect* is the former; the one you *treat as elder* is the latter.' The line of reasoning appears to be as follows. Respect is a quality of the agent and so any action which evinces respect is internal. But whether I treat the man from my village as elder depends on the occasion, and since this is the case my treatment varies according to external circumstances. It, therefore, cannot evince respect which is a permanent disposition. If respect is not involved in all acts which are *yi* then it cannot be the basis of the internality of *yi*.

Mencius replies by providing a new example. One respects one's uncle, but when one's younger brother is acting the part of an ancestor at a sacrifice then one respects one's younger brother. On the surface, Mencius seems to be providing an example of his own which reinforces Meng Chi Tzu's case, but in fact he was undermining the distinction between respecting and treating as elder that Meng Chi Tzu was trying to establish. In his own example Mencius has substituted the younger brother for the fellow villager. There is no question of treating one's younger brother as elder, for even when he is acting the part of an ancestor he is still one's junior. What is due to him in his special position is respect. Thus in Mencius' example, though one's act is still determined by external circumstances, it nevertheless evinces respect. This Mencius explains by the distinction between normal and temporary respect. That the act of treating the man from my village as elder is determined by external circumstances, instead of showing that it does not evince respect, shows only that it evinces temporary respect. Meng Chi Tzu seems willing to accept this distinction between normal and temporary respect but argues that, in that case, acts which are *yi* are external in spite of the fact that they evince respect because they depend on external circumstances. Mencius' reply is that even of

(5) the act of drinking

it is true that it is conditioned by external circumstances:

(5.3) In winter one drinks hot water, in summer cold.

Of (1) which is also conditioned by external circumstances we can equally say:

(1.3) Normally I respect my eldest brother, but in offering wine I give precedence to the man from my village.

Again, by showing that (5.3) can be said of (5) which is indubitably internal, Mencius argues that the fact that (1.3) can be said of (1) does not show that *yi* is external. Furthermore, by drawing an analogy between (1) and (5), Mencius is returning to Kung-tu Tzu's opening remark: 'I put into practice my respect.' As in an act which is *yi* one puts into practice one's respect, so in an act of drinking one is motivated by one's thirst.

The arguments are obviously not conclusive, but this is in part due to Mencius' limited purpose. All he set out to do, in both cases, was to show that his opponents failed to establish the externality of *yi*. He did not attempt to go beyond this and to establish positively that *yi* was internal. The main reason for the inconclusiveness is, however, one we have already touched upon. The dichotomy between internal and external was too simple for the facts of the situation. Such a dichotomy could only work if there was only one characteristic or one set of characteristics which is to be found in one kind of act but not in another. In the present case, there are a number of characteristics, some of which are sometimes present and sometimes absent in acts of the same kind. In the course of the arguments, three such characteristics are mentioned. (1) The motive. In the case of benevolent acts, it is assumed that this is love. In the case of eating and drinking it is assumed to be appetite. According to Mencius, the motive is respect in the case of all acts which are *yi*, and this his opponents either deny or deny to be significant. (2) There are the external circumstances. These are irrelevant to benevolent acts. But in the case of acts which are *yi* these determine the matter of precedence in particular situations. In the case of drink, these decide what we want in different seasons. (3) The relation which the object of respect has to the agent. In the case of *yi*, there need be no special relationship at all. In the case of food, there is no special relationship either. As acts which stem indubitably from what is internal show no uniformity in the possession or otherwise of these characteristics, so acts which are *yi* display an ambivalence in the similarity and dissimilarity they show to these acts. The result is that no conclusion can be drawn from the success or failure of these analogies.

The problem whether *yi* is external in contrast to benevolence which is internal must have been an issue of some importance, as we find that the later Mohists were also interested in it. In the logical chapters of *Mo tzu*, viz., chapters 40 to 45, there are three places where this problem is discussed. I shall quote only the longer passage from the *Ching shuo hsia* chapter, because this is comparatively free from textual difficulties and is a lucid statement of the Mohist position:

> Benevolence is loving; *yi* is benefiting. He who loves and he who benefits are here; he who is loved and he who is benefited are there. Of the one who loves and the one who benefits we cannot say that one is internal and the other external. Neither can we say this of the one who is loved and the one who is benefited. To say[11] that benevolence is internal and *yi* is external is to select the one who loves and the one who is benefited. This is selection with no consistent basis. It is like saying that the left eye goes out and the right eye comes in. (*Ssu pu ts'ung k'an* 四部叢刊 ed., 10.21a-b)

At first sight the Mohists seem to have brought order to an otherwise untidy problem, but on closer examination one sees that this is achieved only by ignoring certain factors that Kao Tzu and Mencius took into account. In defining *yi* in the way they do, the Mohists are looking upon it as exactly parallel to benevolence. As benevolence is a disposition to love, so is *yi* a disposition to benefit others. Both are relations obtaining between an agent and a patient. In respect of the agent both benevolence and *yi* are internal; in

---

[11] Read 爲 as 謂.

respect of the patient both are external. In the view of the Mohists, whoever says that *yi* is external though admitting that benevolence is internal must be guilty of inconsistent selection. He must be taking the patient in the case of *yi* and the agent in the case of benevolence. Though the Mohists were defending the same position as Mencius, the basis for their defence is certainly unacceptable to Mencius. Mencius was quite clear that *yi* was an attribute of the agent and could not possibly be applied to the patient. 'Is it the one who is old that is *yi* or is it the one who treats him as elder that is *yi*?' Mencius knew full well that when both benevolence and *yi* were applied to the agent there was no problem. But he was also aware of the fact ignored by the Mohists that *yi* applied equally to actions, and it was here that a case could be made out for challenging its internality. Part of the conditions for an action being *yi* is that it should be 'fitting', and this means that whether an action is *yi* depends, to no small measure, on external circumstances. It is from this that Kao Tzu and others argued that *yi* was external, and it is also with this that Mencius grappled when he defended the internality of *yi*. For the Mohists to say that the problem rested on the failure to distinguish between agent and patient is both to misrepresent Mencius and his opponents and to distort the usage of the word *yi*. This misrepresentation is due to the refusal on the part of the Mohists to take into account certain factors involved in the problem of *yi* and this refusal is, in turn, due to two features of the Mohist position. Firstly, they define *yi* as benefiting, and by so doing render it independent of the ethical code. A 'fitting' action depends on external circumstances in a way a 'benefiting' action does not. This definition of *yi* is certain to be unacceptable to either Mencius or Kao Tzu. Secondly, by rendering *yi* similar to benevolence, the Mohists were ignoring its applicability to actions and looked upon it solely as an attribute of agents. This emphasis on the agent to the exclusion of actions is a marked feature of Mohist moral thinking. Here are some passages from the logical chapters in which this feature can be clearly seen:

Canon: *Yi* is benefiting. (10. 1a. 6)
Explanation: The will takes the Empire as its responsibility[12] and the ability is capable of benefiting it. There is no need to be in office.[13] (10. 6b. 6)

Some live long, some die young, but they benefit the Empire to the same extent.[14] (11. 7a. 2)

---

[12] Emend 芬 to 分.
[13] Cf. Canon: To be filial is to benefit one's parents. (10. 1b. 1) Explanation: One takes one's parents as one's responsibility (see previous note), and one's ability is capable of benefiting them. There is no need to succeed. (10. 7a. 2-3)
[14] Emend 指若 to 相若.

Even when a man is in as exalted a position as that of an emperor, he does not benefit the Empire to a greater extent than a common man.[15] If two sons serve their parents and one meets with a good year while the other meets with a bad, then the one benefits[16] his parents to no greater extent than the other. As it is not through his action that more has resulted, this does not add to his merit.[17] External circumstances[18] are powerless to add to the benefit for which I am responsible (11. 6a. 2-5).

All these passages show that in the view of the later Mohists external circumstances are irrelevant to the moral assessment of the character of the agent. So long as a man has both the will and the capacity to benefit the world or his parents, whether in fact he succeeds or not is immaterial, because success —and even opportunity—depends on favourable conditions over which he has no control and for which he can take no credit.[19] Thus *yi* is removed from the contaminating influence of external circumstances only through denying it application to action. In this way the problem with which Mencius and his opponents were concerned was by-passed by the Mohists. This hardly justifies their claim that the problem itself rested on confusion and inconsistency.

Not only is one of the problems discussed between Mencius and Kao Tzu also discussed by the later Mohists but the method of argument as well. In the *Hsiao ch'ü* chapter[20] we find logicians of the Mohist school writing on the different methods of argument amongst which is to be found the method of analogy:

Analogy is to put forth another[21] thing in order to illuminate this thing. Parallel is to set [two] propositions side by side and show that they will both do. (11. 8a. 3-5)

Here an analogy drawn between two things is distinguished from one drawn

[15] Emend 正夫 to 匹夫.
[16] Emend 其親也 to 其利親也.
[17] This sentence is obscure, as the text is almost certainly corrupt.
[18] Emend 執 to 埶.
[19] The Mohist position that in moral assessment it is the agent and not the actions that should be emphasized seems to have some relevance to a problem concerning moral goodness in Western philosophy. If we define moral goodness as goodness which is realized only when an agent chooses to do his duty from the motive of dutifulness the question arises whether a man who acts dutifully more often than another necessarily realizes more moral goodness. Those who feel uneasy about returning an affirmative answer may find a certain appeal in the Mohist position.
[20] For a more detailed discussion of the *Hsiao ch'ü* see my 'Some logical problems in ancient China' (*Proceedings of the Aristotelian Society*, Vol. LIII 1952-3, pp. 189-204).
[21] Read 也 as 他.

between two statements. We have seen that both methods were used by Mencius. The analogy between 'That which is inborn is meant by "nature" and 'White is what is meant by "white" ' is an analogy between two statements and would come under "parallel" in the Mohist classification.

The Mohist chapter goes on to discuss the method:

> Things may have similarities, but it does not follow that therefore they are completely similar. When propositions are parallel, there is a limit beyond which this cannot be pushed.[22] (11. 8a. 7-8)

This is a very good description of the method as it was used by Mencius. In his hands the method of analogy was used to throw light on things which were otherwise obscure. It is by proposing analogies and showing in what way they broke down that this was achieved. That the aim was to arrive at the truth can be seen from the fact that it was not always analogies proposed by his opponents that were shown to be inadequate in this way. We have seen a case of Mencius suggesting an analogy to illustrate his opponent's thesis, and this was criticized after his opponent accepted it.

It is perhaps worth pointing out that the use of analogy is often the only helpful method in elucidating something which is, in its nature, obscure. Two examples come readily to mind. Theories about the mind are often presented through the medium of models, and so are physical theories of the atom. In either case the models are not only helpful in enabling us to see something of the 'structure' of the mind or the atom which is not open to inspection by the senses, but also instructive in the way they break down.

I hope enough has been said to show that in the fourth and third centuries B.C. in China the method of analogy, indispensable for certain types of philosophical problems, was in wide use,[23] so much so that the only surviving

---

[22] Emend 正 to 止.

[23] There is a story about the famous sophist Hui Shih in the *Shuo yüan* which illustrates this point:

Someone said to the King of Liang, 'Hui Tzu is very good at using analogies when putting forth his views. If your Majesty could stop him from using analogies he will be at a loss what to say.'

The King said, 'Very well. I will do that.'

The following day when he received Hui Tzu the King said to him, 'If you have anything to say, I wish you would say it plainly and not resort to analogies.'

Hui Tzu said, 'Suppose there is a man here who does not know what a *tan* is, and you say to him, "A *tan* is like a *tan*," would he understand?'

The King said, 'No.'

'Then were you to say to him, "A *tan* is like a bow, but has a strip of bamboo in place of the string," would he understand?'

The King said, 'Yes. He would.'

Hui Tzu said, 'A man who explains necessarily makes intelligible that which is not

treatise on the methods of argument deals with it in some detail. Seen in the light of the Mohist treatise, Mencius was, indeed, a very skilful user of this method, who never failed to throw light on philosophical issues that were discussed. This is an impression somewhat different from the ineffective debater that he is sometimes made out to be.

known by comparing it with what is known. Now Your Majesty says, "Do not use analogies." This would make the task impossible.'

The King said, 'Well said.' (S.P.T.K. edition, 11. 6b-7a)

Hui Shih's explanation of the function of analogy can be seen to be similar to that given in the *Hsiao ch'ü*.

Appendix 6

SOME NOTES ON THE *MENCIUS*[1]

Reprinted from Asia Major, *N. S., Vol. XV (1969) with the kind permission of Princeton University Press.*

References

Bodman   N. C. Bodman, *A Linguistic Study of the* Shih Ming, Cambridge, Massachusetts, 1954.

CCST   Wang Yin-chih 王引之, *Ching chuan shih t'zu* 經傳釋詞, Peking, 1956.

Chiao   Chiao Hsün 焦循, *Meng tzu cheng yi* 孟子正義 (Ssu pu pei yao ed.).

Chu   *Meng tzu chi chu* 孟子集註 (*Ssu shu chi chu* 四書集註, Hong Kong, 1964).

CTCS   Kuo Ch'ing-fan 郭慶藩, *Chuang tzu chi shih* 莊子集釋, ed. by Wang Hsiao-yü 王孝魚, Peking, 1961.

CYSW   Wang Yin-chih, *Ching yi shu wen* 經義述聞 (Basic Sinological Series).

Fukunaga   Fukunaga Mitsuji 福永光司, *Sōshi* 莊子 (Chūgoku Kotensen Series), Tokyo, Vol. II, 1966, Vol. III, 1967.

Graham (1)   A. C. Graham, "Some Basic Problems of Classical Chinese Syntax", *Asia Major*, N.S. XIV/2, pp. 192-216

Graham (2)   A. C. Graham, *The Book of Lieh Tzu* (The Wisdom of the East Series), London, 1960.

GS   B. Karlgren, *Grammata Serica*, Stockholm, 1940.

Hattori   Chiao Hung 焦竑, *Chuang tzu yi* 莊子翼, ed. by Hattori Unokichi 服部宇之吉 (Kanbun Taikei Series), 1911.

Ichikawa and Endō Ichikawa Yasushi 市川安司 and Endō Tetsuo 遠藤哲夫, *Sōshi* (Shinyaku Kambun Taikei Series), Tokyo, 1967.

[1] This article deals with difficulties and points of interest encountered in the course of preparing a new translation of the *Mencius* to be published by Penguin Books in 1970. Most of the points are textual, but some, being concerned with interpretation, are of a grammatical or philosophical nature. It is perhaps worth pointing out that I have not in all cases followed the ideas put forth in this article in my translation, and for facility of exposition the wording of the translations used here is not always identical with that to be found in the complete translation.

Kanaya   Kanaya Osamu 金谷治, *Mōshi* 孟子 (Chūgoku Kotensen
                    Series), Tokyo, 1966.

Kobayashi   Kobayashi Nobuaki 小林信明, *Resshi* 列子 (Shinyaku
                    Kambun Taikei Series), Tokyo, 1967.

Ku   Ku Yen-wu 顧炎武, *Jih chih lu* 日知錄 (Ssu pu pei yao ed.).

KYSC   Wang Nien-sun 王念孫, *Kuang ya shu cheng* 廣雅疏證
                    (Wan yu wen k'u ed.).

Makino   Makino Kenjirō 牧野謙次郎, *Sōshi* 莊子 (Sentetsu icho
                    tsuiho Kanseki Kokujikai Zensho Series), Tokyo, 1914.

MTCS   *Meng tzu chu shu* 孟子注疏 (*Shih san ching chu shu* 十三
                    經注疏), Nanchang, 1815.

Ōta   Ōta Genkyu 太田玄九, *Resshi* 列子 (Sentetsu icho Kan-
                    seki Kokujikai Zensho Series), Tokyo, 1912.

Shih chi   Ssu-ma Ch'ien 司馬遷, *Shih chi* 史記, Chung Hua Shu
                    Chü punctuated edition, Peking, 1959.

Simon   W. Simon, *"Bih=Wey?"*, *Bulletin of the School of
                    Oriental and African Studies*, XII, pp. 781-802.

Sun Yi-jang   Sun Yi-jang 孫詒讓, *Cha yi* 札迻, 1894.

SWKL   *Shuo wen ku lin* 說文詁林, Shanghai, 1932.

Takeuchi   Takeuchi Yoshio 武內義雄, *Mōshi* (Iwanami Bunko
                    Series), Tokyo, 1936.

TSTC   Wang Nien-sun, *Tu shu tsa chih* 讀書雜誌 (Wan yu wen
                    k'u ed.).

Wang Chung   Wang Chung 汪中, *Shu hsüeh* 述學 (Ssu pu ts'ung k'an
                    ed.).

Wang Hsien-ch'ien   Wang Hsien-ch'ien 王先謙, *Shih ming shu cheng pu* 釋名
                    疏證補 (Wan yu wen k'u ed.).

Wang Shu-min   Wang Shu-min 王叔岷, *Lieh tzu pu cheng* 列子補正,
                    Shanghai, 1948.

Watson (1)   Burton Watson, *Chuang Tzu Basic Writings*, New York
                    and London, 1964.

Watson (2)   Burton Watson, *The Complete Works of Chuang Tzu*,
                    New York and London, 1968.

Yang (1)   Yang Po-chün 楊伯峻, *Meng tzu yi chu* 孟子譯註, Peking,
                    1962. (Yang's name appears in this edition but not in
                    the earlier edition in 1960)

Yang (2)   Yang Po-chün, *Lun yü yi chu* 論語譯註, Peking, 1958.

Yang (3)   Yang Po-chün, *Lieh tzu chi shih* 列子集釋, Shanghai, 1958.

Yen   Yen Jo-ch'ü 閻若璩, *Ssu shu shih ti san hsü* 四書釋地三續
                    (Huang ch'ing ching chieh 皇清經解, chüan 23).

Yü (1)   Yü Yüeh 俞樾, *Ch'ün ching p'ing yi* 羣經平議 (Huang

ch'ing ching chieh hsü pien 續編, chüan 1362-96).
Yü (2)　　　　Yü Yüeh, *Chu tzu p'ing yi* 諸子平議 (Basic Sinological
Series).

References to the Classics are to the *Shih san ching chu shu* edition noted
above, and in the case of all other works not listed to the *Ssu pu ts'ung k'an*
edition.

(1) I.A.3 五十者可以衣帛矣……七十者可以食肉矣……七十者衣帛食肉……
Since Mencius has just said that "those who are fifty can wear silk" and
"those who are seventy can eat meat", it is odd for him to go on to say
"those who are seventy wear silk and eat meat" as the wearing of silk applies
as much to those who are fifty as to those who are seventy. In the parallel
passage in I.A.7 the text, instead of 七十者, reads 老者 which seems preferable.

(2) I.A.5 寡人恥之，願比死者壹洒之。
Chao Ch'i 趙岐 offers no gloss for the word 比. Chu Hsi 朱熹, however, says
"比猶爲也."(Chu, p. 6) In the passage 且比化者無使土親膚，於人心獨無恔乎？
(II.B.7), it is not clear at all how Chao understands the text (MTSC 4B.1b),
but Chu repeats the earlier gloss (Chu, p. 57). Professor W. Simon has argued
very persuasively that 比 here should be taken in the sense of "by the time
of". This is, of course, one of the most important uses of the word. Nevertheless, as far as the present passage is concerned, there seems to be room for
dissent, and it is, perhaps, worth reviewing the merits of one of the alternatives.

The Pseudo Sun Shih 孫奭 commentary gives a paraphrase of the present
passage: 今願近死不惜命者一洗除之 (MTCS IA, 12b). Sun's meaning is not
very clear, but at least one thing is certain. He is offering 近 as a gloss of 比.
Yü Yüeh 俞樾 has also independently—because, as has been noticed by
Simon (p. 802, n. 3), he seemed to have had a version of the Sun commentary
which read 爲 in place of 近 —arrived at the same conclusion that 比 ought
to be taken in the sense of 近. He quotes, in support, a passage from the *Ch'i
yü* 齊語：夫管夷吾射寡人中鈎，是以濱於死, and Wei Chao's 韋昭 com-
mentary: 三君皆云，濱近也 (*Kuo yü*, 6.1b). Yü then goes on to add that 比
and 濱 are interchangeable because they share the same initial ('一聲之轉')
(Yü (1), 1393.3a).

Now the glosses of both Sun and Yü give the sense of the expression 比死
者 as "one verging on death". In connexion with Sun's gloss, Simon makes
the following objection:

We shall see that this commentary got very near to what I consider the
correct interpretation of the passage. It operates with a well-known
meaning of *bih*, viz., *bih jinn yee* 比近也 ("close to, near"), which is in

fact the primary meaning of *bih*. However, this meaning "close to" refers usually to space. When referring to time, *bih* has acquired, as we shall see, a very special meaning which is quite different from the meaning of "on the point of, on the verge of" suggested by the Pseudo Suen Shyh's paraphrase. As is well known, the meaning "on the point of" is expressed in Chinese by *jiang* 將 or *chiee* 且 (p. 792).

The main point of the argument seems to be this. When 比 means 近, this refers usually to space. When it refers to time, it has a special meaning, *viz.*, "by the time". Now there does not seem to be any evidence that 比, when it means "close to, near", refers to space. In fact, the gloss 比近也 as given in the *Kuang ya* (KYSC, p. 331) is much more likely to have been intended to be taken in the sense of 親近, just as the *Shuo wen* gloss 比密也 (SWKL, pp. 3651-2) is to be taken in the sense of 親密. In both cases, 比 does not, in the first instance, refer either to space or to time, but to close relationship between persons, as, for example, in the expression 朋比. If we prefer to take 比近也 as referring to space, the meaning would be "close together" rather than "close to". But the meaning of "close to" is, as a matter of fact, not relevant to the example under discussion. As Simon points out, there is an idiomatic use of 比 which means "side by side". One can go further and say that in the construction " 比 x", if x is the object and 比 is taken in a spatial sense, it is natural for the meaning to be taken as "placing the x's side by side", as, for instance, 比肩 means "a line of shoulders" and 比屋 "a line of roofs". Thus by paraphrasing 比死 as 近死, the Pseudo Sun Shih commentary could not have meant this to be taken spatially, but could only have meant this to be taken in the sense of "verging on". The question, then, would simply be this. Does 比 have such a meaning or not? The mere fact that 比 has the special meaning of "by the time" does not rule out the possibility of its possessing, side by side with this meaning, another of "verging on". Again, though it is true that the meaning "on the point of" is expressed in Chinese by 將 or 且 , it does not follow that either 比 cannot also mean "on the point of" or that there cannot be any difference between the meaning of 比 and that of 將 or 且 , even though they all *generally* mean "on the point of". As a matter of fact, a case can be made for differentiating them. 將 means "going to" with no reference to "imminence". The action thus indicated can take place any time in the future. 且 , perhaps, indicates the near future. But 比, in the sense of 瀕, would indicate imminence.

Now the gloss of 瀕 for 比 is worth examining. There is a possibility of a phonetic connexion. 比 is the phonetic in 妣 which is a variant form of 蠙 which, in turn, is a homophone of 瀕. There is a passage in the *Shih chi* 史記 : 又比殺三趙王 where Ssu-ma Chen 司馬貞 glosses 比 as 頻 ("in rapid succession") (p. 407). As 頻 is the same as 瀕, it would seem that 比 has two meanings which are similar to two meanings of 頻.

Now if we follow Simon in taking 比 as "by the time", then 比死者 means "by the time of death". But if we take 比 as "verging on", then the expression will mean "one who is verging on death". Now one of the important features of the construction where 比 is used to mean "by the time", as pointed out by Simon, is that "the end of the time clause is sometimes marked by *jee* 者 or *yee* 也 " (p. 795). This being the case, there is a clear point of difference between the two interpretations and this may prove to be useful in deciding, in a specific case, which is more likely to be right. On Simon's interpretation 者 marks the end of the time clause and cannot, therefore, be at the same time, the indicator of the agent, while on the second interpretation 者 has, precisely, to be taken as an indicator of the agent.

As far as the *Mencius* text is concerned, it is possible to interpret 比 in either way, because the agent of the main verb 願 is still 寡人. Thus, it can either mean "I am ashamed of this and wish, by the time of death, to wash it all away", or "I am ashamed of this and wish [myself as] one verging on death to wash it all away".

There is, however, another text where the expression 比死者 is to be found which seems to have been overlooked by commentators of the *Mencius* but may turn out to be helpful towards the solution of our problem. In the *Yen tzu ch'un ch'iu* 晏子春秋 (1/8) we find 比死者勉爲樂乎 (11a). This example is different from that of the *Mencius* in that 比死者[2] is the agent of the verb and can only mean "Should those verging on death not try their best to enjoy themselves?"[2] This being so, the 者 in 比死者 is an indicator of the agent and this rules out its being, at the same time, the marker of the end of the time clause. To put it in another way, if we insist that 比死者 be taken as a time clause, we are forced to leave the main verb without an agent. Thus whereas the *Mencius* example admits of both interpretations, the *Yen tzu ch'un ch'iu* admits of only the interpretation "one who is verging on death".

Both Yü Yüeh and Simon (pp. 801-2) have pointed out that King Hui of Liang was an old man at the time of his interview with Mencius. If we remember that he, in fact, died not long after the interview, though the interpretation "before I die" is appropriate, "one verging on death" would add a poignant note to the remark.

There remains the interpretation of the passage in II.B.7. On our interpretation, it can be translated rather literally as: "Moreover, one verging on decomposition, not to let the earth come in contact with the skin, does this not afford some satisfaction to the heart of man?" 比死者 is here a nominal

---

[2]We can leave open the question whether 比死者 refers to the speakers or to others, as this does not affect the point at issue, *viz.*, that 比死者 is the agent of the main verb.

unit in the absolute position serving as a point of reference for the word 膚.

(3) I.A.6 " '孰能與之？'

"對曰：'天下莫不與也。王知夫苗乎？七八月之間旱，則苗槁矣。天油然
作雲，沛然下雨，則苗浡然興之矣。其如是，孰能禦之？今夫天下之人牧，
未有不嗜殺人者也。如有不嗜殺人者，則天下之民皆引領而望之矣。 誠如
是也，民歸之，由水之就下，沛然誰能禦之？'"

It is odd that when the question is 孰能與之, in the answer the point to be
repeated is 孰能禦之, 誰能禦之. It seems likely that 與 is a mistake and that
the question should also be 孰能禦之. Thus in the answer Mencius throws
back the original question in a rhetorical form at the questioner. But if we
emend the question, we have to emend the immediate answer as well. Instead
of 天下莫不與也, the text should read 天下莫之能禦也.[3] 莫之能禦 is a cliché
to be found more than once in the *Mencius*. In the next section we find 保民
而王，莫之能禦也. (I.A.7) and in II.A.1 there is 行仁政而王，莫之能禦也. The
example from I.A.7 is of particular interest, as the same wording is often to
be found in sections that form a group dealing with the same topic. Here both
I.A.6 and I.A.7 deal with, amongst other things, the inevitability of the benevolent ruler becoming a true king. Furthermore, there are parallels to the
present section. In VII.A.16 we find 若決江河，沛然莫之能禦也 which
parallels closely the final sentence of the present section. Again, in the *Shuo
yüan* 說苑 6/5 we find 今天油然作雲，沛然下雨，則苗草興起，莫之能禦
(6.5a). Thus we can see that both 孰能禦之 and 誰能禦之 have parallels which
read 莫之能禦. Can it be that in some versions of the *Mencius* the text reads
孰能禦之 and 誰能禦之 echoing the question, while in other versions the text
reads 莫之能禦 echoing the opening words of Mencius' answer?

Is there any good reason why 禦 should have been corrupted to 與? Could
this have come about through some phonetic connexion? According to
Karlgren's reconstruction, 與 was *zio* in Archaic and *iwo* in Ancient (GS 89b),
while 禦 was *ngio* in Archaic and *ngiwo* in Ancient (GS 60p). 能 is *nang* in
both Archaic and Ancient (GS 885a). Now it is quite easy to see how *nang
ngiwo* could easily be corrupted to *nang iwo*, but this could only have
happened after the transition from Archaic to Ancient, and however early we
place this, it is too late for our purposes, as the text was most probably
corrupt by Chao Chi's time. But the *zio* of Karlgren's reconstruction is not
beyond question. It is well known that 與 is often used in ancient texts for
舉. Wang Yin-chih cites Yü Fan's 虞翻 gloss 與謂舉也, and Cheng Hsüan's
鄭玄 commentary to the *Chou li* 周禮：故書舉爲與 (14.5b), and Wang Yi's
王逸 comment on the *Ch'i chien* 七諫：與舉也 (*Ch'u tz'u*, 13.3a). He then goes

---

[3] 天下莫之能損益也 (*Hsün tzu*, 13.7a) is a sentence of similar construction.

on to show other cases where 與 is used for 舉: *Li yün* 禮運，選賢與能 (*Li chi chu shu*, 21.3a); (2) *Chiu chang* 九章，與前世而皆然兮 (*Ch'u tz'u*, 4.12b) and (3) *T'ien chih chung* 天志中，天下之君子與謂之不祥 (*Mo tzu*, 7.10a).[4] Wang Nien-sun also gives an example from the *Wang chih* 王制：制與在此亡乎人 (*Hsün tzu*, 5.18a).[5] There is also an instance of 舉 used for 與, again given by Wang Yin-chih: 豈唯寡君舉羣臣實受其貺 (*Tso chuan*, Chao 3).[6] The array of evidence is impressive, and there is, in fact an example of 與 being used for 舉 in the *Mencius* itself.[7] Now Karlgren gives *kio* for 舉 in Archaic, and it seems possible that 與 also had a guttural initial of some sort. Now if 與 had a guttural initial or at least an initial cluster including a guttural element[8] in Archaic, then we can see how the corruption could have come about.

To return to the text of the *Mencius*, we can see that there is much to be gained in the unity of the argument by adopting such an emendation. Having been told that the Empire would be united by one who was not fond of killing, King Hsiang went on to ask, "Who can stop him?" and Mencius' answer was "No one in the Empire can stop him." What follows will then be just an elaboration on this answer.

(4) I.A.7 我非愛其財而易之以羊也。宜乎百姓之謂我愛也。
According to the traditional interpretation, the major pause is taken after the first 也, and the meaning, then, is "It was not the case that I substituted the lamb for it *through* grudging the expense." But the remark "It is only natural that the people should have thought me miserly" does not, then, follow, for if it is not through grudging the expense that the King substituted the lamb for the ox, why is it natural for the people to have thought him miserly? The first major pause should be taken after 財, so that the negative force of 非 does not extend to the part of the sentence beginning with 而 which serves the same purpose as 然而. This would give the sense, "It was not true that I grudged the expense, but I *did* use a lamb instead of the ox." Thus, it is, indeed, natural for the people to have thought the King miserly.

(5) I.B.16 行或使之，止或尼之。行止非人所能也。吾之不遇魯侯天也。
It is easy to get the impression that Mencius was quite oblivious to all the philosophical activities around him. It is interesting, therefore, to find a case

[4]CYSW, p. 568.
[5]TSTC, 11.11.
[6]CYSW, p. 732.
[7]See (15) below.
[8]For a discussion of the possibility of an initial cluster in such cases, see Bodman, pp. 61-2.

where a seemingly ordinary remark turns out to contain a reference to philosophical problems that very much interested his contemporaries. In chapter 25 of the *Chuang tzu* 莊子 we find Shao Chih asking, 季眞之莫爲，接子之或使，二家之議，孰正於其情，孰徧於其理？ (CTCS, p. 916). ("Of the two theories—the 'nothing does it' of Chi Chen and the 'something causes it' of Chieh Tzu—which has got it right and which is one-sided?") This concerns the problem of the universe. The question is: behind the universe is there a controlling power, a lord, or not? 或使 represents the view that returns an affirmative answer to this question, while 莫爲 answers it in the negative. Furthermore, for Chuang Tzu, the problem whether there is a sovereign lord (*chen chün* 眞君) over the multifarious phenomena in a man's mind is parallel to that about the lord of the universe.

In chapter 38 of the *Kuan tzu* there is a passage dealing with the same question:天或維之，地或載之。天莫之維則天以墜矣，地莫之載則地以沉矣。夫天不墜，地不沉。夫或維而載之末夫。又況於人［乎］。人有治之，辟之若夫靁鼓之動也。夫不能自搖者，夫或搖［emend to 搖］之。夫或者，何若然者也？視則不見，聽則不聞；洒乎天下滿，不見其塞；集於顏色 ［emend to 肌膚］ ，知於肌膚 ［emend to 顏色］ ；責其往來，莫知其時；薄乎其方也，韓乎其圓也，韓乎莫得其門. (13.8b) ("There is something that suspends Heaven; there is something that supports Earth. If there is nothing to suspend it, Heaven would have fallen; if there is nothing to support it, Earth would have sunk. Now if even Heaven and Earth would probably have fallen or sunk unless there is something which suspends and supports them, how much more so with man! There is something which manages a man, just as is the case with the movement of thunder-drums. That which cannot shake itself must have something to shake it. But what is this 'something' like? It cannot either be seen or heard; it fills the world without blocking it up; it permeates the flesh and skin and manifests itself in the complexion of the face. You may demand to know when it comes and goes, but no one knows the time. It is square and it is round, and being round,[9] no one can find the way in.") It is here concluded from the fact that Heaven does not fall and Earth does not sink that there must be "something" which keeps the one from falling and the other from sinking. So we can see that 或維 and 或載 are just instances of 或使.

The parallel with the *Chuang tzu* does not end here. It is further argued that if this is the case with Heaven and Earth it must be even more so with man. There must be "something" which manages man. This presumably refers to the heart (*hsin* 心), as the description "you may demand to know when it comes and goes, but no one knows the time" is the kind of language that is used of the heart. For instance, in chapter 49 of the *Kuan tzu* it is said of the

---

[9] Perhaps the text is corrupt and should read "being square as well as round".

heart that "no one can fathom its going and coming (一往一來，莫之能思)" (16.2b).

Enough has been said to show that the term 或使 is used in the writings of the Warring States period to refer specifically to the "something" which is behind the universe and responsible for its workings. Mencius' use of this term is no exception. Having said that "when a man goes forward, there is something which urges him on; when he halts there is something which holds him back", Mencius goes on to say: "It is not in a man's power either to go forward or to halt. It is due to Heaven that I failed to meet the Marquis of Lu." This mention of the agency of Heaven as opposed to human agency shows that the "something" of 或使 refers, indeed, to Heaven.

It is interesting that Mencius, too, describes the heart in terms similar to those used in the *Kuan tzu*. In VI.A.8, we find Confucius quoted as saying, "Hold on to it and it will remain, let go of it and it will disappear. One never knows the time it comes or goes, neither does one know the direction", on which Mencius comments, "It is perhaps to the heart this refers." Not only does Mencius share with the *Kuan tzu* the view that the heart is elusive but also that it informs the body with its own quality: "That which a gentleman follows as his nature, that is to say, benevolence, rightness, the rites and wisdom, is rooted in his heart, and manifests itself in his face, giving it a sleek appearance. It also shows in his back and extends to his limbs, rendering their message intelligible without words" (VII.A.21). Although as a Confucian, Mencius differs from the *Kuan tzu* in attributing moral qualities to a man's nature, nevertheless there is a great deal of common ground between the two. According to the *Kuan tzu*, the heart is the seat of the *ching ch'i* 精氣 which is part of the *tao* 道, whereas, according to Mencius, man's endowment of incipient moral tendencies is that which links him to Heaven.

We can see, then, that Mencius takes for granted a great deal of the prevalent theories concerning man and his relationship to the universe. The only thing is that he puts a moral complexion on the current theory and harnesses it in support of Confucius' teaching.

(6) II.A.1 德之流行，速於置郵而傳命。
The traditional interpretation takes both 置 and 郵 as nouns—either taking both as meaning relay horses (Chu, p. 35) or taking 置 to refer to post by relay horses and 郵 to refer to post by messengers on foot (Chiao, 6.8a). Construed in this way, 置郵而傳命 would be a nominal unit in which 而 intervenes between the exposed element and the nucleus, and the whole unit would be object to 於 .[10] But there is an alternative way of construing the sentence. 而

[10] See Graham (1), pp. 213-14.

can be taken to be linking two verbal units, in which case 置 has to be taken as a verb and 置郵 would mean "setting up relay stations". The *Lü shih ch'un ch'iu* 呂氏春秋 (ch. 19, part 3) quotes this saying as: 德之速，疾乎以郵傳命 (19.7b), where 以郵 is parallel to 傳命. As the word 以 here is a verb it gives some support for taking 置 in the *Mencius* text as a verb as well.

(7) II.A.2 自反而不縮，雖褐寬博，吾不惴焉。

"If, on looking within, one finds oneself to be in the wrong, then even though one's adversary be only a common fellow coarsely clad . . ." As 惴 means "to be afraid", it is very difficult to make sense of the final clause with its negative. The traditional interpretation ". . . I must not make him afraid", taking 惴 as a causative, is forced. There are two objections. First, as 惴, not being an action verb, normally takes no object, it is difficult to see how it can be used as a causative verb. Second, the negative would normally demand an inversion of the object. It may be argued that this does not happen in this case because 焉 is used as object, but the use of 焉 as object is it itself odd. Yen Jo-ch'ü 閻若璩, though he does not follow this interpretation, nevertheless finds it necessary to explain away the negative. He suggests that 不 should be taken as equivalent to 豈不 (Yen 23.18b), a usage unsupported elsewhere in the *Mencius*.

The only reasonable way of getting out of the difficulty is to take 不 as a mistake for 必, as a confusion between the two characters is not unknown in ancient texts. In the passage in chapter 16 of the *Kuan tzu*: 故曰上無固植，下有疑心；國無常經，民力必竭；數也, (6.2a) Wang Yin-chih says that 必 is a mistake for 不 (TSTC, 7.78) while in the passage in the *Yen tzu ch'un ch'iu* (3/18): 所求于下者，不務于上；所禁于民者，不行于身, (8.18b) he says that 不務 should be 必務 (*ibid.*, 8.122) In a passage in chapter 37 of the *Mo tzu*: 凡出言談則必可而不先立儀而言 (9.10b), Yü Yüeh says that 必 should be 不 (Yü (2), 195).

Neither Wang nor Yü suggests that the confusion is due to phonetic resemblance, though this cannot be entirely ruled out. It is true, the only evidence we have of the archaic pronunciation of 不 points to its being a homophone of 否 *piug and therefore quite different from that of 必 *piêt. But Karlgren remarks, "All the modern dialect readings reveal an Anc. puət, which points to an Arch, *pwət, cognate to 弗 *piwət" (GS, 999). If this is the case, then the confusion with 必 may well be due to phonetic resemblance.

(8) II.A.2 志壹則動氣，氣壹則動志也。今夫蹶者趨者是氣也，而反動其心。

The words 蹶 and 趨 are usually taken to mean "to stumble" and "to hurry" respectively. This gives the sense, "Now stumbling and hurrying *are* the *ch'i* yet in fact palpitations of the heart are produced." Now "stumbling" and "hurrying" may bring on a shortness of breath, but it is odd to say that they *are* the *ch'i*.

In his comments on a passage from chapter 105 of the *Shih chi*,齊郎中令循病，衆醫皆以爲蹷人中，而刺之 (p. 2799), Wang Nien-sun says that 人 should be emended to 入,[11] citing as his evidence the definition in the *Shih ming* 釋名：厥，逆氣從下厥起上行入心脇也.[12] The opening part 厥，逆氣 is also found in the *Shuo Wen*,[13] except that 厥 is there written 瘚. The *Shih ming* definition can be translated, "*Chüeh* is *ch'i* going the wrong way. It rises the wrong way from below and goes up into the heart and the side." We can see from the *Shih chi* text that the character is also written 蹷. This definition fits the Mencius passage very well, for, as 蹷 is *ch'i* "that goes the wrong way", one can see why Mencius says that it is the *ch'i* which, as we have suggested, would be surprising if 蹷 is taken to mean "to stumble". Moreover, this furnishes support to Chao's interpretation of the opening sentences in the passage. He takes 壹 as 噎, meaning "blocked" (Chiao, 6.14a). If the *ch'i* is going the wrong way, then it is, indeed, blocked.

But whether this suggested interpretation of 蹷 can stand or not depends on whether one can find evidence for 趨 , similarly, being the name of an illness connected with the *ch'i* or, at least, for its being a loan for another character with such a meaning, but so far I have not found such evidence, though the word is, in fact, used in the same chapter of the *Shih chi* to describe the 脈氣 (pp. 2814-15). I have included this suggestion here in the hope that scholars knowledgeable on early Chinese medical works may be able to throw light on the matter.

(9) II.A.2 必有事焉而勿正心勿忘勿助長也。
It is difficult to make good sense of this passage. Ku Yen-wu 顧炎武 quotes Ni Ssu's 倪思 theory that 正心 is a corruption from 忘 (Ku, 7.16b). This is surely right, as the passage will then make straightforward sense: "You must work at it and never let it out of your mind. While you must not let it out of your mind, you must not forcibly help it grow either."

(10) II.B.4 求牧與芻而不得，則反諸其人乎？抑亦立而視其死與？
This is one of the forms which alternative questions "Is it . . .? Or is it . . .?" take. Each question ends with a different interrogative particle. This is found again in VI.A.1, 子能順杞柳之性而以爲桮棬乎？將戕賊杞柳而後以爲桮棬也？ The only difference is that in this example 也 is used in place of 與 with which it is interchangeable in such contexts.

---

[11] TSTC, 3.25.
[12] Wang Hsien-ch'ien, p. 396.
[13] SWKL, p. 3325.

The ignorance of this form of alternative questions has given rise to an interesting case of the misinterpretation of a passage in the *Chuang tzu*. In chapter 19 there is a story about a hunchback who never misses when picking cicadas. This led to the following exchange: 仲尼曰，"子巧乎有道邪？" 曰，"我有道也．" In his commentary, Ch'eng Hsüan-ying 成玄英 says, "怪其巧一至於斯，故問其方" (CTCS, p. 640). It is not very clear how he understood the passage, but it is likely that his comment has played a part in misleading subsequent editors and translators into taking the first part as an exclamation. Wang Hsiao-yü 王孝魚, in his edition of the *Chuang tzu chi shih*, puts an exclamation mark after the 乎 and a question mark after the 邪． (CTCS, p. 639). Japanese translators of the *Chuang tzu* have always read this as: Kimi wa takumi naru kana! Michi ari ya.[14] Professor Burton Watson, following this tradition, translates the passage as, 'What skill you have! Is there a special way to this?"[15]

The same passage is also to be found in chapter 2 of the *Lieh tzu* (2.5b). In his modern edition, Yang Po-chün punctuates in the same way as Wang Hsiao-yü, by putting an exclamation mark after the first sentence and a question mark after the second (Yang (3), p. 40). Dr. A. C. Graham, following Yang, translates, "What skill! Is it because you have the Way?" (Graham (2), p. 45) Japanese translators, too, treat this passage in the same way as they do the *Chuang tzu* passage.[16]

Now apart from the *Mencius* examples which show that the *Chuang tzu* passage should also be taken as consisting of alternative questions, there is proof in the *Chuang tzu* itself. In chapter 22, in the story about the buckle maker, we find "子巧與？有道與？" 曰，"臣有守 [emend to 道][17] 也。" Now Wang Hsiao-yü, in face of this, punctuates with two question marks.[18] Japanese translators, however, vary in the way they translate this passage. Both Hattori and Makino relent and translate both as questions with "ka", but both modern translators stick to their guns and persist in "kana" for the first sentence and "ka" for the second (Fukunaga, III, p. 692; Ichikawa and Endō, p. 593). Watson also chooses to follow Fukunaga's lead (Watson (2), p. 244).

In the *Lieh tzu*, as in the *Chuang tzu*, there is a further example of this

[14] *e.g.*, Hattori, 6.38; Makino, p. 68; and, more recently, Fukunaga, II, p. 480; and Ichikawa and Endō, p. 507.

[15] Watson (1), p. 120, Watson (2), p. 199.

[16] Ōta, p. 159; Kobayashi, however, translates, "Shi ga takumi ya michi ari ka?" (p. 93), but shows in his paraphrase which follows, "Anata no sono udemae ni wa nanika tokubetsu no waza demo aru deshō ka?" that he does not understand it as alternative questions.

[17] TSTC, 16.26.

[18] CTCS, p. 760.

question. In chapter 8 we find 孔子問之曰，"[子]¹⁹巧乎？有道術乎？"²⁰
This time Yang Po-chün punctuates with two question marks,²¹ but Graham
ignores his punctuation and translates, "What skill! Have you some special
art?" (Graham (2) p. 166)

Having shown that 子巧乎 must be taken as a question in the context of
子巧乎有道邪, we may, perhaps, go a step further and say that even taken by
itself 子巧乎 can only be taken as a question. 乎 often appears as a final
particle in a rhetorical question or in a sentence expressing a wish—in which
case there is always a modal word like 其 —but it never appears as a final
particle in an exclamatory sentence meaning "How . . .!" In such exclamatory
sentences which, incidentally, are quite rare, 乎 appears after an initial
adjectival unit, usually consisting of a single word, for example 宜乎百姓之謂
我愛也 (I.A.7). ("How natural it was for the people to have thought me
miserly!") In this respect 乎 is similar to 哉 , for instance,大哉堯之爲君
III. A.4). ("How great Yao was as a ruler!") But 哉 differs from 乎 in one
important respect. It can also appear at the end of the sentence, for instance,
管仲之器小哉 (*Analects*, 3/22). ("How small Kuan Chung was in his capacity!") It is perhaps the similarity between 乎 and 哉 that has misled translators into taking the final 乎 as exclamatory.

(11) II.A.12 王庶幾改之！王如改諸，則必反予。
The *Feng su t'ung yi* 風俗通義 quotes this with 之 and 諸 transposed (7.2b).
This is the correct reading. In I.B.1 we find 王庶幾無疾病與！This shows that
sentences with 庶幾 expressing a wish end with an exclamatory particle. The
present text should be no exception. Moreover, there is no good reason why
the first part of the second sentence should end with a 諸 , as it is a straightforward if-clause. The only complication is that further on we find:……天下
之民舉安。王庶幾改之！予日望之. It is very likely that here, too, 改之 was
originally 改諸, and was corrected to 改之 by some misguided editor to bring
it into line with the earlier sentence. after the corruption had crept in. That
the reading should be 改諸 is confirmed by the *Lun heng* 論衡 (chapter 30)
where this is quoted as 民舉安。王庶幾改諸！予日望之. (10.13a)

¹⁹Supplied from parallels in the *K'ung tzu chia yü* 孔子家語 (2.9a) and the *Shuo
yüan* 說苑 (17.16a), as suggested by Wang Shu-mın, 4.25b. See also Yang (3), p. 158.
²⁰Although this story is also to be found in chapter 19 of the *Chuang tzu* (CTCS,
p. 656), the version there seems defective and this question does not appear there. It
seems that there was a genre of story all concerned with people with surpassing skill, and
the crucial point of the story consists in this question as to whether this was skill or
something far beyond skill—the possession of the Way. Although we have only three
extant stories belonging to this genre, there probably were others that have been lost.
²¹Japanese translators, too, take both sentences as questions. Ōta, p. 278; Kobayashi,
pp. 377-8.

(12) III.A.1 今滕 . . . 猶可以爲善國 .

This expression 善國 is awkward. I suspect that the word 國 is an interpolation. 猶可以爲善 is similar in construction to 王由 (= 猶) 足用爲善 in II.B.2 and can be translated ". . . It is big enough for you to do good."

(13) III.A.5 夫夷子信以爲人之親其兄之子爲若親其鄰之赤子乎？

It is obvious that the repetition of 爲 poses a problem. Wang Yin-chih has suggested that the second 爲 should be taken as equivalent to 有 (CCST, p. 60). This is unconvincing. When 以爲 is used to mean "to consider x as y", the object x is always interposed between 以 and 爲, and we only find 以爲 together when the object is not expressed.[22] In the present case, the object 人之親其兄之子 is expressed and there is a 爲 following it, and there is no reason why there should be another 爲 preceding it. The first must be an interpolation. There is one other example of a similar construction in the *Mencius*: 夫公明高以孝子之心爲不若是恝 (V.A.1), and there 爲 appears only after the object.

(14) III.B.1 如不待其招而往何哉。

It is usual to take the pause after 往, though it is not very clear what sense the sentence will make. Both Chao and Chu seem to want the sentence to mean, "How much less can a man go without waiting for his summons!" Yang, however, translates "How would it be if I were to go without waiting for the summons of the feudal lords?"[23] It seems this is an instance of the construction " 如x何 " where x is the object. There are two other instances of this construction in the *Mencius*. (1) 君如彼何哉！ (I.B.14), (2) 吾如有萌焉何哉！(VI.A.9). The first can be translated "What can you do about Ch'i?", and the second as "What can I do with the few new shoots that come out?" The present text should also be translated, "What can one do about those who go without even being summoned?"

The difficulty is with the repetition of this sentence further on with 也 instead of 哉. But as it is difficult to make good sense of the sentence with 也, one must assume that it is a corruption and, if this is so, then it is likely that this is a corruption from 哉 .

(15) III.B.3 不由其道而往者與鑽穴隙之類也。

This sentence is ungrammatical as it stands. There have been various suggestions—that 與 should be read as 歟, that 之 is an interpolation and that 與

---

[22] Or when the expression is followed by a verbal unit, *e.g.*, 一心以爲有鴻鵠將至 (VI.A.9). But this usage does not concern us as it constitutes a separate usage with a different meaning.

[23] 假定我竟不等待諸侯的招致便去，那又是怎樣的？(Yang (1) p. 139)

should be read as 如(see Yang (1), p. 145, n. 12). None of these suggestions seems satisfactory. 與 is here used for 舉.[24] This is supported, on the one hand by the fact that 舉, meaning all, is found six times in the *Mencius*,[25] and, on the other, by the sentence in VII.B.31, 是皆穿踰之類也, which is similar both in grammatical structure and in meaning to the text in question, except that it has 皆which is synonymous with 舉. The sentence, when emended, can be translated, "All those who go without following the right way are no different from the men and women who bore holes in the wall."

(16) III. B.10 三咽然後耳有聞，目有見。

In his *Shih san chiu* 釋三九,[26] Wang Chung 汪中 points out that 三 is often used not in its exact sense of "three" but in the vague sense of "many". Amongst the examples he cites are a number from the *Analects of Confucius*: (1) 焉往而不三黜 (18/2), (2) 季文子三思而後行[27] (5/20), (3) 雌雉三嗅而作 (10/21), (4)令尹子文三仕爲令尹 ... 三已之 (5/19), and also the above passage from the *Mencius*. While he follows Wang's suggestion in his *pai hua* translation in his *Lun yü yi chu*,[28] Yang Po-chün has not followed it in the present passage. Surely Wang's point applies to this as it applies to most of the passages from the *Analects*? There is another example similar to the *Mencius* passage. In a story about another starving man in the *Lü shih ch'un ch'iu* we find 爰旌目三餔之而後能視 (12.5b). If 三 is to be taken to mean "three", it is odd that one starving man should take "three gulps" while another should take "three sips" before either could see.

(17) IV.A.15 存乎人者莫良於眸子。

By using 存在 to gloss 存, Chao seems to be taking the word as meaning察 (see Chiao, 15.9a). This is followed by Yang in his modern translation, "If you examine a man, there is nothing better than examining his eyes."[29] But there is no justification for taking the word in this sense. In VI.A.8 we find 雖存乎人者，豈無仁義之心哉 . Chao again says, 存在也 (II.B.1b), but this time he seems to be taking the word to mean "to be in". If 存means in this instance "to be in", there is no reason to suppose that it should have a

---

[24] For evidence of the words being interchangeable, see (3) above.

[25] I.B.1: 舉疾首蹙頞而相告曰 (twice), 舉欣欣然有喜色而相告曰 (twice), II.B.12: 天下之民舉安 , and VI.A.7: 故凡同類者舉相似也 .

[26] Wang Chung, I.2b.

[27] It is likely that Wang's theory does not apply to this example, for as Confucius commented, "Twice is quite enough." 三 is here contrasted with 再 "twice" and may, in fact, be used in the exact sense of "three".

[28] See Yang (2), particularly p. 4, n. 2.

[29] "觀察一個人，再沒比觀察他的眼睛更好了 ." (Yang (1), p. 177)

different meaning in the passage in question, which can be translated, "there is in man nothing more ingenuous than the pupils of his eyes".

(18) IV.A.22 人之易其言也，無責耳矣。

Chao offers two interpretations of this passage. First, that a man speaks lightly is because he has never been taken to task for saying the wrong things. Second, the reason a man refuses to reprimand the ruler is that he is not in a position of responsibility to offer advice.[30] In his second interpretation he has to introduce a negative element into the first half of the sentence and this is unsatisfactory. Chu follows, with a slight change in wording, Chao's first interpretation.[31] Yü Yüeh offers a new interpretation, "If a man speaks lightly, it is not worth taking him to task."[32] None of these interpretations seems satisfactory, but Chao is right, in his second interpretation, in taking the word 責 as meaning "responsibility" rather than in the sense of "taking someone to task". As the first part of the sentence is concerned with speaking, it is no accident that the expression 言責 "responsibility for offering advice" is, in fact, used by Mencius (II.B.5). If we combine this with the first part of Chao's interpretation, we arrive at a more satisfactory interpretation of the whole passage, "If a man speaks lightly it is simply because he has no responsibility of office." Thus the idea expressed is not very different from Mencius' criticism in III.B.9 of 處士橫議 "people with no official positions being uninhibited in the expression of their views".

(19) V.A.4 而舜既爲天子矣，敢問瞽瞍之非臣如何？

Chao interprets this as meaning, "No one in the Empire is not a subject of the King, yet you say that the Blind Man is not a subject. Why?"[33] Yang translates, "Since Shun was already Emperor, may I ask why the Blind Man was not his subject?"[34] Both interpreters have been misled by the 如 of 如何. Here 如 is used for 而.[35] "非 x 而何" is an idiomatic expression meaning "if it is not x, what is it?" The present text would, then, mean "Now after Shun became Emperor, if the Blind Man was not his subject, what was he?"

(20) V.A.8 "有諸乎？" 孟子曰，"否，不然也。"

V.A.5, 6, 7 all have the same question and answer, except that there is no final 乎. "有諸" is a set formula to be found also in I.A.7; I.B.1, 2, 8; II.B.8,

---

[30] 人之輕易其言，不得失言之咎責。一說，人之輕易不肯諫正君者，以其不在言責之位者也. (7B.10a)

[31] "人之所以輕易其言者，以其未遭失言之責故矣." (Chu, p. 108)

[32] "無責耳矣，乃言其不足責也。猶曰，若而人者，吾無責焉爾." (Yü (1), 1394.3a)

[33] "徧天下循土之濱無有非王者之臣而曰瞽瞍非臣，如何也." (Chao, 9A.10a)

[34] "如果舜既做了天子，請問瞽瞍卻不是臣民又是甚麼道理呢？" (Yang (1), p. 216)

[35] See (28) below for cases of 而 used for 如.

9; and VI.B.2. The present text is not only out of step with the other sections but also grammatically incorrect in having the extra 乎.

(21) V.B.1 伯夷 ... 思與鄉人處，如以朝衣朝冠坐於塗炭也。
This passage is found also in II.A.12, where the text reads, 立於惡人之朝，與惡人言，如以朝衣朝冠坐於塗炭。推惡惡之心，思與鄉人立，其冠不正，望望然去之，若將浼焉。By comparison, we can see that the text in V.B.1 is defective. It is not in the company of a fellow-villager that Po Yi feels as if he were sitting in mud or pitch while wearing court cap and gown. It is being at the court of a bad man and conversing with him that gives him this feeling. Moreover, Po Yi does not object to the company of a fellow-villager as such but to his cap being awry. Even then, all he did was to walk away in disgust.

(22) V.B.1 思天下之民匹夫匹婦有不被堯舜之澤者，若己推而內之溝中。其自任以天下之重也。
The final sentence is obviously incomplete with only a nominal unit. Yang has suggested that the word 此 should be added to the beginning.[36] Thus the sentence would mean "This is because of his taking on the responsibility of the Empire." But this is incorrect, and it so happens there is no need for conjecture. In IV.B.7 the same passage is found except that there are the words 如此 at the end. Thus the sentence means, "It is to this extent that he considered the Empire his responsibility."

(23) VI.A.4 吾弟則愛之，秦人之弟則不愛，是以我爲悅者也 ... 長楚人之長，亦長吾長，是以長爲悅者也。
The character 悅 is not found in the *Shuo wen*, and in the Classics only the character 說 is used. With the philosophers, the position is confused. The *Analects of Confucius* has no 悅 except as a variant reading in 1/1. In both the *Mo tzu* and the *Chuang tzu*, 悅 is to be found, but in the *Hsün tzu* there are only two instances of 悅 and only one of these is used in the sense of to be pleased.[37] Thus it would seem that in ancient works only 說 was used even where the meaning is "to be pleased", and that the occurrence of 悅 in some works is due to later editors, perhaps with a view to helping the reader. The *Mencius* belongs to this category. But it is always possible for an editor to have misunderstood a text and substituted a 悅 where the meaning is, in fact, not "to be pleased". The present passage seems to be a case in point. This does not make good sense unless one reads 說 instead of 悅, in which case it can be translated, "My brother I love, but the brother of a man from

[36] Yang (1), p. 234, n. 3.
[37] The other is, according to Sun Yi-jang 孫詒讓 (6.13a), a loan for 娧.

Ch'in I do not love. This means that the explanation lies in me ... Treating
an elder of a man from Ch'u as elder is no different from treating the elder
of my own family as elder. This means that the explanation lies in their elderliness."

(24) VI.A.11 人有雞犬放，則知求之；有放心而不知求。學問之道無他，求其
放心而已矣。

This passage is found in the *Han shih wai chuan* 韓詩外傳 (4/27) where
between the two sentences there is the added passage, 其 (= 豈) 於 [emend to
以] 心爲不若雞犬哉！不知類之甚矣，悲夫！終亦必亡而已矣。The sentence
不知類之甚矣 is similar to 此之謂不知類也 in VI.A.2 and 弗思甚也 in VI.A.13,
and 終亦必亡而已矣 is also to be found in two other sections-in the same
book.[38] It would seem that the *Han shih wai chuan* has a more complete text.

(25) VI.A.16 今之人修其天爵，以要人爵，既得人爵，而棄其天爵，則惑之甚
者也，終亦必亡而已矣。

Commentators tend to take the final sentence as referring to the loss, in the
end, of the "honours bestowed by man". But grammatically this is difficult,
as 亡 here has no object. Furthermore, this line is to be found also in VI.A.18:
此又與於不仁之甚者也，亦終必亡而已矣。[39] It is difficult here to see what it
is that is supposed to be lost if 亡 is taken to mean "to lose". From Chao
onwards, commentators all take this to refer to "the benevolence he did
practise", but this seems forced. I think that, in both cases, 亡 means "to
perish" and can be translated "in the end he is sure only to perish".[40]

(26) VI.B.7 葵丘之會，諸侯束牲載書而不歃血。

There is doubt as to whether 載 is a verb here or not. Chao comments,但加載
書，不復歃血.[41] The interpretation turns on whether 載書 is taken as a term
which is object to the verb 加 , or whether 加載 is Chao's way of indicating
that 載 is to be taken as a synonym of 加 . Mao Ch'i-ling 毛奇齡 favours the
first while Chiao Hsün favours the second.[42] It seems possible to settle the
point by investigating the usages of 載 and 載書. Cheng Hsüan's 鄭玄 commentary to the *Chou li* says, 載 , 盟辭也 (36.5b), "*Tsai* is the text of the
covenant." Again, Tu Yü's 杜預 commentary to the *Tso chuan* says, 載書,盟
書 (Duke Hsiang 9), which also amounts to saying that 載書 is the text of the

[38] Compare (25) below.
[39] And also in VI.A.11 if we follow the *Han shih wai chuan*. See (24) above.
[40] This applies to the sentence as supplied from the *Han shih wai chuan* referred to in
(24) above as well.
[41] MTCS, 12B.2a.
[42] Chiao, 25.3b-4a.

covenant. Now 載書 appears ten times in the *Tso chuan* and it is always a
single term, never a verb-object construction. There is a case of 載 being used
on its own, 載在盟府，太師職之 (Duke Hsi 26). Even here it is clear that it is
a noun, meaning the "text of the covenant". It would seem that Chiao is
wrong about the meaning intended by Chao. All he was doing was to add the
verb 加 to make the sense of the text clearer, without intending it to be taken
as a synonym of 載. Perhaps he was doing no more than echoing the Ku-liang
commentary which says, 葵邱之盟，陳牲而不殺，讀書加于牲上 (Duke Hsi
9), where the word 加 is used.

(27) VI.B.12 君子不亮，惡乎執。
The word 惡 has two pronunciations. In the level tone, it is an interrogative
word; in the falling tone it is a verb. Traditionally, it has always been taken in
the level tone in the present passage. Chiao, however, quotes Ho Yi-sun 何異
孫 of the Yüan who argued in favour of the falling tone.[43] Amongst modern
commentators Takeuchi Yoshio is the first one I know of who follows this
interpretation. He translates the present passage as: Kunshi no kakawarazaru
wa shū wo nikumeba nari.[44] This is, in fact, mistaken, because the particle 乎
does not intervene between verb and object. The particle that does so is 夫.

Even if we take 惡 in the level tone as an interrogative, there still remains
the question whether 執 is a verb to which 惡 is the object or not. Chao
seems to take it in this way, as he comments, 若爲君子之道，舍信安執之.
("If one were to follow the way of the gentleman, where can one hold on to
if one lets go of fidelity?") (12B.10a). Chu seems to do the same. His comment is, "惡乎執"，言凡事苟且無所執持. ("'*Wu hu chih*' means that in all
things one is easy-going and there is nothing one holds on to firmly.")
(p. 185)

This way of construing the sentence seems to me to be mistaken as well.
惡 in 惡乎 cannot be the object of the verb which follows it. Furthermore,
the word that follows 惡乎 has to be an adjective, not a verb. This is clearly
shown in other examples in the *Mencius*: (1)敢問夫子惡乎長.(II.A.2) ("May
I ask wherein are you strong?") 長 here is an adjective and as an adjective it is
often used in sentences of the form "A 長於 y" ("A is strong in y"), where
" 於 y" occupies the same position in the answer as 惡乎 in the question. (2)
惡乎宜乎？ (III.B.5) ("Wherein would it be suitable?") The expression is used
in the same way in the *Analects*, 君子去仁，惡乎成名. ("If a gentleman
forsakes benevolence, wherein can he be known?")成名, a verb-object construction, is used in place of a single adjective. Thus 執 has to be taken as an

[43] Chiao, 25.asb.
[44] Takeuchi, p. 281; Kanaya Osamu in his recent translation follows Takeuchi in taking
惡 as a verb: Kunshi no makoto narazaru wa torawaruru wo nikumeba nari (p. 425).

adjective. It cannot mean "to hold on to" but has to mean "inflexible". This use of the word is attested in the *Chuang tzu*. We find in chapter 4 將執而不化 (CTCS, p. 141), and in chapter 25 有主而不執 (p. 909). On this interpretation the present passage can be translated, "Other than adherence to his word, wherein can a gentleman be guilty of inflexibility?"

(28) VII.B.3 以至仁伐至不仁，而何其血之流杵也？

The *Lun heng*, in quoting this, is right in having 如何 in place of 而何. This is not the only example in the *Mencius* of 而 used for 如. It has been pointed out by Wang Yin-chih that 而 in 望道而未之見 (IV.B.20), should be read as 如 (CCST, p. 143). The use of 而 for 如 in these two examples is comparable to the use of 如 for 而 noted in (19) above. The present passage can be translated, "How could it be that 'the blood spilled was enough to carry staves along with it', when the most benevolent waged war against the most cruel?"

WORKS CITED

Analects of Confucius trans. D. C. Lau (Penguin Classics, 1979).

Chan kuo shih 戰國史 by Yang k'uan 楊寬 , Shanghai, 1955.

Chan kuo t'se 戰國策 , Huang Shih Tu Wei Chien Shu Chai ch'ung tiao Yao Shih pen 黃氏讀未見書齋重雕姚氏本 , 1803.

Chi Wei Chü hsiao hsüeh chin shih lun ts'ung 積微居小學金石論叢 by Yang Shu-ta 楊樹達 , Peking, 1955.

Ching hsüeh chih yen 經學卮言 by K'ung Kuang-sen 孔廣森 , *Huang Ch'ing ching-chieh* 皇清經解 ed.

Ching yi shu wen 經義述聞 by Wang Yin-chih 王引之 ,WYWK (*Wan yu wen k'u* 萬有文庫) ed.

Chuang tzu 莊子 , *Hsü ku yi tsung shu* 續古逸叢書 ed.

Ch'ün ching p'ing yi 羣經平議 by Yü Yüeh 俞樾 , *Hsü Huang Ch'ing ching chieh* 續皇清經解 ed.

Erh ya chu shu 爾雅注疏 , SSCCS (*Shih san ching chu shu* 十三經注疏 , Nan-chang, 1815) ed.

Feng su t'ung yi 風俗通義 by Ying Shao 應劭 (*Feng su t'ung yi chiao chu* 風俗通義校注 by Wang Li-ch'i 王利器 , Peking, 1981).

Han shih wai chuan 韓詩外傳 by Han Ying 韓嬰 , SPTK (*Ssu pu ts'ung k'an* 四部叢刊) ed.

Hsien Ch'in chu tzu hsi nien 先秦諸子繫年 by Ch'ien Mu 錢穆 , revised and enlarged ed., Hong Kong, 1956.

Hsin hsü 新序 by Liu Hsiang 劉向 , SPTK ed.

Jih chih lu 日知錄 by Ku Yen-wu 顧炎武 , SPPY (*Ssu pu pei yao* 四部備要) ed.

Kuan tzu 管子 , SPTK ed.

Kuang ya shu cheng 廣雅疏證 by Wang Nien-sun 王念孫 , WYWK ed.

Kuo yü 國語 , Shih Li Chü 士禮居 ed.

Li chi chu shu 禮記注疏 , SSCCS ed.

Lieh nü chuan 列女傳 by Liu Hsiang 劉向 , SPPY ed.

Lun heng 論衡 by Wang Ch'ung 王充 , SPTK ed.

Po shu wu hsing p'ien yen chiu 帛書五行篇研究 by P'ang P'u 龐樸 , Shantung, 1980.

Shih chi 史記 by Ssu-ma Ch'ien 司馬遷 , Chung Hua Shu Chü 中華書局 , 1959.

Shih Chia Chai yang hsin lu 十駕齋養新錄 by Ch'ien Ta-hsin 錢大昕 ,WYWK ed.

Shu ching 書經 (*Shang shu chu shu* 尚書注疏|), SSCCS ed.

Shuo wen t'ung hsün ting sheng 說文通訓定聲 by Chu Chün-sheng 朱駿聲 , 1870.

Shuo yüan 說苑 by Liu Hsiang 劉向 , SPTK ed.

Ta Tai li chi 大戴禮記 , SPTK ed.

Three Ways of Thought in Ancient China by Arthur Way, London, 1939.

Tzu chih t'ung ch'ien 資治通鑑 by Ssu-ma K'uang 司馬光 , Peking, 1956.

Wen hsün 文選 , Hsün Yang Wan Shih ch'ung k'an Hu k'e pen 潯陽萬氏重刊
胡刻本 , 1869.

Yi Meng tzu 逸孟子 ed. Li T'iao-yüan 李調元 , *Han hai* 函海 t'ao 25.

Yi Meng tzu 逸孟子 ed. Ma kuo-han 馬國翰, *Yü Han Shan Fang chi yi shu* 玉函
山房輯佚書.

Yin Hsü pu tz'u tsung shu 殷虛卜辭綜述 by Ch'en Meng Chia 陳夢家 , Peking,
1956.

INDEX OF PROPER NAMES

Bandit Chih, III. B. 10.
Blind Man, the, IV. A. 28; V. A. 2, 4; VI. A. 6; VII. A. 35. See Appendix 4.

Chang Tzu, IV. B. 30, i.e., K'uang Chang.
Chang Yi, III. B. 2.
Ch'ang Hsi, V. A. 1; V. B. 3.
Chao Meng, VI. A. 17.
Ch'ao Wu, I. B. 4.
Chen, the, IV. B. 2.
Ch'en, VII. B. 18, 37.
Ch'en Chen, II. B. 3; VII. B. 23.
Ch'en Chia, II. B. 9.
Ch'en Chung, VII. A. 34, i.e., Ch'en Chung-tzu.
Ch'en Chung-tzu, III. B. 10.
Ch'en Hsiang, III. A. 4.
Ch'en Liang, III. A. 4.
Ch'en Tai, III. B. 1.
Ch'en Tzu, II. B. 10; VI. B. 14. This is Ch'en Chen, according to Chao Ch'i.
Cheng, IV. B. 2, 24; V. A. 2; VII. B. 37.
Ch'eng Chien, III. A. 1.
Chi, the, III. A. 4.
Chi, IV. B. 29. i.e., Hou Chi.
Chi family, the IV. A. 14.
Chi Huan, V. A. 8.
Chi Huan Tzu, V. B. 4.
Chi Jen, VI. B. 5.
Chi Sun, II. B. 10.
Chi Tzu, VI. B. 5, i.e., Chi Jen.
Ch'i, V. A. 6. See Appendix 4.
Ch'i, I. B. 5.
Ch'i, I. A. 5, 7; I. B. 1, 10, 11, 13, 14; II. A. 1, 2; II. B. 1, 2, 3, 5, 6, 7,

8, 11, 12, 13, 14; III. B. 5, 6, 10; IV. A. 24; IV. B. 31, 33; V. A. 4, 8; V. B. 1; VI. B. 5, 6, 8; VII. A. 34, 36; VII. B. 17, 23, 29.
Ch'i, the, VI. B. 6.
Ch'i, Viscount of Wei, VI. A. 6. See Appendix 4. See also Viscount of Wei.
Ch'i Chou, IV. B. 1.
Ch'i Liang, VI. B. 6.
Chiao Ke, II. A. 1; VI. B. 15.
Chieh, I. B. 8; IV. A. 9; V. A. 6; VI. B. 2, 6, 9, 10.
Chih, VII. A. 25, i.e., Bandit Chih.
Ch'ih Wa, II. B. 5.
Chin, I. A. 5; II. B. 2; III. B. 3; IV. B. 21; V. A. 9; VII. B. 23.
Ch'in, I. A. 5, 7; V. A. 9; VI. A. 4, 12; VI. B. 4.
Ch'in Chang, VII. B. 37.
Ching, III. A. 4; III. B. 9. Another name for the state of Ch'u.
Ching-ch'ou family, the, II. B. 2.
Ching Ch'un, III. B. 2.
Ching Tzu, II. B. 2.
Chou, I. B. 3; II. A. 1; II. B. 13; III. A. 3; III. B. 5; IV. A. 7; V. A. 4, 6; V. B. 2, 4.
Chou, II. B. 11, 12.
Chou, Marquis of Ch'en, V. A. 8.
Chou Hsiao, III. B. 3.
Chu Feng, IV. B. 1.
Ch'u, I. A. 5, 7; I. B. 6, 13; II. B. 2; III. A. 1, 4; III. B. 5, 6; IV. B. 21; VI. A. 4, 12; VI. B. 4.
Ch'u Tzu, IV. B. 32; VI. B. 5.
Chuan Fu, I. B. 4.
Chuang, III. B. 6.

Chuang Pao, I. B. 1.

Chuang Tzu, I. B. 1, i.e., Chuang Pao.

Ch'ui Chi, V. A. 9.

Ch'un-yü K'un, IV. A. 17; VI. B. 6.

Chung Jen, V. A. 6. See Appendix 4.

Ch'ung, II. B. 14.

Ch'ung Yü, II. B. 7, 13.

Chü, I. B. 3.

Ch'ü, V. A. 9.

Confucius (551–479), I. A. 4, 7; II.
A. 1, 2, 3, 4, 7; III. A. 2, 4; III. B.
1, 3, 7, 9; IV. A. 2, 7, 8, 14; IV. B.
10, 18, 21, 22, 29; V. A. 4, 6, 8; V.
B. 1, 4, 5, 7; VI. A. 6, 8; VI. B. 3,
6; VII. A. 24; VII. B. 17, 19, 37,
38. See Introduction.

Duke Ching of Ch'i (reigned 547–
490), I. B. 4; III. A. 1; III. B. 1; IV.
A. 7; V B. 7.

Duke of Chou, II. A. 1; II. B. 9; III.
A. 1, 4; III. B. 9; IV. B. 20; V. A. 6;
VI. B. 8. See Appendix 4.

Duke Hsiao of Wei, V. B. 4.

Duke Huan of Ch'i (reigned 685–
643), I. A. 7; II. B. 2; IV. B. 21; VI.
B. 7.

Duke Hui of Pi, V. B. 3.

Duke Ling of Wei (reigned 534–
493), V. B. 4.

Duke Mu of Ch'in (reigned 659–
621), V. A. 9; VI. B. 6.

Duke Mu of Lu (reigned 415-383),
II. B. 11; V. B. 6, 7; VI. B. 6.

Duke Mu of Tsou, I. B. 12.

Duke P'ing of Chin (reigned 557–
532), V. B. 3.

Duke P'ing of Lu (reigned 322-303),
I. B. 16. See Appendix 1.

Duke Ting of T'eng, III. A. 2.

Duke Wen of Chin (reigned 636–

628), I. A. 7; IV. B. 21.

Duke Wen of T'eng, I. B. 13, 14, 15;
III. A. 1, 3.

Earl of Ke, III. B. 5.

East Sea, IV. A. 13; VII. A. 22.

Eastern Mount, VII. A. 24.

Fan, VII. A. 36.

Fang Hsün, III. A. 4; V. A. 4, i.e.,
Yao.

Fei Lien, III. B. 9.

Feng Fu, VII. B. 23.

Five Leaders of the feudal lords, VI.
B. 7; VII. A. 30.

Fu Ch'u, IV. B. 31.

Fu Hsia, IV. B. 1.

Fu Yüeh, VI. B. 15. See Appendix 4.

Hai T'ang, V. B. 3.

Han, VII. A. 11.

Han, the, III. A. 4, III. B. 9.

Hao-sheng Pu-hai, VII. B. 25.

Ho Nei, I. A. 3.

Ho Tung, I. A. 3.

Hou Chi, III. A. 4.

Hsi, III. B. 1.

Hsi Po, IV. A. 13; VII. A. 22, i.e.,
King Wen.

Hsi Shih, IV. B. 25.

Hsia, I. B. 4; II. A. 1; III. A. 3; IV. A.
2; V. A. 6, 7; V. B. 4. See Appendix
4.

Hsiang, V. A. 2, 3; VI. A. 6. See
Appendix 4.

Hsieh, III. A. 4. See Appendix 4.

Hsieh Liu, II. B. 11; III. B. 7. See
also Tzu-liu.

Hsien-ch'iu Meng, V. A. 4.

Hsin, III. A. 4.

Hsiu, II. B. 14.

Hsü Hsing, III. A. 4.
Hsü Pi, III. A. 5.
Hsü Tzu, III. A. 4, i.e., Hsü Hsing.
Hsü Tzu, III. A. 5, i.e., Hsü Pi.
Hsüeh, I. B. 14; II. B. 3.
Hsüeh Chü Chou, III. B. 6.
Hsün Yü, I. B. 3.
Hu He, I. A. 7.
Hua Chou, VI. B. 6.
Huai, the, III. A. 4; III. B. 9.
Huan Ssu-ma, V. A. 8.
Huan Tou, V. A. 3.

Jan Ch'iu, IV. A. 14.
Jan Niu, II. A. 2.
Jan Yu, III. A. 2.
Jen, VI. B. 1, 5.
Ju, the, III. A. 4.

Kao T'ang, VI. B. 6.
Kao Tzu, II. A. 2; VI. A. 1, 2, 3, 4, 6.
Kao Yao, III. A. 4; VII. A. 35; VII.
  B. 38. See Appendix 4.
Kau Tzu, II. B. 12; VII. B. 21, 22.
Kau Tzu, VI. B. 3; II. B. 12; VII. B.
  21, 22.
Ke, I. B. 3, 11; III. B. 5.
Ke, II. B. 6.
King of Ch'i, VII. A. 36, i.e., King
  Hsüan of Ch'i.
King of Sung, III. B. 6. See Appendix
  1.
King Hsiang of Liang (reigned 318-
  296), I. A. 6. See Appendix 1.
King Hsüan of Ch'i (reigned 319-
  301), I. A. 7; I. B. 2-11; IV. B. 3;
  V. B. 9; VII. A. 39.
King Hui of Liang (reigned 370-319),
  I. A. 1-5; VII. B. 1.
King Li (reigned 857-842), VI. A. 6.
King Wen (d. 1027), I. A. 2; I. B. 2,

3, 5, 10; II. A. 1, 3; III. A. 1, 3; III.
  B. 9; IV. A. 7, 13; IV. B. 1, 20; VI.
  A. 6; VI. B. 2; VII. A. 10, 22; VII.
  B. 19, 22, 38. See Appendix 4.
King Wu (reigned 1027-1005), I. B.
  3, 8, 10; II. A. 1; II. B. 12; III. B. 9;
  IV. A. 9; IV. B. 20; VI. A. 6; VII. A.
  30; VII. B. 4, 33. See Appendix 4.
King Yu (reigned 781-771), VI. A. 6.
Kou Chien, I. B. 3.
Ku Kung Tan Fu, I. B. 5, i.e., T'ai
  Wang.
Kuan Chung, II. A. 1; II. B. 2; VI. B.
  15.
Kuan Shu, II. B. 9.
K'uang Chang, III. B. 10; IV. B. 30.
  See Appendix 1.
K'uei Ch'iu, VI. B. 7.
K'ung Chü-hsin, II. B. 4.
Kun, V. A. 3. See Appendix 4.
K'un tribes, I. B. 3.
Kung chih Ch'i, V. A. 9.
Kung Kung, V. A. 3.
Kung Liu, I. B. 5. See Appendix 4.
Kung-hang Tzu, IV. B. 27.
Kung-ming Kao, V. A. 1.
Kung-ming Yi, III. A. 1; III. B. 3, 9;
  IV. B. 24.
Kung-shu Tzu, IV. A. 1.
Kung-sun Ch'ou, II. A. 1, 2; II. B. 2,
  6, 14; III. B. 7; IV. A. 18; VI. B. 3,
  13; VII. A. 31, 32, 39, 41; VII. B.
  1, 36.
Kung-sun Yen, III. B. 2.
Kung-tu Tzu, II. B. 5; III. B. 9; IV. B.
  30; VI. A. 5, 6, 15; VII. A. 43.
Kung-yi Tzu, VI. B. 6.
Kuo, V. A. 9.

Lady Chiang, I. B. 5.
Lai Chu, VII. B. 38.

Lang Yeh, I. B. 4.
Li Lou, IV. A. 1.
Liang Mountains, I. B. 15.
Ling Ch'iu, II. B. 5.
Liu Hsia Hui, II. A. 9; V. B. 1; VI. B. 6; VII. A. 28; VII. B. 15.
Lu, I. B. 12; II. B. 7; III. A. 2; IV. B. 21; V. A. 8; V. B. 1, 4; VI. B. 6, 8, 13; VII. A. 24, 36; VII. B. 17, 37.
Lung Tzu, III. A. 3; VI. A. 7.

Meng Chi-tzu, VI. A. 5.
Meng Chung-tzu, II. B. 2.
Meng Hsien Tzu, V. B. 3.
Meng K'e, I. B. 16, i.e., Mencius.
Meng Pin, II. A. 2.
Meng Shih-she, II. A. 2.
Mi Tzu, V. A. 8, i.e., Mi Tzu-hsia.
Mien Chü, VI. B. 6.
Min Tzu, II. A. 2, i.e., Min Tzu-ch'ien.
Ming T'iao, IV. B. 1.
Mo, III. B. 9; VII. B. 26, i.e., Mo Ti.
Mo Chi, VII. B. 19.
Mo Ti, III. B. 9.
Mo Tzu, VII. A. 26, i.e., Mo Ti.
Mount Chi, V. A. 6.
Mount Ch'i, I. B. 5, 14, 15.
Mount Ch'ung, V. A. 3.
Mount T'ai, I. A. 7; II. A. 2; VII. A. 24.
Mount Yü, V. A. 3.
Mu Chung, V. B. 3.
Mu Palace, V. A. 7.
Mu P'i, VII. B. 37.

Nan Ho, V. A. 5.
Nan Yang, VI. B. 8.
North Sea, I. A. 7; IV. A. 13; V. B. 1; VII. A. 22.

Ox Mountain, VI. A. 8.

P'en-ch'eng K'uo, VII. B. 29.
P'eng Keng, III. B. 4.
P'eng Meng, IV. B. 24.
Pi Chan, III. A. 3.
Pi Ying, IV. B. 1.
Pin, I. B. 14, 15.
P'ing Lu, II. B. 4; VI. B. 5.
Po, III. B. 5; V. A. 6, 7.
Po Kuei, VI. B. 10, 11.
Po Yi, II. A. 2, 9; III. B. 10; IV. A. 13; V. B. 1; VI. B. 6; VII. A. 22; VII. B. 15.
Po-kung Ch'i, V. B. 2.
Po-kung Yu, II. A. 2.
Po-li Hsi, V. A. 9; VI. B. 6, 15.
Prince Pi Kan, II. A. 1; VI. A. 6. See Appendix 4.
Prince Tien, VII. A. 33.

River, the, III. A. 4, i.e., the Yangtse River.

San Miao, V. A. 3.
San Wei, V. A. 3.
San-yi Sheng, VII. B. 38.
Shang, IV. A. 7.
Shang Kung, VII. B. 30.
Shen Hsiang, II. B. 11.
Shen Nung, III. A. 4.
Shen T'ung, II. B. 8.
Shen Tzu, VI. B. 8.
Shen-yu Hsing, IV. B. 31.
Shih Ch'iu, VI. B. 4.
Shih K'uang, IV. A. 1; VI. A. 7.
Shih Tzu, II. B. 10.
Shu, III. A. 4; III. B. 9.
Shun, II. A. 2, 8; II. B. 2; III. A. 1, 4; III. B. 4, 9; IV. A. 1, 2, 26, 28; IV. B. 1, 19, 28, 32; V. A. 1, 2, 3, 4, 5, 6, 7; V. B. 1, 3, 6; VI. A. 6; VI. B. 2, 3, 8, 10, 15; VII. A. 16, 25, 30,

35, 46; VII. B. 6, 33, 37, 38. See Appendix 4.

Snow Palace, I. B. 4.

Ssu, the, III. A. 4.

Ssu-ch'eng Chen-tzu, V. A. 8.

Sun Shu-ao, VI. B. 15.

Sung, II. A. 2; II. B. 3; III. A. 1, 2, 4; III. B. 5; V. A. 8; VII. A. 36.

Sung K'eng, VI. B. 4.

Sung Kou-chien, VII. A. 9.

T'a, the, III. A. 4.

Tai, III. B. 10.

Tai Pu-sheng, III. B. 6.

Tai Ying-chih, III. B. 8.

T'ai Chia, V. A. 6; VII. A. 31. See Appendix 4.

T'ai Kung, IV. A. 13; VI. B. 8; VII. A. 22.

T'ai Kung Wang, VII. B. 38, i.e., T'ai Kung.

T'ai Ting, V. A. 6.

T'ai Wang, I. B. 3, 5, 14, 15. See Appendix 4.

Tan Chu, V. A. 6.

T'ang (Yao's dynasty), V. A. 6.

T'ang, I. B. 3, 8, 11; II. A. 1, 3; II. B. 2, 12; III. B. 5; IV. A. 9; IV. B. 20; V. A. 6, 7; VI. B. 2, 6; VII. A. 30; VII. B. 33, 38. Founder of the Yin Dynasty. See Appendix 4.

T'ang, VII. B. 23.

T'ao Ying, VII. A. 35.

Tchou, I. B. 8; II. A. 1; III. B. 9; IV. A. 9, 13; V. A. 6; V. B. 1; VI. A. 6; VII. A. 22. See Appendix 4.

T'eng, I. B. 13, 15; II. B. 6; III. A. 1, 3, 4; VII. B. 30.

T'eng Keng, VII. A. 43.

Ti tribes, I. B. 14, 15, i.e., Hsün Yü.

Three Dynasties, III. A. 2, 3; IV. A. 3;

IV. B. 20. See Appendix 4.

Tieh Tse Gate, VII. A. 36.

Tsai Wo, II. A. 2.

Ts'ai, VII. B. 18.

Tsang Ts'ang, I. B. 16.

Ts'ao Chiao, VI. B. 2.

Tseng Hsi (younger son of Tseng Tzu), II. A. 1.

Tseng Hsi (i.e. Tseng Tien, father of Tseng Tzu), IV. A. 19; VII. B. 36, 37.

Tseng Tzu, I. B. 12; II. A. 2; II. B. 2; III. A. 2, 4; III. B. 7; IV. A. 19; IV. B. 31; VII. B. 36, i.e., Tseng Ts'an.

Tseng Yüan, IV. A. 19.

Tsou, I. A. 7; I B. 12; III. A. 2; VI. B. 1, 2, 5.

Tuan-kan Mu, III. B. 7.

T'ung, V. A. 6; VII. A. 31.

Tung-kuo family, the, II. B. 2.

Tzu-ao, IV. A. 24, 25; IV. B. 27, i.e., Wang Huan.

Tzu-ch'an (d. 522), IV. B. 2; V. A. 2.

Tzu-chang, II. A. 2; III. A. 4.

Tzu-chih, II. B. 8.

Tzu-chuo Ju-tzu, IV. B. 24.

Tzu-hsia, II. A. 2; III. A. 4.

Tzu-hsiang, II. A. 2.

Tzu-k'uai, II. B. 8.

Tzu-kung, II. A. 2; III. A. 4,

Tzu-liu, VI. B. 6.

Tzu-lu, II. A. 1, 8; III. B. 7; V. A. 8, i.e., Chung Yu.

Tzu-mo, VII. A. 26.

Tzu-shu Yi, II. B. 10.

Tzu-ssu, II. B. 11; IV. B. 31; V. B. 3, 6, 7; VI. B. 6.

Tzu-tu, VI. A. 7.

Tzu-yu, II. A. 2; III. A. 4.

Viscount Chien of Chao (reigned

517-458), III. B. 1.

Viscount of Chi, II. A. 1. See Appendix 4.

Viscount of Wei, II. A. 1. See also Ch'i, Viscount of Wei.

Wai Ping, V. A. 6.

Wan Chang, III. B. 5; V. A. 1, 2, 3, 5, 6, 7, 8, 9; V. B. 3, 4, 6, 7, 8; VII. B. 37.

Wang Huan, II. B. 6; IV. B. 27. See also Tzu-ao.

Wang Liang, III. B. 1.

Wang Pao, VI. B. 6.

Wang Shun, V. B. 3.

Wei, VII. A. 11.

Wei, IV. B. 24, 31; V. A. 8.

Wei, the, IV. B. 2.

Wei Chung, II. A. 1.

Wu, I. B. 3; IV. A. 7.

Wu-lu Tzu, VI. B. 1, 5.

Wu Ch'eng, IV. B. 31.

Wu Huo, VI. B. 2.

Wu Ling, III. B. 10.

Wu Ting, II. A. 1.

Yang, III. B. 9; VII. B. 26, i.e., Yang Chu.

Yang Ch'eng, V. A. 6.

Yang Chu, III. B. 9. See also Yang Tzu.

Yang Hu, III. A. 3.

Yang Huo, III. B. 7.

Yang Tzu, VII. A. 26. See also Yang Chu.

Yangtse River, III. B. 9; VII. A. 16. See also the River.

Yao, II. A. 2; II. B. 2; III. A. 1, 4; III. B. 4, 9; IV. A. 1, 2; IV. B. 32; V. A. 4, 5, 6, 7; V. B. 1, 6; VI. A. 6; VI. B. 2, 8, 10; VII. A. 30, 46; VII. B. 33, 37, 38. See Appendix 4.

Yellow River, II. A. 2; III. B. 9; VI. B. 6; VII. A. 16.

Yen, I. B. 10, 11; II. B. 8, 9.

Yen, III. B. 9.

Yen Ch'ou-yu, V. A. 8.

Yen Hui, II. A. 2; III. A. 1; IV. B. 29.

Yen Pan, V. B. 3.

Yen Tzu, I. B. 4; II. A. 1.

Yi, III. A. 4; V. A. 6. See Appendix 4.

Yi, IV. B. 24; VI. A. 20; VII. A. 41.

Yi Chih, III. A. 5.

Yi Ch'iu, VI. A. 9.

Yi Tzu, III. A. 5, i.e., Yi Chih.

Yi Ya, VI. A. 7.

Yi Yin, II. A. 2; II. B. 2; V. A. 6, 7; V. B. 1; VI. B. 6; VII. A. 31; VII. B. 38. See Appendix 4.

Yin, II. A. 1; II. B. 9; III. A. 3; IV. A. 2, 7; V. A. 6; V. B. 4; VII. B. 4. See Appendix 4.

Yin Kung chih T'uo, IV. B. 24.

Yin Shih, II. B. 12.

Ying, II. B. 7.

Yu, III. B. 5.

Yu Chou, V. A. 3.

Yu Hsin, V. A. 7.

Yu Jo, II. A. 2; III. A. 4.

Yu Pi, V. A. 3.

Yung Chü, V. A. 8.

Yü (Shun's dynasty), V. A. 6.

Yü, II. A. 8; III. A. 4; III. B. 9; IV. B. 20, 26, 29; V. A. 6; VI. B. 11; VII. B. 22, 38. Founder of the Hsia Dynasty. See Appendix 4.

Yü, III. B. 5.

Yü, V. A. 9; VI. B. 6.

Yü Kung chih Ssu, IV. B. 24.

Yüeh, IV. B. 31; VI. B. 3.

Yüeh, III. B. 6.

Yüeh-cheng Ch'iu, V. B. 3.

Yüeh-cheng Tzu, I. B. 16; IV. A. 24, 25; VI. B. 13; VII. B. 25.